Pitt Series in Policy and Institutional Studies

Japanese Prefectures and Policymaking

Steven R. Reed

University of Pittsburgh Press

Published by the University of Pittsburgh Press, Pittsburgh, Pa. 15260
Copyright © 1986, University of Pittsburgh Press
Feffer and Simons, Inc., London
Manufactured in the United States of America

Library of Congress Cataloging in Publication Data

Reed, Steven R., 1947–
  Japanese prefectures and policymaking.

  (Pitt series in policy and institutional studies)
  Bibliography: p. 181.
  Includes index.
  1. Local government—Japan.   2. Environmental
policy—Japan.   3. Housing policy—Japan.   4. Education
and state—Japan.   I. Title.   II. Series.
JS7373.A3R44   1986   352'.00047   85-22528
ISBN 0-8229-3527-9

Contents

Tables

Acknowledgments

In the course of preparing this book I incurred many obligations. While I cannot thank everyone who deserves it, I do wish to acknowledge several specific debts.

First, the research on which this book is based was made possible by funding from the United States Educational Commission in Japan (Fulbright Commission) and the Social Science Research Council. The cooperation and patience of the many Japanese officials in Saga, Chiba, and Saitama prefectures, the Ministries of Home Affairs and Construction, and the Environment Agency who answered my strange foreign questions were also necessary for the successful completion of this research.

I have received comments and suggestions from several colleagues, including Thomas J. Anton, Jack Walker, Robert Cole, and Robert Putnam, but I owe a special debt to John Creighton Campbell, whose editorial comments have made this a much better book and me a much better writer. His substantive comments are woven into the work and my thinking so closely that it is now impossible to recognize all his contributions. I have depended on John for advice and support and would never have been able to finish this book without his help.

Finally, my wife Michiko deserves a vote of thanks for enduring the vagaries of an academic career. Her unfailing common sense has helped keep everything in perspective. Her support has kept me going and just the knowledge that Michiko is watching has motivated me to do my best.

Japanese
Prefectures and
Policymaking

1

Influence in Intergovernmental Relations

*I*N READING the literature on local government in various countries, one is struck by the degree to which the terms *local autonomy* and *centralization* are politically value-laden. Probably the most common usage of these terms occurs in political debate and the image invoked depends on the issue at hand. One's reaction to arguments about local autonomy depends a great deal upon whether the image invoked resembles a New England town meeting or a small-town southern sheriff, a rural community or a big-city machine. Political bias pervades the use of these terms. In the United States and Great Britain local autonomy is identified with a conservative persuasion, while in France, Italy, and Japan the slogan belongs to the left. In fact, local autonomy tends to be a slogan used by the "outs" at the national level to oppose the policy initiatives of the "ins" (Gourevitch, 1977).

Centralization and local autonomy are value-laden terms, but they are also the most obvious starting points for comparing how levels of government interact in different political systems (Kesselman and Rosenthal, 1974; Ashford, 1975, 1976). If we are to use these concepts analytically, we must avoid images of local government either as the representative of a natural community defending freedom from the octopus of central control or as the backward strongholds of traditional privilege. While political scientists should participate in these debates, they should not be captured by them.

How, then, shall we characterize subnational governments? For present purposes we shall limit the discussion to examples from relatively industrialized democracies. Although many of the generalizations may apply to less industrialized and nondemocratic countries, we gain a great deal by limiting the scope of inquiry. Given these two limitations,

3

we can reject the image of local governments as representatives of "natural" communities (Fesler, 1965). In industrialized countries, states, departments, counties, prefectures, and so forth, seldom coincide with anything resembling a sociological community. The population tends to be highly mobile and the boundaries are changed too seldom to adjust to changing social and economic realities. We must, therefore, reject the image of subnational governments as independent social systems each with its own political and economic subsystems (Rose, 1973). The developed nations have become far too integrated for some part of the nation to stand apart as a system in its own right. In particular, policymaking has become highly integrated. [1]

Even if subnational governments are not complete systems, they are governmental systems, organizations that make public policy. Even the most "unnatural" units gain legitimacy over time and serve important functions. There is no "natural" way to organize the functions of a central government but bureaus and ministries prove quite capable of maintaining their "unnatural" boundaries. Subnational governments are equally capable of maintaining their integrity no matter how irrational their boundaries may seem. One need not posit a social system to discuss a governmental or policymaking system. We begin, therefore, with the simple image of a subnational government as a governmental unit responsible for a broad range of public policy within a geographically defined area.

A Policymaking Approach

I have chosen to focus on intergovernmental policymaking. Centralization and local autonomy are basically power concepts: who decides, who controls, who has influence? These questions can be asked at many levels of abstraction, but the many problems associated with the concept of power can be minimized by making such questions as concrete as possible. Therefore, I will investigate influence over public policy decisions in specific cases of intergovernmental policymaking. My specific focus will be on three Japanese prefectures during 1976–1977.

Relations among levels of government is an important topic in the study of policymaking for at least two reasons. First, it has become increasingly apparent that one cannot explain how subnational policy is made without reference to the influence of other levels of government. In the United States, the early community power studies and comparative studies of state and urban government have tended to assume that subnational governments are independent social systems, that their politics and policies can be explained by subnational factors alone. This assumption has proved untenable, however, as vertical dimensions of community power were discovered (Walton, 1968). When attempts were made to replicate U.S. studies in other countries, the assumption of subnational autonomy could not be made so easily (Rosenthal, 1968). Statistical comparisons of subnational government decisions and policies are not valid if effective decision making takes place at other levels of government. Some attempts have been made to include intergovernmental aid as a determinant of subnational policymaking (Strouse and Jones, 1974), but more important is the finding by Lawrence Gary (1973) that state governments make some policy decisions while others are effectively determined by federal grant formulas. This kind of contextual knowledge of intergovernmental policymaking is necessary for meaningful interpretation of statistical findings. In other words, investigation of subnational autonomy in policymaking logically precedes comparisons of the policies that are made at the subnational level.

The second reason for choosing to focus on intergovernmental policymaking is the less widely recognized fact that one cannot understand national policymaking without reference to subnational governments and the relationships among levels of government. Since policies may be made at several levels, one cannot know what "national" policy is by looking exclusively at central government policy. A central government may not need to enter a policy area if subnational governments are performing satisfactorily. When the central government does enter a new field, it may well find some subnational governments already active there. Policies developed by subnational governments often serve as models for national policies. Subnational governments also influence national policymaking directly by joining together to form interest groups to lobby the central government. More generally, the structure of the intergovernmental system affects how national policy is made.

Unfortunately, few scholars have compared the vertical aspects of political systems. The only area to have received attention has been the differences between federal and unitary states. Most studies have analyzed the constitutional distribution of authority in federal states (Maas, 1965; Wildavsky, 1971).[2] However, this focus on constitutional law has not proven fruitful. The distinction between federal and unitary systems is unclear and does not explain much about relations or policymaking among levels of government (Riker, 1969; Ashford, 1977). Recent studies in unitary, and presumable highly centralized states has demonstrated a surprising degree of local autonomy in making policy (Sbragia, 1974, re Italy; Milch, 1974, re France). In fact, intergovern-

mental policymaking looks remarkably similar in both unitary and federal states. The focus on concrete cases of policymaking is designed to
get at problems of centralization and local autonomy while avoiding a
dependence on constitutional or other legal interpretations.

Common Characteristics of
Intergovernmental Systems

Recent work on local government in industrialized democracies reveals a consistent set of findings.[3] One finds terms like *bargaining* and
negotiation stressed over *power* and *authority*. Taken together, these findings can be summarized under four generalizations and a few corollaries.

*Generalization 1: Intergovernmental relations take place in many different
arenas and the balance of power among levels of government in each one tends
to be fairly even.* We often picture intergovernmental relations as taking
place between *the* central government and *a* local government. Actually, it is rare for a single local government to deal with the whole
central government. Policy is made among various levels of a nation's
government in two basic situations: when a local government faces an
agency of the central government and when the central government
faces all local governments collectively, perhaps represented by some
organization of local officials. Other situations occur. The central government deals with a subsets of local governments defined regionally or
by some particular problem salient to the group. Others are harder to
classify, but the distinction between local and national arenas is a good
place to start.

In local arenas, policy is made for one local government: whether a
grant proposal should be funded or not, or how the local government
will respond to a new law or some central guideline. The proximate
policymakers are normally limited to local officials, the staff of a central
government agency, and often the national representatives from the
local district. Sometimes the central agency does have a great deal more
legal and financial resources than the local government, but the agency
must deal with many local governments and cannot afford to spend too
much time and energy trying to control any one. Normally, an issue in
a local arena commands a higher priority in the local government and
thus a higher proportion of its time and energy (Gyford and James,
1983: 147). Local governments often have trouble getting the central
agency to attend to its special problems, but seldom have to worry
about effective or detailed monitoring. If the local government does

have trouble with the agency, its national representative often proves an effective channel of influence.

Sometimes the balance of resources favors the local government, not the agency. Large cities are often special cases. For example, Stockholm had little trouble getting the Swedish national government to amend a law to allow it to pursue an active housing policy (Anton, 1975). Chicago under Mayor Daley often proved a special case because of its importance in Democratic party politics. For example, the mayor was able to get a federal welfare administrator changed to someone whose philosophy was closer to his own and thus avoid implementing the spirit of the law (Greenstone and Peterson, 1973). When one adds political resources, time, energy, and control over information, to legal and financial resources, the balance of power in local arenas is seldom very skewed and local governments are never powerless.

In the national arena, policy has national scope and the proximate policymakers are normally central officials, but if local government interests are at stake local officials will become actively involved and try to influence the outcome. Organizations of local officials are powerful in many countries, including the United States (Haider, 1974, and Beer, 1976), Sweden (Anton, 1975), France (Kesselman, 1967), and Great Britain (Griffith, 1966; Gyford and James, 1983, ch. 6). Political channels of influence are also important. Grodzins (1963) argues that because of the American party system, members of Congress tend to play the role of state representatives ensuring that all national legislation meets with the approval of most states. In France most National Assembly members are also mayors of communes, making it extremely difficult to pass legislation detrimental to communal interests (Kesselman, 1974). The relationship between elected officials who share overlapping electoral districts has not been well studied, but national legislators must play the role of local representative to some extent (Schlesinger, 1965).

Generalization 2: Levels of government are fundamentally interdependent. This generalization is an extension of the findings of the literature about implementation: implementation is a complex process requiring a large number of actions to become effective and authority for all these action seldom lies with any one level of government. This generalization also follows Arthur Maas's (1959) analogy between the "areal division of powers" among levels of government and the "capital division of powers" among branches of the central government: in the same sense that the president cannot enact any legislation without Congress, central governments cannot effectively pursue many policies without the cooperation of subnational governments. This generalization summarizes the findings of many studies. No matter what any particular policy area looks like, the overall relationship is one of interdependence; even if it seems that one level of government dominates some policy, it needs the cooperation of other levels in so many other areas that it cannot ignore them. This "simple" generalization is really the key point, for several important corollaries flow from it.

Corollary 1: Cooperation is the dominant mode of intergovernmental relations but conflict is also inevitable. Scholars who take a positive (often idyllic) view of local autonomy, and see the penetration of the central government into local affairs negatively, look for conflict and find it. However, most intergovernmental relations are noncontroversial and mutually beneficial. Officials at all levels share an overriding interest in keeping the machinery of government operating. High levels of conflict result in a breakdown of governmental services and few issues are worth that price. On the other hand, interdependence breeds conflict. Conflict comes from differing perspectives, varying priorities, and the tension between the necessity of both uniformity and diversity in policy results. Conflict over the terms of sharing, who will pay for joint endeavors and how political responsibility for successes and failures will be apportioned, is endemic to any intergovernmental system. Interdependence also creates "the frustration produced by the inability of decision-makers in one government to produce action at their own discretion: other governments must also be moved" (Grodzins, 1963: 14). This frustration explains why officials at each level complain so much about what is fundamentally a mutually beneficial relationship.

Corollary 2: Intergovernmental disagreements tend to be resolved through bargaining. This corollary summarizes empirical findings from many different countries: most of the interactions among levels of government are literally processes of bargaining, negotiation, and persuasion. Even when the central government issues authoritative commands, those commands will normally anticipate the reactions of subnational governments, anticipations based on predecision consultations. The central government is seldom in a position simply to demand immediate compliance.

Interdependence makes bargaining necessary. In the long run, the only alternative to cooperation is inaction, which is politically unacceptable. Interdependence also defines the character of intergovernmental bargaining. As is not true of commercial or international bargaining, neither party can opt out: there are no other suppliers or allies. Again, the bargaining situation is analogous to that between the U.S. president and Congress. Each level of government has a monopoly on goods needed by the other. Interdependence is unavoidable.

Noncooperation and the breakdown of intergovernmental policy-making does sometimes occur. Eisenhower sending the national guard into Arkansas to enforce federal school desegregation legislation comes to mind. Many countries have specified procedures for such crises, ways in which duly elected mayors can be removed from office or duly enacted local policies can be reversed. Such intergovernmental confrontation is rare and deserves more study. Under normal circumstances, the threat of such a confrontation is an effective weapon that can be used by governments at any level. Noncooperation changes the positive-sum game of intergovernmental policymaking into a zero-sum (or even negative-sum) game of confrontation. Participants in intergovernmental policymaking soon learn to avoid confrontation.

Generalization 3: Areas of exclusive jurisdiction do exist, but generally any level of government can intervene in the affairs of any other level, producing shared jurisdiction. Most policymaking involves all levels of government, but activities carried out independently by one level alone can be found. In order to find these independent activities, one must define "activities" rather specifically, speaking not of "education" but of "hiring teachers" or "choosing textbooks," for example. These areas of exclusive decision making do exist, but their continued existence depends on the acquiescence of the other levels of government.

Central governments can intervene into local affairs in various ways: they can enact a law regulating local activities, establish a grant program to make some policy cheaper for local governments, or simply proclaim a national goal or identify a national problem. The last option is clearly a matter of persuasion, but often has a significant effect on local policymaking. Such national policy statements place the issue on all local agendas simultaneously, often with impressive results.

Subnational governments have fewer options for intervention into central affairs, but they still can and do intervene. Collectively, they can organize and lobby to change a law. Widespread noncompliance can force revisions of the law. The law can be implemented vigorously, passively, or for different purposes than intended. Local governments can establish guidelines on top of legal requirements or concerning how the law will be implemented. A great deal of discretion can be found within the law or in the process of implementation. More positively, subnational governments can respond creatively to social problems and set the pattern for central policy. Innovative local policies can embarrass a reluctant central government into action. Diffusion occurs not only among subnational governments but also back and forth between central and subnational levels.

As each level of government intervenes into the affairs of the others, fewer independent activities remain and the scope of intergovernmental policymaking expands. This process seems to have accelerated since World War II. In many countries this phenomenon has been interpreted as centralization, but the expansion has occurred among levels of government, not at the center. The level of interaction has risen, making it harder to ignore the interdependence that has been there all along (Elazar, 1967). Increased interaction may have changed the shape and style of intergovernmental relations, but it does not necessarily indicate increased central control.

Generalization 4: Governments often try to avoid responsibility for policymaking. Subnational governments are particularly capable of avoiding policymaking and become active policymakers only under extraordinary circumstances. Making policy is a difficult business. It is easier to avoid problems than to solve them. Even active governments tend to choose a few high-priority issues to deal with and avoid controversy in other areas as much as they can. Because central governments are the final arbiters even in federal states, subnational governments are in a good position to avoid policymaking; they can often simply wait until the central government makes the policy for them. Particularly in unitary states, subnational governments can often deflect citizen demands by claiming to lack autonomy (Sbragia, 1974).

Small local governments often avoid conflict by stressing community harmony and avoiding policymaking as much as possible. A remarkably similar picture of inactivity emerges from studies done in the United States (Vidich and Bensman, 1960), France (Kesselman, 1967), Germany (Dolive, 1976), and Japan (Beardsley, Hall, and Ward, 1959). This nearly complete avoidance of policymaking seems possible only in very small local governments, but larger subanational governments are also inactive most of the time. Rose points to the relative inactivity in the American states: "For most states political activity is regular but not strenuous. . . . But if the national pattern becomes dysfunctional, then states need to become systems. The 1929 crash and the contemporary school busing issue are perhaps instances" (Rose, 1973: 1171). Larger subnational governments tend to avoid policymaking by hiding behind the cover of expertise. The myth of nonpartisan, nonpolitical local government insulates them from demands just as the myth of community harmony insulates smaller local governments from the same kinds of pressures. Subnational governments tend to become active, political policymakers only under extraordinary conditions.[4]

These four generalizations summarize many of the findings of the literature on local and intergovernmental policymaking. After reviewing this literature, I find it most useful to conceive of intergovernmental relations as one overarching bargain. For most policies, the bargain is noncontroversial and cooperation prevails. Conflict occurs only at the margins. Winning or losing a particular conflict shifts the bargain in favor of one level or the other. The record indicates the direction of change but is a poor indicator of the level of centralization. Jerry Hough (1975) points out that it is often more important to know the content of the conflict than who won and who lost. He uses a football analogy: it is more important to know that the ball is on my five-yard line than to know that I just gained three yards. In the 1960s and 1970s subnational governments lost several battles in the United States and won several in Japan. But the American federal government was fighting battles won long ago by the Japanese central government. Japan is still more centralized than the United States, even though the won-loss record of the past twenty years would tend to imply the reverse.

Wins and losses show the direction of change, while the substance of the conflict indicates the level of centralization. In both cases the key piece of evidence is intergovernmental conflict. Relations among levels of government in industrialized democracies have a great deal in common, but our goal is comparison. The basic similarities form a necessary background for comparison but it is the differences that interest political scientists.

Influence in Intergovernmental Relations

In a situation of unavoidable interdependence, what determines the distribution of influence? We can distinguish six basic hypotheses found in the literature: they concern the distribution of authority, finances, and information, electoral politics, policy substance, and the principle of least interest. In this section I will discuss each of these hypotheses and make a preliminary evaluation of each one based on the comparative literature. Each hypothesis finds some support in the literature. Indeed, it would be surprising to find that any one of these factors does not have an impact on influence. The hypotheses cannot be phrased as simple dichotomies: impact or no impact. Rather, we must ask under what conditions will a particular factor be more or less important. We must analyze the structure of causality.

The Distribution of Authority Hypothesis. In an ideal bureaucratic world, the distribution of influence would follow the distribution of authority perfectly. All influence would be legitimized by law and there would be no other sources of influence. We do not live in such a world, but examining where authority is located would seem a good starting point for investigating influence. The evidence suggests, however, that the relationship between authority and influence is far from simple. One cannot, for example, simply divide authority into central and local spheres.

Authority for any particular policy or project is rarely located exclusively at any one level of government. Each level normally has authority over some decisions necessary for the successful implementation of any given policy. There are very few purely central or local functions; most functions are shared. Kurt Steiner (1965) has amply documented this "muddle of functions" in Japan. Morton Grodzins (1963) described this phenomenon in the United States with his famous "marble cake" analogy, and the validity of his findings have been further documented in the literature about implementation. Fritz Scharpf and his associates have found "a prevailing pattern of joint decision making, in which the typical policy making process will usually involve all three levels of government" (1978: 57) in the Federal Republic of Germany. J.A.G. Griffith's (1966) detailed study of the division of authority in Britain leads to similar conclusions. Shared functions is another reflection of the interdependence of the levels of government.

Even when one can divide authority into central and local components, authority is a poor indicator of actual influence over policy. It is not difficult to find examples in which other resources have overwhelmed authority. Scharpf's group studied a change in the constitutional distribution of authority in Germany. They found "no evidence of an increase in Federal control capacity in line with its intended effects" (in Garlichs and Hull, 1978: 144). Jerome Milch (1974) found that one mayor in France was able to exert considerable influence over housing policy in his city even though local governments in France have no direct authority over housing policy. Authority is not even a necessary condition of influence.

Even if influence is not directly proportional to authority, authority often produces some influence over policy. In fact, authority is often the basic currency of intergovernmental bargaining: "Unless you perform that action over which you have authority, I will not perform this action over which I have authority." Milch concludes that in France, "Formal powers are more significant than one might gather by reading the municipal code. They can be used to achieve policy objectives in ways that were never intended by the state" (1974: 157). A reading of Edward Banfield (1961) and Martha Derthick (1970) leads to similar conclusions for the United States.

This review of the literature leaves us with many questions. How authority is distributed is not a reliable indicator of influence nor even a necessary condition of influence. Yet authority sometimes proves important. The problem is to determine under what circumstances authority produces influence.

The Distribution of Finances Hypothesis. Political scientists are familiar with the idea that actual influence may diverge from formal authority, but the distribution of finances seems to offer a measure that is at once more precise and more reliable. Moreover, data on the distribution of finances come neatly prepackaged in budgetary documents. The availability of data has led several scholars to use indices of financial centralization in statistical analyses (Sherwood, 1969; Davies, 1970; Wilensky, 1975; Randall, 1976). A review of the literature reveals, however, that the relationship between financial contribution and influence is as problematic as that between authority and influence.

Despite the superficial precision of such accounting procedures, one cannot divide expenditures into central and local components. First, there are many technical problems (Crispin, 1976). How, for example, should one classify transfers of funds from the central to subnational governments? Both levels spend the money. Who controls how the money is spent, the first or the last to spend it?

Another problem is substituting monies at one level with those from another. If the central government subsidizes a program that the local government would have pursued without the subsidy, central monies have been substituted for local monies, actually increasing the flexibility of local budgeting (Porter, 1973). The literature on the influence of federal grants in the United States has not been optimistic about using this mechanism to gain local compliance with federal goals. Robert Stein concludes, "Even in instances where administrations engage in overt and specific targeting of aid, there is little evidence to support the success of their efforts" (1981: 335).

We tend to assume that the central government is giving the money and must therefore be buying something with that money. Actually, both levels are buying something with their money. When a jointly funded program is carried out, the only thing we can say for certain is that both levels of government agreed on the project and on the terms of financial sharing. Neither is it necessarily the case that the central government is "giving" the money; subnational governments may be "taking" it. General revenue sharing in the United States would seem to be a case of state and local governments taking federal money with no concomitant increase in federal control (Beer, 1976). Essentially, state and local governments act as pressure groups and manage to get their subsidy through Congress on a strictly political basis.

Students of public policy tend to assume that governments buy influence over policy outputs with their money, but they may well be buying something else. A local government may be buying increased revenues as when a mayor wants a big project to be his "record" for electoral purposes and any highly subsidized project will do. The central government may be buying reelection for one of its legislators by funding a pork-barrel project. The U.S. Army Corps of Engineers implements federal projects that are fully funded by the federal government, but often locally conceived and controlled. Governments deal in many more types of resources than authority and money; politics cannot be ignored.

There is no necessary relationship between an entity's financial contribution and influence over policy. The relationship does not even hold between policy areas within a single country. In Britain the central government exercises more direct control over capital investments than over current expenditures even though they provide few loans and many grants (Davey, 1971). In the end, we return to Maas's analogy between the central and areal division of powers: except for the availability of intergovernmental accounting figures, it is no easier to classify expenditures as central or local than it would be to classify central expenditures as presidential or congressional.

Influence over policy is not proportional to financial contributions. The relationship between finances and control is much more complex. In fact, there are two hypotheses concerning finances that would seem more probable than the financial contribution hypothesis. One would expect the marginal contribution to be more important than the absolute contribution. One should, for example, examine the demand and supply of funds for particular programs. If local demands are greater than central supplies, one should expect central control. If, however, supply exceeded demand, one should expect local discretion, no matter which level supplies the greater proportion of the funds. Another hypothesis is that subnational governments with fewer slack resources should be easier to control than those with greater flexibility. Slack resources should provide the subnational government with options other than dependence on central funds. Alberta Sbragia (1974) argues that the relative affluence of Milan was a necessary condition for its autonomous housing policy. Again the question is, what financial factors affect influence over policy, and under what circumstances?

The Control over Information Hypothesis. Information is one resource that can sometimes prove decisive even when opposed by seemingly overwhelming financial and authority resources. Garlichs and Hull (1978) present a stark example in their study of highway planning in the Federal Republic of Germany. Highway planning is a case in which the federal government has a dominant authority position, provides all the finances, and uses a highly sophisticated cost-benefit approach to choosing projects and yet, the authors conclude, the federal government has been unable to control the process because it depends on the states to provide all of the data necessary for planning. They further suggest that there is a relatively low ceiling on the degree of centralization that can be acheived in projects, like highway construction, that require detailed long-range planning and both legal and political negotiations among many different actors, both public and private. Sbragia (1974) reaches similar conclusions about housing in her study of Italy. One can find support for the information hypothesis in Milch (1974) and Pressman and Wildavsky (1973).

Control over the detailed information necessary for implementing a program is a power source often overlooked and underestimated. However, there is another aspect of information that generally favors the central government: expertise. Expertise is a kind of detailed information necessary for implementing policy, but this information comes not from deep familiarity with local conditions but from broad knowledge of theory and practice. In order to build a bridge in New York City, one must not only know something about New York but also know how to build a bridge. Usually the central government has an advantage in expertise that can prove decisive. In France, one of the key aspects of centralization is that the small communes depend on the prefectural and ministry field staffs for technical advice. The city of Lyons, for example, did not create its own department for public works and urban planning until 1962. Before that time they depended completely on the ministry field staffs for expertise in this area (Webman, 1977: 39–42).

We may expect that control over knowledge of local conditions and control over expertise will work in opposite directions, the former generally favoring the local government and the latter favoring the central government. It will be necessary to ask about the demand and supply for both kinds of information. How necessary is detailed local knowledge for the implementation of a program? How hard is it to obtain the necessary data? How much technical knowledge is required? How many people have the necessary expertise and for whom do they work? Finally, we must ask: under what circumstances will information and expertise produce influence and under what circumstances will it prove unimportant?

The Electoral Politics Hypothesis. Ironically, political scientists have virtually ignored political factors in intergovernmental relations.[5] I am using electoral politics in the broadest sense as anything that might affect the outcome of an election. I only wish to distinguish electoral from bureaucratic politics. In fact, one goal of this research has been to identify the types of intergovernmental politics that occur. I certainly wish to include not only political parties but also the distributive politics of obtaining pork-barrel projects that help incumbents get reelected.

When a mayor, a state legislator, and a national legislator share an electoral district, which one has the most influence over the voters? Aside from a stimulating discussion by Joseph Schlesinger (1965) and a few specific examples, political scientists have not dealt with this question. In Mayor Daley's Chicago it was clear that members of Congress and state legislators were representatives of the local party organization run by the mayor (Snowiss, 1966). It seems equally clear that in Britain the dominant influences on elections are national, not local (Butler and Stokes, 1971). Why the differences? What differences in intergovernmental policymaking are produced by such differences in the vertical dimensions of electoral politics? This is an important but virtually unexplored area.

The Policy Substance Hypothesis. Political debates often seem to focus on issues of centralization and local autonomy, but the argument that any given decision should be made at some other level of government is usually based on the unspoken premise that if it were to be made at that level, the decision would reflect different substantive preferences. Politics often seems to be electioneering and electioneering only, but parties and politicians also fight over the substance of policy. Just as lawyers tend to argue substance when they have a strong case, and legalities when their case is weak, politicians whose cases are weak tend to argue procedural and electoral politics. These "purely political" arguments do not always win. The substantive aspects of policy can overwhelm all others.

The civil rights movement in the United States is a case in point. Those who opposed it argued for local autonomy because they knew that integration would not occur if reform were left up to local governments. Proponents argued for the substance of the case and the centralization that occurred in this area occurred not because the central government was stronger than local governments, but because the substantive case for civil rights won the day. Politicians seldom vote against their substantive preferences in order to preserve such abstractions as local autonomy. Many politicians are genuinely concerned about intergovernmental issues, but they seldom rank these concerns above more concrete ones.

If the issue of local autonomy is often used to block central policy initiatives, the issue of national uniformity is often used to block local initiatives. In Britain, business often prefers to be regulated by the central government (Scarrow, 1971); local government regulation is often tougher, so businesses argue that regulations should be uniform across the country. In the United States, local governments find it difficult to pursue policies detrimental to local business interests (Peterson, 1981) and local autonomy tends to produce conservative results. How and why do different levels of government produce different policies? How and under what circumstances does the substance of a policy overwhelm the procedural and other barriers erected in intergovernmental relations?

The Principle of Least Interest. George Homans (1974) has suggested a theory of influence that seems particularly appropriate for relations of unavoidable interdependence: "The party least interested in a joint venture has the greatest control over its content." If officials at each level of government share an overriding interest in keeping the machinery of government operating, the level of government most willing to risk a breakdown of governmental services has the bargaining advantage; it is in no hurry, while the other participants tend to be anxious to get under way. The least interested party tends to get its way on many of the "details" of the policy in return for allowing implementation to proceed more smoothly and rapidly.

Milch (1974) found that local interest in increasing their housing supply explained the differences in policies between two French cities.

One city went along with the central government's housing program. The other city was not interested in housing construction and gradually increased its control over the housing that was built within its boundaries. Central officials made substantive policy concessions in order to get some housing built. Alberta Sbragia (1974) shows that the major controls exercised by the Italian central government over housing policy in Milan were negative ones. Owen Hartley's study of central-local disagreements in four local governments over a forty-year period in Britain also supports the hypothesis. He concludes: "Positive action can be controlled eventually, but inaction is not so easily handled by central departments" (1971: 450). In housing policy at least, the principle of least interest seems to apply quite well. Will it apply as well to Japanese housing policy? What is it about housing policy that makes this principle applicable? Under what conditions will the least interested party prove influential?

In this section I have outlined six basic hypotheses about influence in intergovernmental policymaking. In each case the question is: under what circumstances will this particular factor prove important? To summarize briefly:

(1) *The Distribution of Authority:* the party with greater authority over a decision will have greater influence over it.

(2) *The Distribution of Finances:* the party that contributes the greater proportion of the finances to a program will have greater influence over it.

(3) *Control over Information:* the party that has access to more of the information necessary for implementing a policy will have more influence over the content of that policy.

(4) *Electoral Politics:* the party that influences election outcomes will also influence policy.

(5) *Policy Substance:* the party with the stronger technical arguments will have more influence over policy.

(6) *The Principle of Least Interest:* the party least interested in the completion of a joint project will have greater influence over its contents.

The Plan of Study

My basic research strategy is to use comparative case studies. I conducted over one hundred interviews with Japanese officials, both from the prefectural and and the central levels of government, and supplemented this research with government documents and prefectural newspapers. I chose to focus on prefectures, not cities, because to have focused on municipalities would have involved dealing with interactions among three rather than just two levels of government. The design is meant to produce four different kinds of evidence: across prefectures, across policy areas, across time, and across countries.

The first type of evidence comes from comparing prefectures. I chose three prefectures that were very different in economic and political character. I selected one rural, agricultural prefecture, Saga, at the southwest extremity of Japan, and two urban, industrial prefectures, Chiba and Saitama, just to the southeast and northwest of Tokyo, respectively. Statistically, Chiba and Saitama are quite similar, ranking near each other on most economic and financial indicators. (See table 1.) However, Chiba has a conservative governor and an assembly dominated by the conservative Liberal Democratic party (LDP), while Saitama has a progressive governor and a somewhat more balanced assembly.

Comparing these three prefectures should help answer questions about the relationships among wealth, politics, and intergovernmental policymaking in Japan. If financial factors influence policy, influence should vary between rich and poor prefectures. If electoral politics

TABLE 1
The Three Prefectures

	Saga		Chiba		Saitama	
Population	838	(41)	4,149	(9)	4,821	(7)
Population in DIDs[a]	20	(44)	239	(10)	311	(8)
Personal income	747	(42)	4,021	(9)	5,149	(7)
Expenditures	131	(42)	334	(8)	328	(9)
Financial strength[b]	.290	(45)	.771	(12)	.806	(10)
LDP % assembly seats	76.2	(6)	67.1	(13)	63.9	(17)
LDP % Diet votes	58.1	(12)	42.8	(33)	35.8	(41)

Source: Nihon Tōkei Nenkan, various years.

Note: Figures in parentheses are the rank of the prefectures out of a total of 47 prefectures. All figures are for 1975 except for financial strength which is for 1974. Population figures are in thousands of people. Income and expenditures figures are in billions of yen.

a. DID: densely inhabited district, as defined by the census. This figure is the best available estimate of urbanization.

b. Financial strength refers to the ratio of standard demand to standard revenues. See chapter 2, "Intergovernmental Finance," on the local allocation tax.

makes a difference, intergovernmental relations should differ in conservative and progressive prefectures. Maximizing economic and political variation should also maximize variation in policies pursued. For the purposes of this study, however, I am less interested in explaining the variations in prefectural policies than in analyzing these variations to gauge the boundaries of local influence over policymaking. The amount and types of subnational policy variation is a key piece of evidence in assessing influence. Central influence should produce either uniformity or neatly patterned variation. Local-level influences should produce variety along many different dimensions.

In each of the three prefectures I studied three policy areas—pollution control, public housing, and high school education—yielding a total of nine case studies. The three policy areas differ in several important ways. Pollution control is primarily a regulatory area, whereas both housing and education policy involve services. Since a regulatory issue is based more on policy and less on finances, comparisons should help us distinguish between the hypotheses concerning authority and financial influence. I will also analyze relatively expensive and relatively inexpensive aspects of each policy area. All three policy areas have become political issues, but pollution and education divide the political parties more clearly. Comparison of these policy areas should allow us to discuss the effects of electoral politics and controversy on intergovernmental policymaking.

The ideal type of evidence is gathered across time. One would like to be able to show that a change in some hypothesized variable was followed by a shift in influence. The problem is that time-series data are difficult to collect; and in fact, my interviews produced very little depth on the time dimension. Japanese bureaucrats tend to change jobs every two or three years, so my informants seldom knew the details of past policymaking. Nevertheless, I made every effort to probe for changes over time. In Japan local officials tend to have little sense of the history of their organizations, but the outlines of policy development are usually well documented. I found both academic and bureaucratic materials useful in this regard. While published documents could not fill in all the gaps, they do make some longitudinal comparisons possible.

Finally, the policy areas were all chosen to facilitate cross-national comparisons. For each of these policy areas, much has been written about Europe and the United States. Truly comparative policy studies are rare, but I will try to place this study in as comparative a context as possible.

My discussion will be divided into policy areas. Before we proceed to the detailed analysis of policymaking, however, some background is necessary. Chapter 2 will describe local government in Japan in comparison to other countries. Chapter 3 will focus on changes over time within Japan. The key phenomenon to be described and explained is the great increase in local innovation that occurred in the late 1960s and early 1970s. Chapters 4, 5, and 6 will cover pollution control, housing, and high school education, respectively. In the last chapter I will attempt to evaluate the six hypotheses in the light of the findings.

2

Japanese Local Government in Comparative Perspective

*H*OW SHOULD one compare systems of local government? What are the basic dimensions of such systems? Little has been written on this question, but there are some traditional areas of concern that can serve as starting points: structure and size, distribution of authority, and the sources of local finances.

Structural characteristics include the number of levels of subnational governments, the variety of special districts in use, and the internal organization of local governments. A major issue in the reform of local government has been what should be the proper size for subnational units (Dahl, 1967). Though the evidence is thin, policymakers have generally assumed that smaller local governments allow more democratic participation and that larger ones are more efficient and have greater capacity to make and implement policy.

Both bureaucrats and politicians are involved in intergovernmental relations. We should therefore analyze the vertical links among both sets of actors and ask which of the two channels is more important.

In analyzing relationships among central and local bureaucrats, James Fester (1967) makes a key distinction between areal and functional lines of authority. A local bureaucrat has two superiors. The mayor or governor represents the areal authority, and is responsible for the muncipality or region as a whole. However, local bureaucrats must also pay attention to their functional superiors in the central government. Local health officials must be responsive to national health officials. If functional lines of authority dominate, local administration becomes vertically fragmented. The Japanese call it *tate-wari gyōsei* (vertically split administration) (Samuels, 1983: 245).

The literature on intergovernmental politics is sparse. If however, we take American machine politics, exemplified by Mayor Daley's Chicago, as one pole and the nationalized local politics of Britain as the other pole, we can begin to put Japan into a comparative perspective. Two excellent studies of British and French intergovernmental relations, by Jerry Webman (1977) and Douglas Ashford (1982), provide a basis of comparison for both political and bureaucratic linkages.

Tarrow (1977) contrasts the French bureaucratic system with the Italian political system. In France, a local government seeking a grant, an exception from some rule, or some other consideration from a central agency, is better advised to concentrate on filling out the forms correctly and making a rational case. In Italy a local entity should focus its efforts on mobilizing its elected officials at all levels and getting signatures on a petition. Is Japan more like Italy or France?

Finally, I will describe the major actors in the Japanese national arena: the Ministry of Home Affairs (MOHA) and the national organizations of local government officials, in particular the National Conference of Governors *(Zenkoku Chijikai)*.

Structure and Size

Japanese local government is organized on two levels, prefectures and municipalities, the latter categorized as cities, towns, or villages. All parts of Japan are part of a municipality as well as a prefecture; there are no unincorporated areas. Although there are "special public bodies," Japan has relatively few special-purpose governments (Steiner, 1965: 194ff.). In this respect, it is more like Britain than France or the United States. Each general-purpose subnational government is headed by an elected chief executive, a mayor for municipalities and a governor for prefectures, and each has a popularly elected assembly. The election of governors was a major innovation of the occupation period. In contrast to the national parliamentary system, local governments are organized on a presidential model.

The organization of local governments is uniform, with two major exceptions. Tokyo's prefectural and municipal governments are combined into a single organization and this combined government is administered under several special provisions.[1] Second, several of the largest cities, including Tokyo, contain wards *(ku)* as a third level of government. These "designated cities" are also given many powers normally assigned to prefectures. Generally, prefectures are superior to municipalities, and all communications between the central government and municipalities must pass through the prefecture. Designated cities represent something of an exception to this rule, but none of the prefectures in this study contains such a city, so we will not deal with these exceptions here.

The structure of Japan's intergovernmental system is typical of medium-sized industrial democracies. Though different from the United States, Canada, or Australia, Japan is quite similar to Britain, France, and Germany.

Japan is about the size of California and is divided into forty-seven prefectures, making prefectures much smaller than most American states and somewhat smaller than most European intermediate levels of government. Hokkaido, by far the largest prefecture, is somewhat larger than Maine but smaller than Indiana. The second largest prefecture, Iwate, is bigger than Connecticut but smaller than New Jersey. The smallest prefectures are only half the size of Delaware. Compared to the Federal Republic of Germany, Hokkaido is bigger than Bavaria but the next largest German states are three or four times larger than the next largest Japanese prefectures. This is primarily a function of the smaller number of German states. Similarly, Italian regions are somewhat larger than Japanese prefectures because Italy has fewer regions. Britain and France have no comparable units.

Japanese prefectures make up in population what they lack in land area. Tokyo Prefecture has a population similar to that of Pennsylvania or Illinois. The smallest prefecture, Tottori, is about the size of Vermont or Delaware in population. Prefectural populations are similar to those of German states or Italian regions both in absolute terms and in the range of sizes represented.

Japanese prefectures are somewhat smaller than the international norm geographically but are about average in population size. If the central government had its way, however, prefectures would be much larger. The Ministry of Home Affairs has been pushing for consolidation of prefectures throughout the postwar period without success (Samuels, 1983). Prefectures have proven more resistant than municipalities, where several successful waves of consolidation have occurred.

The Distribution of Authority

The postwar constitution in Japan contains a section, absent in the old imperial constitution, giving local governments a general grant of authority: "Local governments may . . . enact ordinances within the limits of the law" (art. 8, sec. 94). The Local Government Law further specifies the grant of authority: "General local governments may enact ordinances with respect to their functions and not in conflict with the law" (art. 3, sec. 14, para. 1). This law also adds the police power to local functions. Before the war, local governments were allowed to perform only "proper functions," to provide services with no abridgement of individual freedoms, and to perform "assigned functions" *(i'nin jimu)* specified by law. The postwar local Government Law adds "administrative functions" *(gyōsei jimu),* which are essentially general police powers.

This constitutional grant of authority is generous relative to that of other unitary states. In Britain local governments have no general grant of powers; local governments can do only what Parliament has specifically allowed. In France the general grant of powers is narrower and is not written into the constitution; it is simply set down in a statute. On the other hand, the constitutional powers of Japanese local governments do not approach those of federal countries such as the United States, Germany, Canada, and Australia. American states legislate on a whole range of issues that are administered by the central government in Japan: criminal law, banking, the legal drinking age, marriage and divorce, insurance, and many more. Japanese find it incredible that in the United States the punishment for a murder should depend on which side of a state line it was committed. In fact, the basic difference between a federal state and a unitary one may well be a bias toward uniformity or diversity in policymaking. In Japan uniform policy is assumed unless a good case can be made for allowing diversity. In the United States diversity is assumed and uniformity imposed only when necessary.

The language of the constitutional grant of authority is less important than the interpretation of phrases like "within the limits of the law" and "not in conflict with the law." Britain is the best example of the gap between principle and practice. British local governments have no constitutional authority but operate more autonomously than those in France or Italy. In Japan the central ministries have broad authority to interpret the law in the absence of court decisions, and they guard their authority jealously. Each time a local government has attempted to enact an innovative policy, the concerned ministry has argued that the ordinance conflicts with the law and is therefore illegal. This pattern has been particularly evident when the local ordinance involves use of the police power. In fact, local police powers have been challenged, though unsuccessfully, on constitutional grounds.[2]

The dominant interpretation has come to allow ordinances in areas not covered by the law and in areas covered by the law in two special cases: when the ordinance regulates the same activity as the law but for different purposes, or when the ordinance regulates different activities for similar purposes (Narita, 1964). Again, however, the ministries have the authority to interpret the law unless they are taken to court, so the official interpretation tends to be narrow. Laws always preempt ordinances unless otherwise stated in the law. This situation does not differ greatly from that in other unitary countries. In federal states, the courts play a bigger role and central ministries a lesser one.[3]

A major issue in Japan concerning the distribution of authority has been assigned functions, which serve as mechanisms for implementing national programs through local governments. The central government theoretically provides finances for the implementation of these functions proportionate to the national interests involved. Assigned functions come in two forms. Entity-assigned functions *(dantai i'nin jimu)* are assigned to the local government as a whole. In practice, these functions are more delegated than assigned and they are not particularly controversial.

The controversy focuses on agency-assigned functions *(kikan i'nin jimu)* in which a national function is assigned to the local chief executive.[4] In performing these functions, the elected mayor or governor technically becomes an agent of the central government subject to the supervision of the assigning ministry. The local assembly has no authority over these functions. The number of agency-assigned functions has been rising rapidly since the early 1960s (Kuroda, 1974). Estimates of the proportion of time spent on these functions run around 80 percent for prefectures and between 30 and 75 percent for cities (Yamauchi, 1972). These percentages sound high, but Japan does not seem particularly out of line with other unitary states. In Sweden 60 to 80 percent of local budgets are spent on state activities (Hansen, 1981: 167). In the Federal Republic of Germany two-thirds of all municipal activities are prescribed by federal or *Land* legislation and these activities account for over 90 percent of local current accounts (Schafer, 1981: 230). Moreover, the problem of assigned functions is not limited to unitary states. In the United States, "mandating" has become an issue in intergovernmental relations (Neiman and Lovell, 1981).

The distribution of authority in Japan is similar to that of other unitary states. If anything, Japanese local governments have somewhat more authority than local governments in a typical unitary state.

Intergovernmental Finance

The sources of local revenue are reported in table 2. Local taxes account for less than a third of local revenues, a fact celebrated in the phrase, "one-third autonomy" *(san-wari jichi)*. The transfer tax *(jōyozei)* is, in principle, a local tax collected by the central government and returned to the local government in which the tax was collected. The local allocation tax *(kōfuzei)* is a form of general revenue sharing. The MOHA calculates the demand for a long list of services that local governments provide, subtracts the actual revenues of the local government, and supplies the difference up to a total representing a fixed percentage of three national taxes. These three sources are considered general revenues, or revenues with no strings attached. The remaining sources come with specified purposes for which the money must be spent.

Grants are given for purposes defined by the central government. Local borrowing is subject to MOHA approval, and for prefectures approval is based on a project-by-project review. The requirement that prefectures get MOHA approval for borrowing was a temporary provision of the local finance law that has become permanent (Takehara, 1976). Other revenues consist primarily of service fees such as for utilities, but also include revenues from public property and public enterprises. Some revenues from public enterprises, gambling enterprises, for example, go directly into the general fund and are included in general revenues.

TABLE 2
The Structure of Local Government Revenues, 1975
(in $ millions)

	Amount	*Proportion (%)*
General revenues		
Local taxes	$40,774.0	31.3
Transfer tax	1,241.0	1.0
Allocation tax	22,355.5	17.2
Total	64,320.0	49.4
Grants	29,411.5	27.6
Borrowing	15,899.5	12.12
Other	20,541.0	15.8

Source: MOHA, *Chihō Zaisei Hakusho, 1977 (Local Finance White Paper, 1977)*, p. 9.

Note: Figures are calculated at 200 yen to the dollar.

In comparative terms, Japan's "one-third autonomy" looks pretty good. As shown in table 3, local governments in many industrial democracies collect less than one-fifth of total government revenues. Japan is near the median in this set of nine countries, and the only unitary state in which local governments have a larger share of revenues is Sweden.[5]

More important than the sources of revenue is the flexibility of revenue sources. Can a local government raise more revenues when necessary? We can distinguish two types of flexibility. First, a local government needs short-run flexibility for sound financial management. One must be able to raise revenues in response to changes in the environment. Second, local politicians would like the financial autonomy to raise revenues over the long run to pay for large projects or for a significantly higher level of services. Japanese local governments have plenty of short-run but very little long-run flexibility.

The obvious place to look for financial flexibility is local taxes, or "independent revenues" (jishu zaigen). In Japan, however, the taxes a local government may impose are determined by law and the rates of local taxes may vary only within a limited range. While regulation of local taxes is common in unitary states, the Japanese system seems particularly restrictive.

For major local taxes, the Ministry of Home Affairs sets a standard

TABLE 3
The Distribution of Revenues in Nine
Industrialized Democracies, 1980

	Percent Revenues Subnational
Canada	50.4
United States	40.2
Sweden	37.0
Japan	32.7
Australia	18.6
France	12.3
United Kingdom	11.7
Italy	4.8
The Netherlands	2.9

Source: Yearbook of National Account Statistics, 1981, vol. 1, pt. 1, Individual County Data (N.Y.: United Nations, 1981).

Notes: Calculations are based on the "taxes, fees and contributions" with "social security funds" excluded.

and a maximum tax rate. Formally, local governments are free to raise rates up to the maximum, subject only a requirement that they inform MOHA. In practice, the standard rates are followed except in times of financial stress like the recession following the 1973–1974 oil shock. During that period all but three prefectures raised corporate taxes to the maximum rate, typically for a period of five years. Personal taxes were not raised for fear of the electoral consequences. The time limit set on the raised rate clearly indicated the local government's intention to use the increased revenues for short-term purposes. Theoretically, it could keep reenacting the raised rate every five years or so, but to do so might prove politically unpopular and would reduce the prefecture's financial flexibility.

Local governments can, with the approval of the MOHA, levy new taxes not listed in the law. However, approval is forthcoming only when a special need can be demonstrated. For prefectures, the only new tax approved (except for the special case of Okinawa) has been a tax on nuclear fuel for those prefectures with nuclear power plants (*Nihon Keizai Shinbun,* June 13, 1978). New taxes have not be used for long-run purposes.

The local tax system is well designed for short-term flexibility and sound financial management. Local taxes provide a flexibile tool for longer-range policy, but only by lowering, not raising taxes. Local governments have a great deal of discretion for lowering taxes for specific purposes. This discretion is most useful in promoting local businesses and attracting new industry. The structure of local taxes makes "conservative" policies easy, but makes "progressive" policies, like bigger welfare programs and increased services, difficult.

Another strategy for raising revenues is to maximize central grants. Two factors limit the usefulness of this strategy. First, the Japanese grant system is highly systematized and coordinated. Although Japanese complain about the bewildering maze of central grants, compared to the United States the system is simple. As is not true of the United States, there is little room for creative grantsmanship and very few loopholes.[6] The total to be gained from a grant maximization strategy is not large. Second, trying to get more grants forces the local government to accede to the priorities of the central ministries. A local government can participate selectively in grant programs without abandoning its own priorities, but the only way to receive more grants is to do what the ministries want done.

A third strategy for increasing local revenues is through borrowing. As in most unitary states, local borrowing is regulated. The norm is to regulate only the total volume of local borrowing. Britain, for example, uses a waiting-list system (Ashford, 1978). Japanese prefectures, however, must get project-by-project approval. This requirement is based on a "temporary" provision of the local finance law, but there is no reason to expect a change in the foreseeable future.

The Ministry of Home Affairs reviews requests for loans to check for extravagance and often cuts the amount requested. Its main concern, however, is to prevent "irresponsible" borrowing and to promote sound financial management. For example, a local government whose tax rates are below the standard rate cannot borrow money to construct public facilities. If, over the last three years, borrowing has accounted for 20 percent of a local government's general revenues, borrowing for unsubsidized projects, social welfare facilities, and other designated expenditures will be restricted. If this ratio reaches 30 percent, borrowing is permitted only for disaster reconstruction and specified special projects (Takehara, 1976). The ultimate means of enforcing financial responsibility is to designate a local government a "financial reconstruction body" *(saiken dantai)*. Those governments so designated must develop a plan for financial reconstruction and have the plan approved by MOHA. In return, the central government provides funds to help pay the interest on the necessary loans. One hundred local governments were designated financial reconstruction bodies in 1965, but by 1975 the number had fallen to nine (Ministry of Home Affairs, 1977: 82–83).

Local governments cannot rely on borrowing to increase long-run revenues, and increased borrowing brings increased central regulation. The loan-approval system also reinforces other aspects of central control, creating an incentive to maintain the standard tax rates, for example. The system adds an incentive to grant programs, since loans for subsidized programs are always approved. To deny approval would put MOHA into direct conflict with other ministries and, from the ministry's viewpoint, grant programs are financially sound because the local government's share is smaller. The loan approval system gives the ministry ample means to enforce its definition of responsible borrowing upon local governments.

There is one way a local government can fund a major program: by setting up a formally private corporation. In this way, a local government can borrow and spend money without any restrictions from the MOHA, or from the local assembly for that matter. Similar corporations are used for similar purposes in France (Webman, 1977: 44). Such borrowing is called "black market borrowing" *(yami sai)* (MOHA, Secretariat, 1974). There are limits to this "loophole," however. First, the finances of such a corporation depend upon its ability to attract private investment. Thus, only financially sound projects can be financed in this way. Second, such semiprivate corporations pose many problems of control and coordination. Finally, unsuccessful projects create a financial burden as surely as borrowing through normal channels and local officials are aware of cases of financial trouble brought on by the overuse of such corporations (Fukumaru, 1971).

Miscellaneous revenues provide municipalities with a limited but important means of increasing revenues. Gambling enterprises such as race tracks are particularly popular. This strategy is less useful for prefectures or larger municipalities. The best long-run strategy for increasing revenues is to increase the tax base, and the allocation tax reduces the potential of this strategy. The allocation tax formula subtracts revenues from needs and makes up 80 percent of the difference. Growth in local tax revenues produces a drop in the allocation tax. If the substitution ratio were 100 percent, the net gain from increasing the tax base would be zero. As it is, local governments keep only 20 percent of an increase in local tax revenues.

The Japanese intergovernmental finance system is oriented toward fiscal responsibility. Local governments are prevented from taxing much more heavily than the average or from going too deeply in debt. The Ministry of Home Affairs strictly enforces fiscal responsibility, but there has been little local resistance to this central control. Most local governments accept the ministry's definition of sound financial management. The Minobe administration in Tokyo was, however, an exception. Governor Minobe declared a "financial war" on the central government, trying to break MOHA's hold on local finances. One battle in this unsuccessful war was a suit alleging that the loan approval system is unconstitutional. An *Asahi Shinbun* survey of prefectures and designated cities found little support for abolishing the system outside of Tokyo (October 6, 1977). Moreover, a survey conducted by the National Governors' Conference found only six prefectures registering complaints about the restriction of borrowing based on the financial situation of the prefecture (MOHA unpublished materials). Fiscal orthodoxy weighs heavily only on the most active progressive administrations. In the end, the Minobe administration dropped the suit.

One aspect of fiscal responsibility is a significant bias toward capital expenditures and against consumption expenditures—that is, in favor of economic development policies and against welfare policies. Remember also that the only way around MOHA's fiscal controls is a semipublic corporation, and that mechanism can be used for economic growth policies but not welfare policies. The basic complaint Japanese leftists have with the system is that local governments cannot expand their welfare programs into showcases for what a progressive government would do at the national level if they were in control. Progressives want the long-term financial flexibility the system does not provide.

In comparative terms, I would guess that Japanese local governments have less long-run financial flexibility than most. If one posits a solid local majority in favor of increased services, a local government in Japan would have more trouble raising the funds to implement the local mandate than would an American, British, German, or even a French local government.[7] On the other hand, the Japanese system is well designed to enforce fiscal responsibility. The probability of a local government going bankrupt or getting itself in severe financial difficulties is probably less than in North America or Western Europe. France is a possible exception because there the prefect enforces fiscal responsibility. Japan is like France in the sense that the central government takes responsibility for enforcing proper financial practices on local governments. In other countries this responsibility lies more with the local electorate and the banking system. The difference between France and Japan is that in France this central control is exercised through the prefectoral *tutelle,* while in Japan it is exercised through impersonal rules and regulations.

Links Between Central and Local Bureaucracies

Bureaucracies are organized according to function. Each unit is responsible for some particular function like housing or education. Local governments are organized by area. Each unit is responsible for all functions within specific geographic boundaries. Functional lines of authority are identified with expertise, while areal lines of authority are identified with coordination. One may also identify functional authority with centralization and areal authority with local autonomy (Fesler, 1965). In any case, this distinction is a key to comparing the administrative systems of different countries. The basic question is whether local bureaucrats are primarily responsive to their prefectural or municipal superiors or to their functional superiors in the central ministries.

We can begin with the traditional distinction between generalist and specialist bureaucrats. France tends to emphasize expertise, while Britain tends to trust the generalist. Japan is more like Britain in this respect. Central officials do stay in a single ministry for most of their careers, but move around within it. Local bureaucrats move around within the whole local government, not just a single department. The generalist character of local officials can make them more susceptible to ministerially defined expertise. When local officials move into areas in which they have no experience, central regulations and standards are their only guidelines. On the other hand, local officials do not develop functional loyalties that can overcome the basic areal loyalty to the prefecture or municipality. Overall, the system favors areal lines of authority.

Britain and France also differ in the location of expertise. "The British higher civil service not only resists acquiring the planning and technical expertise of the French administrator, but its members probably could not perform most of the tasks of local government" (Ashford, 1982: 9). In Britain, the field offices depend on the local government's expertise. British field officers simply check to see if central standards have been met (Webman, 1977). French municipalities have very little technical expertise and even large cities depend on ministerial field offices. Japan is somewhere between Britain and France in this respect.

Japanese bureaucrats in the central administration are generalists like the British, but unlike the British they know how local governments operate and could perform the functions of local government if required. Most line ministry officials have worked in prefectural governments. Local experience is a standard part of the apprenticeship in many ministries, especially Home Affairs and Construction. Japanese ministries are repositories of expertise, as in France, but as is not true in France, field officers are relatively unimportant. Japanese field officers operate more like the British, checking standards, than the French, actively participating in local policymaking. As in Britain, Japanese local governments have their own experts, but the distribution of expertise is more balanced than in either Britain or France. Imbalances do occur, of course. In particular, new policy areas tend to be dominated by the ministries until local governments learn the ropes.

In France central expertise is communicated to local governments through field offices. In Britain this task is performed by functionally organized professional associations. Similar associations exist in Japan but play a lesser role. A major means of transferring expertise is to lend central personnel to local governments. After the apprenticeship period when young central officials work in the prefectures to learn the ropes, central officials may become prefectural bureau chiefs or department heads. These transfers are particularly common in areas where central expertise is needed. Construction is the most obvious example, but in Japan financial management is also included in this category.

In 1975 thirty of the forty-seven prefectural finance division chiefs were MOHA officials; fifteen prefectural general affairs departments were headed by MOHA officials. A total of forty prefectures had a MOHA official in a pivotal position in their budgeting process (Chihō Zaimu Kyōkai, 1975). These figures would seem to indicate extreme central control, but one must remember that these central officials come to the prefecture at the request of the governor. Prefectures invite central officials for their expertise and because their connections make them more effective advocates for the prefecture (Park, 1978). Even Governor Ninagawa of Kyoto, a progressive known for his high-handed control of personnel policies, made good use of MOHA officials. The only prefecture that does not make extensive use of central officials is Tokyo, presumably because it has sufficient access to expertise without resort to the central government.

I should also note that central officials also go to a prefecture later in their careers, and at higher levels, especially as vice-governors, and use these positions as stepping stones into prefectural politics. As of 1984, ten of the forty-seven governors were ex-MOHA bureaucrats who had served as vice-governor. The trend toward MOHA governors that roused political commentators in the 1970s seems to have tailed off somewhat (Kaminogō, 1978).

Although Japanese officials and scholars complain about functional fragmentation *(keiretsuka),* in a comparative context, the areal lines of authority are relatively strong. Japan is certainly no more subject to the evils of fragmentation than are other industrial democracies.

Links Between Central and Local Politics

The literature on intergovernmental politics is sparse. If however, we take American machine politics, exemplified by Mayor Daley's Chicago as one pole and the nationalized local politics of Britain as the other, we can begin to put Japan into perspective.

Local and intergovernmental politics takes two forms, distributive and partisan. In distributive politics, vertical linkages are based on the exchange of benefits. The local government is a unitary actor, a supplicant to the national government. Partisan differences are put aside so that the local government can present a united front. Partisan politics, on the other hand, divides local governments on the issues. Partisanship on local issues does occur, but division on national issues is more common. The nationalization of local politics has gone further in Britain than in other democracies (R. W. Johnson, 1972; Butler and Stokes, 1971; Cain et al., 1984).

The distinction between distributive and partisan politics is analogous to the administrative distinction between area and function. Just as local administrators must decide whether to respond primarily to areal or to functional lines of authority, politicians must decide whether primarily to represent their constituencies or their party. Distributive politics is areal in the sense that the local government is the unit represented. Partisan politics is functional in the sense that the issues are normally divided into the same functional areas that organize bureaucracies: housing, education, and so on.

Japan does not have nationalized electoral politics like Britain. There have been no studies of the uniformity of the swing in Japanese elections, so no direct comparisons can be made. Nevertheless, the style of Japanese elections makes nationalized electoral results unlikely. Party organization is weak, especially at the local level (Foster, 1982). The basic electoral organization is the *kōenkai,* or candidate support organizations, not the party organization (Curtis, 1971). Local elections are dominated by independents who adopt a party label only when it seems advantageous (Amakawa, 1974; Yanagihashi, 1981). Leftist parties do not do as well in local as in national elections. The smaller the electoral district, the less partisan the election. In local elections distributive politics is more important than partisan politics. Each area prefers a representative who can deliver a bigger share of the benefits being distributed to one who represents them on the issues of the day.

Local politics is often more concerned with who than what. Great battles are fought over who shall be chairman of the assembly, but there are no policy differences among the candidates. Policy is left up to the mayor or governor. Elections for chief executives are more politicized, but the ideal mayor or governor is someone above politics, someone more concerned with technically correct policies than politically popular ones. In a 1946 poll 75 percent preferred a governor who was a "civilian" over party politicians or bureaucrats (Steiner, 1965: 445n). In a more recent poll 44 percent preferred capable administrators to a little over 30 percent favoring politicians (Toki, 1983: 33). Local chief executives, especially incumbents, are often elected without opposition and are supported by all parties.

Japanese local politics has a strong tendency toward nonpartisanship. In assembly elections, partisanship is seen as getting in the way of distributive politics. In mayoral or gubernatorial elections, candidates strive to appear above politics, as administrators, not politicians. This style of local politics would seem to preclude British-style nationalized politics but appears to be fertile ground for local political machines on the Chicago model.

Japan does have local political bosses called *yūryokusha* (Curtis, 1971), but they do not fit the Daley mold. Instead of the mayor being the boss of the machine with congressmen as followers, as in the United States, the Diet member is the leader and local bosses are lieutenants. Although it is not well documented, the conventional wisdom in Japanese politics is that Diet members lead coalitions of local politicians. In prefectural and city assemblies, the conservatives are organized into factions based on their connections to particular members of the Diet (Tokyo University Social Science Research Group, 1965; Asahi Shinbun, Utsunomiya Branch, 1982). Perhaps the best evidence of the effectiveness of these vertical linkages among politicians was the degree to which the voting in the LDP's first presidential primary mirrored the factional alignment at the national level (Tsurutani, 1980; Reed, 1984). The preferences of Dietmen determined the votes of rank-and-file voters through a vertical factional structure.

Japan is more like the United States than Britain in that intergovernmental politics is based primarily on distributive politics. Unlike the situation in the United States, however, intergovernmental alliances in Japan are led by national, not local, politicians. However, it is important to remember than this comparison between Japan and the United States rests on very little evidence. The U.S. data consist of several case studies of city machines. We have no way of knowing how typical these cases are. Some cases of vertical factions led by national politicians have been noted in the American South (Key, 1949). The Japanese data are based primarily on journalistic usage, naming local factions on the basis of the Dietman they presumably support. How strong is the Dietman's leadership? Are there cases of factions led by local politicians? Intergovernmental politics is an unexplored area in both countries.

Perhaps the most telling indication of the weakness of Japanese parties is the limited usefulness of a party nomination. A nomination does help, but it is not necessary. Conservative candidates often run first as independents to prove their vote-getting ability. In every election several of these "independents" are elected and join the party after the fact. The British system of electoral apprenticeship requires candidates to run in a hopeless district to show the party flag. If they do well, they are rewarded with a chance to run in a winnable district. In

Britain one gets ahead by serving the party. In Japan, as in the United States and France, one is more likely to win by building up a local electoral base. It should not be surprising to find that in the latter countries national politicians spend more time and effort on policies designed to help their constituents.

Finally, we should ask about the degree to which national parties have penetrated local politics. Surprisingly, nonpartisan local government has persisted in Britain. In 1973 only two-thirds of the councils in England and Wales were under party control (Ashford, 1982: 157). Nevertheless, local issues are subordinated to national ones and local party policy is largely a reflection of the national platform (Peterson and Kantor, 1977). In France, by contrast, the local electoral system is based on the assumption that the mayor will assemble a team from several parties. In Webman's words, "A skilled local politician can make and dissolve local coalitions or create a personal image quite distinct from any partisan affiliations he might have" (1977: 106). Once a team is assembled, the parties close ranks to represent the municipality as a whole in dealing with the central government. Only in big cities does party politics penetrate to the local level (Kesselman, 1967; Machin, 1981).

Japan falls somewhere in between France and Britain here, but is probably somewhat closer to France. Most local elections are won by candidates running as independents. The parties' penetration of local government has fluctuated over the postwar period (Amakawa, 1974). All-party coalitions supporting a particular mayor or governor typically account for 10–20 percent of the prefectural administrations. Most local elections are won by conservatives, whether running as independents or under the LDP banner. Although conservatives try to maintain an image of being above politics and welcome the cooperation of the center parties, their administrations are partisan in the sense that they exclude the left-wing parties. Progressives do win mayoral and gubernatorial elections, but about half of the governors elected with the support of progressive parties move to the center and become essentially all-party coalitions. The dominant picture is, like that of France, one of nonpartisan local government. This picture is broken by partisan electoral contests and, less frequently, by partisan administrations. And, more like Britain, partisan local elections are often fought over issues of national concern having major implications for national policy.

Overall, Japanese local politics seems normal, while Britain is the exception. Again, however, we must remember that these comparisons are based on minimal information. If we had more comparative information, we could do more than simply contrast Britain with the other democracies and some distinctive features of Japanese local politics would probably become manifest.

Political versus Bureaucratic Channels

Tarrow (1977) contrasts the bureaucratic system in France with the Italian system, which is more political. In Italy partisan, factional, and personal connections at the center make a significant difference in the distribution of central grants and favors. In France, however, the mayor is well advised to ignore political channels and concentrate on filling out the forms properly. Communist mayors got maybe even more than their share of central grants from the Gaullist regime because they used the bureaucratic mechanisms of the grant process more actively and more skillfully (see also Webman, 1977: 46ff.; Milch, 1978: 487ff.; Ashford, 1982: 222ff.). Japan is more like France than Italy. Although exceptions can be found, the basic distributional system is bureaucratic. Many will find this conclusion hard to believe. The Japanese press and many academics criticize the government for being too political. However, all my findings point to a bureaucratic distribution of grants and favors in Japan. Because this finding contradicts the conventional wisdom, I looked for test cases in which politics should have made a difference.

In 1976 Settsu City sued the central government for grant money owed them (Inoue, 1971). At issue was the problem of "overburdening" *(chōka futan)*. In order to avoid an open-ended commitment, the central grant programs pay a fixed percentage of a standard cost, not the actual cost. When inflation or rising service levels increase the actual cost, but the central government does not increase the standard cost, local government claim they are being "overburdened," that the central government has failed to live up to its legal commitments. Settsu City sued to make the bureaucracy live up to the promises made by the Diet.[8] Some within the city government predicted financial retaliation, but the immediate results were positive as the Ministry of Health and Welfare reformed some of the practices complained about in the suit in order to strengthen its legal case. The central government won the legal battle, but the suit stimulated reforms and Settsu City suffered no ill effects from the confrontation (Inoue, 1971).

A second case involved the designation of new industrial towns. I was alerted to this case by claims in the literature that this was a case of politics overruling bureaucratic rationality (Aqua, 1980; Matsubara,

1968; Ide, 1972). Political lobbying by local governments did have one major effect on the program: the number of designations had to be increased to meet demand. This seems to have been a common fate among similar programs aimed at concentrating central funds into "development poles" in Britain, France, and Italy (Hayward and Watson, 1975). However, amid all this hectic lobbying the progressive governor of Oita refused to go to Tokyo to lobby for his prefecture's case.[9] He also refused to go to the airport to greet a high central official, in violation of common practice. While these political sins embarrassed the prefectural government, Oita still received its designation as a new industrial town. Examination of the other nominations and designations reveals no obvious pattern of discrimination.

I found only one clear case of the central government using its financial clout and that involved approval for local borrowing. In 1969 the Minobe administration ignored central administrative guidance and gave its employees their raises one month before central officials received theirs (*Asahi Shinbun*, December 1969–January 1970). The result was a drastic cut in the amount of loans approved for Tokyo. The cost of the early raises was estimated at 3.9 billion yen and Minobe's loan requests were cut by approximately 10.2 billion yen. The Home Affairs Ministry was clearly trying to discipline the Minobe administration.

Two comments made during this episode in Minobe's "financial war" with the central government indicate that the cuts were the exception that proved the rule. A MOHA official stated that some in the ministry wanted to cut more, but "had to approve those projects for which the state has some responsibility" (*Asahi Shinbun*, May 4, 1970). Discretion was limited to unsubsidized projects. To cut subsidized projects would undercut the efforts of other ministries. The second comment came from a Tokyo official who noted that they had never before had any project rejected completely (*Asahi Shinbun*, May 5, 1970). The norm is cost-cutting, not project evaluation.[10]

One persuasive argument for the effectiveness of politics in central grant distribution and one of the most visible aspects of Japanese intergovernmental relations is the flood of local groups petitioning the central government to fund their pet projects. During the central government's budgeting process, central officials are kept busy meeting delegations, often "introduced" by a Diet member and usually led by a local politician. If politics makes no difference, what are all these people doing?

First, there are cases in which failure to petition vigorously could result in rejection of a grant proposal. When demand so exceeds supply that objective factors fail to narrow choices sufficiently and central officials are looking for places to cut, petitioning demonstrates "sincerity." Petitioning may have an effect in other cases as well, enough to sustain a belief in the practice, but the effect is to supplement, not supplant, the bureaucratic distribution process. Moreover, petitioning goes on even when the danger of a project getting cut is all but academic.

The fact is that each of the participants in this hectic process has something to gain even if the final results are affected only slightly or not at all. The actors that benefit most from petitioning are local politicians and Diet members. Petitioning provides politicians with a chance to demonstrate their support for popular projects and interest group demands, even if the support is largely symbolic. Their participation also sets up a claim to the political credit for any project that gets funded, even if intervention had actually been irrelevant.

Administrators also benefit from the process. If there is any possibility of local conflict over a project, organizing a petition group can give proponents the jump on potential opponents.[11] Petitioning also gets all the important local actors on bandwagon, resolving or suppressing objections before implementation begins. Central administrators can feel confident that a petitioned-for project will not suffer unnecessary delays in implementation. For central officials, the petition process generates an enormous amount of information about both objective local needs and subjective local priorities. Central officials do not enjoy the petitioning, but they do benefit by it. Thus, petitioning continues even though it has little or no effect on the distribution of central monies.

In Japan, as in France, bureaucratic channels to the central government are more important than political ones. Political connections do not significantly affect the overall pattern of distribution of favors.

The National Arena

When a law affecting local governments is being considered by the central government, organizations of local governments become interest groups. Such organizations can be very powerful in this role, as in the United States (Beer, 1976; Haider, 1974), Britain (Gyford and James, 1983), and France (Kesselman, 1967). Japanese organizations of local governments do play this interest group role, but are not particularly influential in it.

Japanese local officials are organized into six national bodies, one each for governors, prefectural assembly chairmen, city mayors, city assembly chairmen, town and village mayors, and town and village assembly chairmen. Local officials are also organized along functional lines. However, only the National Governors' Conference *(Zenkoku Chijikai)* and the National Conference of City Mayors *(Zenkoku Shichōkai)* have much influence. The six national organizations of local officials focus primarily on financial matters. Like other Japanese organizations, they tend to operate by consensus, and the only issues on which all local governments can agree are financial ones. Once a consensus is reached, these organizations can create substantial pressure on the central government, but they seldom play the kind of role in developing policy and reviewing the administrative details of proposed laws that similar organizations play in Britain or France.

In making demands on the central government, the organizations of local officials are normally allied with MOHA, because it serves as the spokesman for local financial interests within the central government. They seldom go beyond MOHA policy and often appear dependent on the ministry. There are exceptions, however.

The National Governors' Conference has actively and successfully promoted policies to aid depopulating areas and rapidly urbanizing areas, in fighting against financial "overburdening," and in getting a grant program for high school construction enacted. In 1977 and 1978 it tried to organize a campaign to force the government to change local tax laws by simultaneously enacting identical ordinances in all prefectures *(Asahi Shinbun,* December 13, 1977; *Nihon Keizai Shinbun,* January 29, 1978). The effort was the boldest ever undertaken by the organization, but it failed. Nevertheless, the National Governors' Conference did take an active policymaking role in the 1970s.

Two partial organizations of local officials, the National Conference of Progressive Governors *(Zenkoku Kakushin Chijikai)* and the National Conference of Progressive City Mayors *(Zenkoku Kakushin Shichōkai)* take more active positions on more issues, but they have little direct influence. Any influence they have operates through the mass media or by prodding the full conference into action. Central officials grant little legitimacy to partial organizations. They like to wait until a consensus has been reached among all local governments before deciding their response. These two progressive organizations have, however, helped to activate the full conferences and have provided support to active local governments.

National organizations of local officials in Japan are important interest groups, but do not have the influence attributed to such organizations in Europe. The most powerful representative of local governments in the national arena is the Ministry of Home Affairs, and that representation is limited primarily to financial matters. The ministry is responsible for the financial health of local governments. This means exercising fiscal control over local governments but also means preventing other ministries from assigning functions to local governments without also providing financing. The MOHA is effective in demanding that adequate financial provision be made for assigned functions and in grant programs, but on other issues it is just another ministry. Its commitment is to efficient local government; there is no commitment to local autonomy or local democracy.

Summary

Japanese prefectures are similar to subnational governments in other industrial democracies, being somewhat smaller than the norm geographically but near the norm in population. Japan is a unitary state, so local governments have less authority than in federal states. Compared to other unitary states, however, Japanese local governments have a somewhat larger grant of authority than is the norm. Japanese local governments have a stronger financial base than those in most unitary states but have less long-run financial flexibility. Japan is like France in that the central government takes responsibility for local finances.

The Japanese system of intergovernmental administration is much like that of other unitary states. The distribution of expertise is more balanced than in Britain, where local officials have more specialized knowledge and knowhow than central authorities, or France, where such knowledge is concentrated at the center. Japan is somewhere between these extremes. Local governments are not immune from the evils of functional fragmentation but do seem better able to respond to areal lines of authority than do most local governments in other countries.

In intergovernmental politics, Britain, with its nationalized politics, is the exception and Japan is like the other industrial democracies, which have relatively nonpartisan local politics. Japanese electoral machines tend to be led by Diet members, as does not occur in the United States where mayors are more common, but the political machines seem similar. Despite the presence of machines, Japan is more like France than Italy in the distribution of central grants: bureaucratic channels are more important than political ones. Politicians take credit for local pork-barrel projects, but have relatively little influence over them.

Finally, Japanese local governments are relatively weak in the national arena. Organizations of local government officials are not particularly powerful and local governments must depend on the MOHA to represent their interests in national policymaking.

The Japanese intergovernmental system is typical of those of most unitary states. Taking all the above characteristics together, intergovernmental relations in Japan would look like France in some respects, Britain in others, and Germany in others. Statistically, Japan could be somewhere in the middle of Europe.

3

The Evolution of
Japanese Local Government

*F*ROM THE Meiji Restoration of 1868 to the end
of World War II, local government in Japan was conceived of primarily
as a means of unifying the nation, of undermining localism and pene-
trating society with public administration (Steiner, 1965: chs. 2–6).
Though some important crosscurrents exist in prewar thinking about
local government, the dominant themes come from French (Napole-
onic) and Prussian thought. Local government was a matter of administration, to be insulated from politics. The organization of local government was prefectural on the French model with an official of the Home
Ministry appointed governor of each prefecture. Authority was concentrated in the offices of local chief executives, leaving local assemblies
almost functionless.

After World War II the U.S. occupation attempted to decentralize
Japanese government based on the idea that local autonomy serves as a
check on tyranny and would thus prevent a recurrence of Japanese
militarism. The Home Ministry (*Naimushō*, literally, Ministry of Internal Affairs) was abolished and replaced by a much more limited Local
Autonomy Board, which eventually evolved into the present Ministry
of Home Affairs (*Jichishō*, literally Ministry of Local Autonomy). Prefectural governors were to be elected instead of being appointed officials of the Home Ministry. Direct elections replaced indirect at the
municipal level. At both the prefectural and the municipal levels, the
authority of the chief executive was reduced and that of the local assemblies increased. Referendum, recall, and initiative were instituted to
further democratize local government. Local governments were given
new and expanded authority and responsibilities, most particularly for

44

police and compulsory education, the traditional functions of local governments in the United States.

After the war Japan's economy was in a shambles. Economic problems, combined with occupation-inspired decentralization, caused severe financial problems for most local governments. Mayors were put in the impossible position of having to build many new schools and to create a police force with no money to spare. When occupation controls were loosened, the conservatives in power at the center began the "reverse course," a policy of reversing many of the occupation reforms. Police forces and education were recentralized, though not to prewar levels. Because of the local financial problems, resistance to these recentralizing policies came not from local governments but from opposition parties at the national level.

With the consolidation of conservative power in the Liberal Democratic party (LDP) and the economic growth policies that came soon thereafter, virtually all local governments followed the central lead in promoting industrialization. Some mayors even switched from progressive parties to the LDP in order to improve their chances of obtaining public works projects that might attract new industry to their areas. During this period there was an increase in the level of formal centralization effected through increasing the number of "agency-assigned functions" (Kuroda, 1975). Local governments put up little resistance to this trend, and indeed seldom pursued policies that brought them into conflict with the central government.

The 1950s and 1960s were characterized by a widespread consensus that industrial development should be the goal of both central and local policies, and this consensus explains the relative lack of resistance to centralization and innovative local programs. Local opposition parties also supported development policies, on the assumption that industry would mean unionization and urbanization, both of which would eventually bring more progressive votes. Because all parties essentially agreed on the type of local policies that should be followed, there was no occasion for either central control or local resistance.

Only one prefecture took exception to the policies of economic growth through big business: Kyoto under the Ninagawa administration (Kyoto Prefectural Administration Study Group, 1973; Shima, 1974; Krauss, 1979, 1980). Ninagawa was the only progressive governor of this period to survive more than a couple of terms. Having been head of the Small and Medium Enterprises Agency before being elected governor, he resisted the introduction of major industries and favored small businesses. The Ninagawa administration also pursued a distinctive policy in education, emphasizing equality over competition. But Kyoto stood alone, especially in its development policies.

The 1960s were years of rapid economic growth and industrialization, both of which brought new problems to Japan. Urban congestion was matched by depopulation of less-developed areas, and rapid industrialization produced severe environmental pollution. In both cases, the problems were faced first by local governments. Pollution in particular caused problems that could not be handled by the dominant public works approach to local government. Neither could the pollution problems be ignored. Dynamic and successful local responses to this problem played a key role in breaking the pattern of local passivity and produced a spurt of local innovation in the late 1960s.

The Pollution Issue

A good part of the industrialization of the 1960s took place in the construction of *kombināto,* vertically integrated industrial parks based on petrochemicals and steel, often located on the sites of old military depots or on land reclaimed from the sea. Concentration of industry in a limited area was economically rational, but made pollution more visible, particularly air pollution and land subsidence caused by excessive use of subterranean water. The initial response to air pollution was to build higher smokestacks, which reduced the concentration of pollutants by spreading it over a wider area, but this policy proved only a temporary solution. Because pollutants rapidly increased in volume, the environment eventually could not absorb them.

Land subsidence proved somewhat easier to deal with, but policymaking was hindered by a general reluctance to regulate industry in a way that might affect local or national economic growth. Active pollution control policies developed first in highly urbanized areas where the problems were most evident and where the need for more economic growth was less pressing. Tokyo, Kanagawa, Osaka, and Fukuoka prefectures all had pollution control ordinances on the books in the 1950s that focused primarily on smoke, odors, and noise, but they were not always effectively enforced (Tobiki, 1970A, 1970B; Mori, 1970; Kawai, 1973).

One major issue was the problem of whether and to what degree local ordinances could regulate industry. At this time no central law regulated pollution, and the authority of local governments to act on their own in such matters had not been well established. The academic community generally agreed that local governments could regulate industry even without a specific grant of authority, but uncertainty about the legal status of local regulation hindered diffusion to more local governments. Local governments tended to demand central action and wait for the the central government's guidance.

The central government entered the field of pollution control in 1958 with two laws regulating water pollution, continuing in 1962 with an air pollution control law, and then the Basic Pollution Law in 1967. The enactment of these laws raised the question: had the central government preempted and thus invalidated existing local ordinances? The issue was first raised in Osaka City in 1961 with respect to the city's authority to regulate the use of subterranean water. Land subsidence was increasing the probability of typhoon damage to a degree that was hard to ignore. The response of Osaka's policymakers reveals much about the tenor of the times: they studied the legal issues and wrote articles in national publications arguing that local governments do have the authority to regulate industry. However, in the end, they did not amend Osaka's ordinance to do so. Instead, the publicity given their case resulted in a revision of the national law that served their purposes sufficiently (Kawai, 1973). But pressures were building for stronger pollution control policies, and such an indirect and time-consuming approach would soon prove inadequate.

Pollution incidents were giving rise to a new political phenomenon: citizens' movements. At first, groups directly affected by pollution organized to demand compensation for damages from specific polluting factories. Their demands soon came to include pleas for governmental action. Though pressure tended to be directed toward the central government in the belief that only it had the necessary authority, demands were also made on local governments (Akimoto, 1975). Local governments had often been key agents in bringing industry to their areas and were pursuing many policies designed to support and attract industry; hence they found it difficult to avoid responsibility for pollution problems. The demands of antipollution movements were hard to ignore, for many of the participants were defending not only their economic interests but also the health of their families.

Pollution-caused diseases spread and came to be recognized for what they were. Mercury poisoning in Minamata City, Kumamoto Prefecture, and again in Niigata Prefecture, and then cadmium poisoning in Toyama Prefecture, all stirred public fears (Huddle and Reich, 1975; Smith and Smith, 1975). In Yokkaichi City, people complained of asthma caused by air pollution. In each case, the citizens' movements eventually turned in desperation to the courts, a move considered extreme in Japanese political culture (McKean, 1981: ch. 2). Pollution consciousness was growing. In 1962–63, citizens' movements entered a new stage when groups in and around Mishima City, Shizuoka Prefecture, succeeded in their attempt to stop the construction of a *kombināto* in their area (Nishioka, 1970; Nishioka and Yoshisawa, 1970; Lewis, 1974; Simcock, 1974). For the first time a city had turned down economic growth out of fear of polluting the environment. The dominant theme of postwar public policy had been rejected. The consensus on economic growth was beginning to break down.

As the environmental problem grew, progressive scholars and parties began to put the problem into a Marxist perspective (Simcock, 1974; Miyamoto, 1975). They argued that big business was, in effect, stealing the air and water from people and that the LDP was its accomplice in this crime. The argument was attractive enough to turn pollution into a highly populist issue: big business versus the man in the street. From the latter half of the 1960s, opposition parties began to win more mayoral and gubernatorial elections on platforms featuring pollution control. Citizens' movements often supported progressive candidates for mayor or governor, though they avoided close ties with political parties. Progressive local executives began pursuing more active pollution control policies, even in the face of central government opposition.

The first breakthrough occurred when Yokohama, under the leadership of Asukata Ichio, a socialist mayor, forced industry moving to the city to sign pollution control agreements as part of their land sale contracts (Narumi, 1970). Soon thereafter Asukata and the progressive governor of Tokyo, Minobe Ryōkichi, extended this practice to existing factories. The idea of pollution control agreements began to diffuse rapidly. An agreement negotiated directly with particular factories represented a way around legal problems. Though the Ministry of International Trade and Industry (MITI) protested, arguing that such agreements had no legal force, it could do little because agreements are not ordinances; they could not be illegal because they are "extralegal" and "private" agreements. The legal status of such agreements is still a matter for debate, but their effectiveness has been proven (Harada, 1970A). However, such pollution control agreements were effective in regulating only a few large firms. There is a limit to the number of agreements that a local government can negotiate. The need for comprehensive and legally enforceable regulations remained.

As the central government undertook to control pollution, the issue came to focus on coverage. The central laws took a "designation ap-

proach," regulation becoming effective only in areas specifically designated by the central ministries. While it was generally agreed that local
governments could regulate factories in undesignated areas, could they
regulate factories in designated areas too small to be covered by law and
impose stricter regulations than the law? These questions were answered
firmly in the negative by the central ministries (Kawai, 1973).

Local governments had been demanding central action and welcomed the new laws for the clear authority they offered. However, as
the time for implementation of the Air Pollution Law approached,
Tokyo and Osaka officials realized that under the dominant legal interpretation their existing antipollution ordinances would become void in
the designated areas. Some smaller factories would be freed from regulation because the new law only applied to larger plants. Becoming a
designated area would actually result in weakened regulation. When
Tokyo and Osaka protested, it proved politically difficult to backtrack
on pollution control. The central government amended the law even
before it went into effect.

Kanagawa Prefecture took the next step by amending its ordinance
to include a permit system for new polluting facilities (Kawai, 1973).
The law provided for a weaker, after-the-fact approval system. The
Kanagawa ordinance thus enforced a stricter standard and challenged
the central government's interpretation of the limits of local authority.
Nevertheless, the issue was avoided until Tokyo again took the lead
with its 1969 ordinance. This ordinance challenged the law in several
ways and became the object of much comment (Noma, 1970; Kawakami, 1970; Harada, 1970B).

One controversial provision gave the governor the authority to issue recomendations *(kankoku)* and requests *(yōsei)* to polluting factories.
These measures extended the governor's activities beyond his legal authority, but since they were not legal orders and entailed no sanctions
for noncompliance they are similar to pollution control agreements in
their "extralegal" character. How could anyone argue that a governor
should not be able to make requests of private industry? On the other
hand, why include provisions for "informal" requests in an ordinance if
they were actually meant to be informal? The legal status of requests
and recommendations remains unsettled but, like pollution control
agreements, they have proven effective (Tomisawa, 1970).

While the enactment of this Tokyo ordinance created a great deal of
controversy and did indeed represent a giant step forward in symbolic
terms, in terms of effective authoritative regulation the ordinance was
no more than an incremental addition to the Kanagawa ordinance,

which itself was only one step ahead of the law. In fact, most of the changes in the Tokyo ordinance made the ordinance more, not less, compatible with the legal framework. Neither did Tokyo ignore the ministries' legalistic arguments. A provision that would have allowed the governor to cut off the electricity and water of chronic polluters was removed from an early draft because the Ministry of International Trade and Industry argued that such a provision would overstep local authority (Yasue, 1975).

In less metropolitan areas of the country, the legal limitations on ordinances were taken still more seriously. The Toyama Prefectural Assembly rejected a draft pollution ordinance presented by a popular initiative, arguing that ordinances cannot impose stricter standards than the law (Kawai, 1973). This incident illustrates the difficult position of many local governments, caught between growing popular demands and their lack of authority.

In the context of the times, Tokyo's incremental step toward stronger pollution control policies was a significant act. It challenged not only the strict interpretation of local authority, but also the central government's position on substantive issues. Governor Minobe in Tokyo and Mayor Asukata in Yokohama were advertising the weakness of the LDP-controlled central government's pollution policies. The substantive issues were finally resolved by changing the law, giving local governments the authority to impose stricter regulations than those provided for by the law. In 1970 the Diet enacted fourteen laws concerning pollution, responding to popular demands, sharp criticism from the opposition parties, and the challenge offered by leading local governments.

In Japan, 1970 was the "year of pollution." The newspapers were filled with pollution-related stories and, paralleling the central government's legislative activity, ten different prefectures enacted new pollution ordinances. This was also the year in which national pollution policy "caught up" with the leading local policies and surpassed them in many ways Local governments continued to enact policies beyond the boundaries of the law, but since 1970 the central government has pursued pollution control actively without the reluctance it had earlier displayed. The central government had decided not to try to get the popular "illegal" ordinances declared void in court. The conflict between illegal ordinances and the law was resolved by changing the law.

By 1970 the central government had caught up on most pollution issues but local governments have retained the initiative. One outstanding issue remains: assessing the potential environmental impact of new industries. The Environmental Agency (EA) has proposed a bill to require environmental assessments for large-scale projects every year since 1976, but has failed to get the bill passed because of opposition from MITI, the Ministry of Construction (MOC), big business groups, and parts of the LDP (*Yomiuri Shinbun,* August 9 and 29, 1984). Kawasaki City officials decided not to wait any longer and enacted their own program in 1977, followed the next year by Hokkaido Prefecture (*Nihon Keizai Shinbun,* May 19 and July 19, 1978). As of 1980, two additional prefectures and one additional city had implemented assessment programs through extralegal guidelines, and 80 percent of the prefectures and larger cities had plans to enact similar programs (*Yomiuri Shinbun,* October 2, 1980).

The development of pollution control policy continues to include a large role for local governments, though intergovernmental conflict has shifted from arguments over direction to arguments over timing and the degree of control over environmental programs. More generally, the spurt of local innovation that began in the area of pollution control soon spread to other policy areas.

The Spurt of Activity in Other Areas

Encouraged by their success in fighting pollution, local governments began to attack other problems. For example, many urban municipalities have actively pursued land use control policies, and the most common means of implementing these controls is through the extralegal device of "guidelines" *(yōko)* (Kuze, 1973; Harada, 1974; Masago, 1975). These guidelines typically require a developer to provide areas for recreation, to leave some percentage of the land in natural vegetation, and often to donate land for public facilities, especially schools.

Innovation has also occurred in local social welfare programs, an area close to the hearts of progressive politicians. In 1968, the Minobe administration in Tokyo extended subsidies to day-care centers "unrecognized" by the Ministry of Health and Welfare (MacDougall, 1975; Yasue, 1975; Muramatsu, 1975), and began providing free medical care for the elderly in 1969 (Campbell, 1977). In the latter case, the ministry had just failed to enact a national program and Governor Minobe decided to wait no longer, telling reporters, "If the central government will not do it, Tokyo will have to do it on its own" (*Asahi Shinbun,* August 27, 1969). Many local governments followed Tokyo's lead and the resulting political pressure on the LDP to equal Tokyo's commitment to the elderly proved irresistible. The central government soon found itself again following the lead of local governments, enacting a similar national program in 1972. Thereafter, local governments continued to supplement the program with their own independent policies.

Many of these innovations challenged the central government politically without challenging the law directly. Conflict over authority was avoided by using extralegal devices. Moreover, legal problems are less serious when local governments provide services, as in the social welfare programs just mentioned, than when they regulate private citizens, as in pollution control. Local governments have, however, directly challenged central authority on regulatory issues. The most direct confrontation occurred in 1970 when Tagawa City, Fukuoka Prefecture, ignoring a Ministry of Justice circular, approved changes in the official registration of fourteen Korean nationals from Kankoku to Chōsen, a move that enabled the Koreans to choose between the North and South of their divided country (MacDougall, 1975; Sakata, 1972). The ministry almost took the case to court, but then relented. A compromise allowed the ministry to save face while the substantive victory clearly went to Tagawa.

The Tagawa case is often cited as an example of the evils of "agency-assigned functions" and of "administration by circular," but it more clearly illustrates the weakness of both. Regarding an agency-assigned function, the ministry's authority over the mayor was clear. The substantive content of that particular circular was questionable, however, and Tagawa challenged its constitutionality. The ministry was trying to use a circular to extend its authority beyond the letter of the law and failed.

Progressive organizations across the country supported Tagawa. In fact, a coordinated campaign to oppose the circular had been planned. Several local governments planned to change the registrations of groups of resident Koreans simultaneously. This planning indicates that many progressives feared the authority of the ministry, but events proved their fears had been exaggerated. The factor they had forgotten was politics. Although a bureaucrat might be willing to take a popular mayor to court, elected officials, particularly the governor who would have to implement any such procedures, were more reluctant.

In cases of regulatory policies, a pattern had developed: a local government would enact an "illegal" ordinance; the ministry involved would point out the potential conflict with the law; after some maneuvering on both sides, the law would be amended to make the local policy clearly legal. This pattern occurred several times in the development of pollution control policy. For example, in 1971 Nagano Prefecture enacted a Protection of Nature ordinance that contained some "illegal" provisions, but the problem was resolved when the Law for the Preservation of the Natural Environment was enacted in 1972.

One case unfolded during the research period. In 1976 Kumamoto Prefecture enacted an ordinance regulating "medium-sized" retail stores (*Asahi Shinbun*, October 1, 1976). Retail chain stores have been spreading rapidly throughout provincial cities in Japan and often cause hardship among the established small businesses. In 1973 a law was enacted to regulate the establishment of stores with over 1,500 square meters of floor space. The law was effective enough to motivate business owners to evade it. Provincial cities began to see more "medium-sized" stores not quite large enough to come under the provisions of the law. Sometimes a chain would build two such stores side by side.

Several local governments enacted guidelines to cover these cases, but Kumamoto enacted an ordinance including provisions for fines (*Saga Shinbun*, October 31, 1976). MITI had endured the extralegal guidelines but publicly objected to Kumamoto's ordinance. It asked for a formal opinion from the Cabinet Legislation Bureau. Five months later MITI, the Legislation Bureau, and the Ministry of Home Affairs arrived at the government's "unified opinion": the ordinance could not be considered illegal (*Saitama Shinbun*, March 27, 1977). Two years later the law was amended to include medium-sized stores (*Asahi Shinbun*, October 21, 1978).

The medium-sized stores case follows the familiar pattern, but two differences should be noted. First, Kumamoto could not be called a progressive prefecture. Its governor was a conservative. The prefecture is not large, rich, or urbanized, and it has no particular tradition of active government. That Kumamoto would challenge MITI on an issue of policy suggests that the early examples of innovative policymaking had been watched closely and learned from. Even conservative administrations find it more and more difficult to avoid policymaking responsibility by passing the buck to the central government.

The second important difference in the medium-sized stores case is that the Kumamoto ordinance was proposed not by the governor but by twenty assemblymen from three parties. Although member bills are rare in Japanese local assemblies and seldom pass (Abe, 1974), even though the governor's public stance was neutral, this ordinance was passed unanimously (*Asahi Shinbun*, October 1, 1976).

This pattern was repeated in Saga, the second prefecture to enact a medium-sized store ordinance, and the conservative agricultural prefecture included in my research. The issue was raised when Takeo City passed a weak ordinance, without enforcement provisions, introduced by seven assemblymen (*Saga Shinbun,* March 17, 1977). Ōmachi Town followed with a mayoral bill (ibid., June 23, 1977), but the assembly again took the lead at the prefectural level: the administration was studying a set of proposed guidelines when the LDP and the Socialist party presented a joint bill (ibid., July 20, 23, and August 6, 1977). This was the first administrative (police power) bill ever proposed by the Saga Prefectural Assembly and the first time in seventeen years that the assembly invited representatives of concerned groups to present their opinions (ibid., August 4 and 15, 1977).

In both Kumamoto and Saga, policymaking regarding medium-sized stores followed an extraordinary process. This process was highly political, but not partisan: both assemblies were unanimous. The issue was controversial in that consumer representatives were concerned that the ordinance would be used to protect inefficient businesses indefinitely and deny consumers convenient shopping. The vote calculus was, however, quite clear: the bill benefits small businessmen, who are many and well organized, while offending only the chains, who would have little representation in the city until one of their stores opened there. Consumers might be hurt by slowing the process of retail modernization, but they are unorganized and their costs consist of lost potential benefits; they would be unlikely to perceive such costs and thus unlikely to vote on this issue. These prefectural assemblymen were responding to cries for help from a well-organized interest group. The lines were drawn not between parties, but between doing something and waiting for the central government to act. In the past the LDP had usually been found on the side of inaction, but this time the conservatives decided not to wait.

The Present

At this point I risk leaving the impression that the dam has burst and local innovation dominates the scene in Japan. This is not the case. Innovative policies are not made daily, or even yearly, in any local government. Moreover, when the central government catches up with the leading local governments by amending the law, the result is an agency-assigned function. Amending the law reestablishes uniformity by bringing all local governments up to the level of the leaders. The restoration of uniformity means that any further innovation will again face criticism and doubts of its legality from the concerned ministry. Remember that conflicts between ordinances and laws have been resolved by amending the law. No court has ruled on the ministries' narrow interpretation of local authority. That interpretation remains essentially intact, saved mainly, one presumes, by prudent retreats from confrontation. Amending the law allows the ministries to maintain their position without testing it.

The spurt has ended. The LDP and the central ministries have coopted the issues of the 1970s and reestablished their policy leadership. The "stars" of the spurt, Minobe of Tokyo and Asukata of Yokohama, have passed from the local scene.[1] In the "low-growth" atmosphere following the 1973–1974 oil shock, the ministries have even made some progress in rolling back some of what they considered the "excesses" of the 1970s. The Ministry of Home Affairs has had some success in getting local governments to reduce their commitments to free medical care for the elderly (*Yomiuri Shinbun,* August 16, 1982) and the Ministry of Construction is trying to get cities to loosen their land use control guidelines (ibid., August 8, 1983). However, despite a reassertion of ministerial authority and worsening finances, local governments continue to innovate. The level of local policymaking activity has fallen off sharply, but not to 1950s levels. Today's issues are not as dramatic and seldom result in confrontations, but local governments have not returned to the passivity of the 1950s.

The most recent case developed over ordinances regulating local freedom of information *(jōhō kōkai),* in particular, whether such ordinances can cover assigned functions (Imaihasi and Takayose, 1982). Technically, information about assigned functions comes under the jurisdiction of the concerned ministry. Since a high percentage of local government activities are assigned functions, local freedom of information ordinances would be ineffective if information regarding such functions could not be released to the public. The development of this issue has proceeded rather slowly and confrontation has been avoided. Kanagawa Prefecture was the first to enact an ordinance and other local governments were not far behind (*Yomiuri Shinbun,* July 3, 18, and August 7, 1982, and July 9, 1984). The Home Affairs Ministry has expressed the opinion that local governments can apply their ordinances to assigned functions and other ministries have yet to object (*Asahi Shinbun,* April 16, 1982).

Other local innovations include an ordinance to require the recycling of drink cans (*Yomiuri Shinbun,* August 6, 1980, September 24 and 28, 1981), various administrative reorganization policies (ibid., August 7, 1981 and March 15, 1982), mental health programs (ibid., August 17, 1982), resolutions to make cities "nuclear-free" (ibid., March 24, 1981), and political ethics ordinances (ibid., February 26, 1983). Local government resolutions *(ketsugi)* and opinions *(ikensho)* have become an important means of influencing the central government. Interest groups organize national campaigns to secure many such local actions in order to influence central policymaking (Toki, 1983).

At the same time, MOHA and the Ministry of Finance have been waging a campaign to get local governments to reduce their independent welfare programs *(Yomiuri Shinbun,* May 25 and August 6, 1982). This campaign is aimed primarily at local finances, but would also have the effect of reestablishing national uniformity. The biggest independent welfare program has been free medical care for the elderly, and this issue provoked a left-right battle in Tokyo. Governor Suzuki Shunichi, the conservative who replaced Governor Minobe, had originally promised to "review" the policy, but found it politically unwise to challenge it in his first year (ibid., July 11, 1981). In his second year, however, he did manage to push through a bill requiring the elderly to pay a part of their medical costs, a reflection of similar legislation at the national level (ibid., August 28 and September 30, 1983). This "retreat" was viewed with alarm by progressives but it left Tokyo's independent program intact. In other policy areas where significant financial commitments are necessary, the Home Affairs Ministry, aided by a slowed rate of economic growth, has managed to persuade many local governments to "retreat" from the promises they made in the 1970s. They have not managed to reestablish uniformity nor have they been able to stop local governments from entering new fields.

In terms of intergovernmental relations, the spurt of local policymaking of the late 1960s and early 1970s shifted the overall balance in favor of local governments. Before this time, local governments were perceived to be virtually powerless, a perception shared by academics, central officials, local officials, and, most important, the public. No one would have considered demanding a solution to a political problem from a local government because it was assumed it could do nothing. Local governments actually made a lot of policy, but they kept a low profile and seldom came into confrontation with the central ministries because they believed they could not win. Local policymaking remained within the parameters set by the ministries. This quiescence was supported by the consensus on economic growth. (The only major exception to this quiescence and consensus was education policy, to be discussed in chapter 6.) The overall intergovernmental bargain was basically that local governments could only enact policies within the law and that the ministries were the judges of what was allowed by the law.

The spurt of local innovation changed the bargain. Local governments are now perceived to be potentially powerful. Concerned residents may make demands on them, especially if other institutions fail to respond, because they can be effective policymakers. Local officials now know that they can do a lot and need not fear the ministries so much. They now claim the right to exercise their independent judgment on central policies. Central officials are much less cavalier in handling local policy initiatives. The automatic negative reaction has been replaced with more circumspection and even appreciation. The standard interpretation of what conflicts with the law has loosened considerably.

The changes are real, but they represent only incremental shift from the previous bargain. To use the football analogy, local governments have moved from their ten-yard line to maybe their twenty. Local policymaking is still granted much less legitimacy than central policymaking. National uniformity is still the norm, and local deviations require specific justification.

Explaining the Spurt of Local Activity

The marked increase in innovative local policymaking during the 1970s was a big surprise to students of Japanese local government. No one thought that local governments could do what they did. Japanese scholars began talking about a "rediscovery of local autonomy" (Takayose, 1975) and a "turning point for local government" (Satō, 1976). American students of Japanese politics also began to revise their ideas (Steiner, Krauss, and Flanagan, 1980; Reed, 1982). The puzzle is basically a time-series problem. In the 1950s and early 1960s, Japanese local governments were docile and inactive. In the late 1960s and 1970s, they were active and influential. What changed? Which of our six hypotheses best explains the spurt in local policymaking?

Two hypotheses clearly fail to explain it: the distribution of authority hypothesis and the principle of least interest. The first hypothesis, that authority is the basis of influence, fails to explain the spurt. No major changes in the distribution of authority occurred during this period; indeed, what changes did occur were in the direction of greater centralization. The number of agency-assigned functions increased, and many new national public corporations were created as alternatives to implementation through local governments. A forecast based on the authority hypothesis would have predicted the opposite of what actually occurred: less, not more, influence by local governments. Local governments exercised influence without authority by using extralegal instruments and even proved influential in areas of exclusive central authority by enacting "illegal ordinances."

The events described in this chapter support the converse of the authority hypothesis: rather than an increase in authority leading to an increase in influence, an increase in influence is followed by an increase in authority. Local governments received specific grants of authority, normally in the form of agency-assigned functions, to do what they were already doing extralegally or illegally. Changes in the distribution of authority do not explain the spurt of activity, but the sudden increase in local policymaking does explain some changes in the distribution of authority.

The principle of least interest does not explain the phenomenon either. This hypothesis predicts that the least interested will have influence, but in this case the most active proved the most influential. Perhaps we should not be surprised that this principle does not apply when the public is demanding action. The hypothesis is meant to apply only to "joint projects," and we may interpret this to mean that it applies not to broad policies like pollution control but to specific projects like building a bridge or a dam.

All the remaining hypotheses are helpful in explaining the spurt of innovative policymaking. I shall discuss each hypothesis in reverse order of importance: finances, information, policy substance, and politics.

The hypothesis that influence depends on financial resources has been formulated in many different ways. Some prove more useful than others. There were no structural changes in the intergovernmental finance system that could explain the increased innovation at the local level. Any hypothesis based on the way intergovernmental finances are administered—the grant system, the hidden incentives in the revenue-sharing formula, central control over borrowing, and so on—cannot explain the spurt. Similarly, there was no particular trend in the proportion of local revenues coming from local taxes. Those interpretations that suggest that "he who collects the revenues, calls the tune" must also be rejected.

The financial hypothesis that does help suggests that affluent governments tend to innovate. Local government revenues were growing at an unprecedented rate during the 1970s. Economic growth provided local governments with slack resources that could be allocated to new programs and affluence released them from their single-minded pursuit of development. It makes eminent sense to argue that economic growth and increased revenues were necessary conditions for the spurt of innovative local policymaking, providing local governments with the wherewithal to respond creatively to new needs and demands.

The access to information hypothesis produces a second necessary condition. In the 1950s local governments seldom had the confidence to act contrary to the advice of the central government. A more balanced distribution of expertise was a necessary condition of local innovation. Both pollution control and land use planning require technical expertise. Expertise had been concentrated in the central government and was often used to retard the development of local policies. The development of a countervailing expertise at the local level, often using personnel from local high schools and universities, proved significant in several cases. More important, the quality and self-confidence of prefectural and big-city civil servants rose rapidly during these years.

A major factor in creating and maintaining the power and prestige of the central bureaucracy has been the fact that it has been staffed by an educational elite, winners in the highly competitive Japanese educational system. In the latter 1960s, the prefectural and municipal bureaucracies began to attract better-qualified applicants (*Yomiuri Shinbun,* January 6, 1982). This phenomenon is caused partly by the rising educational levels throughout Japanese society, partly by the trend toward returning to one's home prefecture after going to college in Tokyo, and partly by the growing perception that local policies could make a difference.

The education gap between central and local bureaucrats narrowed signficantly during this period and local governments developed greater expertise, although the balance of technical knowhow still remained tilted in the central government's favor. The increase in expertise at the local level may well have been a necessary condition for the spurt of local innovation, but other kinds of information were more important in creating the impetus for active policymaking. Because the need for better pollution control and urban policies developed at the grass-roots level, the demand for solutions to local problems was more evident and critical to local leaders than to national officials.

Both pollution and urban problems were geographically concentrated. Many municipalities faced particular problems too severe to be ignored. National officials could ignore these problems because they were not nationwide problems and the officials had more important matters to worry about. Local officials could not use either excuse; they found themselves the first to recognize and deal with the problems of their locality.

By the 1970s, the distribution of expertise had become less skewed in the central government's favor, giving local governments the confidence to act independently. Information on the severity of new problems was concentrated in particular areas. The information hypothesis does help to explain the increased local innovation in policymaking, but the two hypotheses that best explain it are the policy substance and electoral politics hypotheses.

The policy substance hypothesis—that the arguments pro and con on the substance of the issue determine whether a policy will be adopted or not—fits these events perfectly. It was not that local governments were strong and therefore were able to force new pollution control and urban policies on the central government. It was rather that the substantive case for stronger pollution and urban policies won the day and local governments found themselves on the winning side. Both the technical case that stronger policies were needed and the political case for responding to citizens demands were strong and persistent and could not be ignored forever. Those institutions, particularly local governments and the courts, that responded to the new needs and demands gained influence.

The increase in local policymaking is a clear case of substantive arguments dominating procedural ones. The best examples are the illegal ordinances. The legal arguments were clearly in favor of the central ministries. Anyone knowledgeable about Japanese local government before these events would have confidently predicted defeat for any local government that would enact such an ordinance. The ordinances stood and were thereafter written into law because they were good policy and good politics. The policies responded to real problems and deficiencies in the law. Central bureaucrats could not argue that the policies were inferior; they could only argue that proper procedure had been violated. The ordinances were also good politics and LDP politicians soon recognized the fact and coopted the policies.

The mechanism through which these substantive arguments were articulated included court cases and the normal process of evaluating policies within the bureaucracy. The key mechanism for bringing the arguments to the fore, however, was electoral politics.

The spurt of local activity was definitely a political phenomenon. It coincided with a jump in the number of progressive mayors and governors (Steiner, 1980). Progressive chief executives were often among the first to enact new policies and two progressives, Mayor Asukata of Yokohama and Governor Minobe of Tokyo, were the most visible proponents of local activism.[2] These two dominated media coverage even when they did not dominate the actual policymaking. Both consciously developed policies to challenge and embarrass the LDP at both the local and national levels. The competition between the progressive mayors and governors on the one hand and the LDP-dominated central government on the other became the major political contest of the period and a major impetus for the rise in local policymaking activity.

The political debate of this period was partly a debate between central and local power, the LDP and the ministries trying to maintain control over restive local governments whether progressive or conservative. The debate was also partly between left and right, conservatives trying to maintain the focus on economic growth against progressive demands for more investment in social infrastructure. The combination of these two cleavages resulted in a contest between the LDP in the central government and the progressives in local government.

The vertical dimension of this political competition was caused by differences in access to information, local government perceiving the problems more clearly than the central government, and by different political pressures. The demands for more effective policies were organized in a peculiarly local form, the "citizens' movement" (*jūmin undō*, see Lewis, 1980; McKean, 1976, 1980). Citizens' movements were organized around single concrete problems. Particularly in the early stages, they tend to be nonideological and to avoid entanglements with political parties. Thus their demands tended to be more often directed toward local than national governments (Akimoto, 1975: 150). Even when the object of protest was a central government project, their concerns were local. Central bureaucrats found it extremely difficult to deal with citizens' movements. The Japanese central bureaucracy is elite and small. National bureaucrats deal with problems rationally and from a distance. Citizens' movements demand that they deal with the details of their problems politically. Local officials are much better equipped to deal with such demands. Mayors and governors tend to emerge in disputes between citizens' movements and the central government.[3] Some comparative evidence from Australia supports the hypothesis that demands organized in this way create pressures for decentralization (Roddewig, 1978).

The horizontal competition, left versus right at all levels of government, was initiated by the built-in incentive of the "outs" to attack the "ins." The LDP had identified themselves with economic growth. The new issues of pollution and urban congestion offered the opposition a way of turning the economic issue against the LDP. The issues could even be presented with a leftist and populist slant: "Big business is stealing your air and water."

The horizontal dimension of the competition muted the vertical dimension somewhat, but did not dominate politics at either level. On the local level, conservatives found themselves faced with serious pollution problems and active citizens' movements. The central government was no help. The policies developed by other local governments, even if identified with progressives, were the only helpful ideas available. Local conservatives were under political pressure to deal with the new issues or lose office. Local conservatives were subject to cross-pressures and tended to take compromising or vague positions.

At the national level, it was the progressives who faced a dilemma. The new issues had one major defect, from the progressive parties' point of view: they did not fit the normal left-right dochotomy between management and labor. In particular cases, the conflict was more often between a company, both management and labor, and inhabitants of the surrounding area, both rich and poor. The ideology of class struggle did not apply. Such problems confused ideologues and kept the unions from taking a strong stand on the new issues. Progressives at the national level were cross-pressured between their ideology and their major support group on the one hand and the electoral incentive to attack the LDP with a popular issue on the other. Japanese opposition parties tend to be dominated by ideologues and unions and thus were not able to exploit the new issues effectively (Tsurutani, 1977). Progressives find it easier to follow electoral incentives at the local level. Progressive governors and mayors tend to be more pragmatic and freer of organizational ties once elected, and thus are better able to exploit the new issues (Reed, 1981B).

The opposition is also hampered by divisions at the center but can be unified at the local level, if only temporarily and provisionally, behind a mayor or governor. At the national level, the opposition has little influence over policy and can take little credit for the influence it does have. Local governments provide the opposition with their only real chance to make policy.

Local conservatives and central progressives were cross-pressured and thus effectively taken out of the debate. The remaining contestants were the national LDP, defending economic growth and rational planning, versus local progressives who argued for greater attention to "quality of life" issues. The spurt of innovative local policymaking in the 1970s was the result of this political competition. The next three chapters will examine in detail three important policy issues affected by this phenomenon.

4

Pollution Control Policy

IN THE 1960s the industrialized countries came to recognize the hazards of environmental pollution. Pollution control became a high-priority agenda item. As we have noted, Japan had one of the worst pollution problem in the world, if not the worst. High levels of industrial activity concentrated into a small land area created enormous problems. The governmental response to these problem was slow and halting, but by the mid-1970s Japan had developed one of the most effective systems for pollution control in the industrialized world (OECD, 1977; Reed, 1981A). Chapter 3 has described some of the troubled history of establishing pollution control policy. This chapter will analyze the system in operation.

Japan's system for controlling industrial pollution consists of four activities: setting environmental standards, monitoring the environment, setting emissions standards, and monitoring emissions standards. (1) Environmental standards represent the level of concentration for each type of pollutant that is considered "desirable for the protection of human health and the conservation of the living environment" (Basic Law for Environmental Pollution Control, art. 9, para. 1). Environmental standards set the administrative goals toward which the other activities are aimed. (2) Monitoring the environment entails gathering information on the levels of pollutants in the environment for two purposes: to identify problem areas and to detect emergency situations. Problems arise both where environmental standards are not being met and where pollution levels are rising. Even in areas where emissions normally meet environmental standards, accidents or weather conditions may cause emergency situations that pose health hazards. Such situations call for immediate, if temporary, countermeasures to minimize damages. (3) Emission standards set legal limits on the concentration or amount of pollutants that can be discharged by particular sources. These standards are the primary means by which environmental protection is to be achieved. (4) To enforce emission standards, officials periodically inspect pollution sources and order improvements when necessary.

These four activities represent the basic system for controlling industrial pollution in Japan. It is applied to all types of pollution with little variation. This system is the core of Japan's approach to pollution control, but it certainly does not exhaust the nation's policies. Two other activities will also be discussed. Japanese governments give aid to small businesses that cannot afford to put in necessary but expensive pollution control equipment. The greatest part of this aid takes the form of low-interest loans. Although aid violates the principle that the polluter should pay and is considered a temporary cushioning device for small businesses, it plays a vital role in making the system work.

Finally, in most areas of Japan, meeting water quality standards depends as much on constructing public sewer systems as upon regulating industry. Japan is far behind other industrialized nations in sewer construction and this activity assumes a larger role in Japanese pollution policy than it does in other industrialized countries.

Pollution Control in the Three Prefectures

Saga Prefecture is agricultural. Having little industry means that Saga has only a little pollution. The environmental problems Saga has experienced have been precisely the kind that have either been ignored or treated as special one-time cases in Japan and elsewhere. Yet Saga is pursuing an active pollution policy.

Saga's official consideration of pollution began in 1969 with a study by the prefectural Commission on Pollution Control. The commission concluded that, while no pressing problems existed, the experience of other parts of Japan indicated that problems were likely to develop in Saga. In June 1970 the governor asked the commission to consider a pollution control ordinance, which was enacted in August of that year. The ordinance was more a response to national than to local factors. Forty-three of the forty-seven prefectures had already enacted ordinances and 1970 was the "year of pollution" throughout Japan (Mori, 1970). The prefectural government was also responding to rising pollution consciousness within the prefecture, a consciousness clearly reflected in the rising numbers of citizen complaints about pollution (see table 4). The sixfold increase in complaints in one year cannot be explained by local factors. Mass media coverage of problems in other parts of Japan raised pollution consciousness even in Saga. National forces put pollution on Saga's policy agenda.

Since the enactment of the 1970 pollution control ordinance, Saga's pollution policy has consisted primarily, though not exclusively, of using the central government's legal structure. The prefecture does make use of extralegal pollution control agreements, but by 1970 these were standard tools of local governments. Saga officials interpret the prefecture's role narrowly. In response to a question by an assemblyman concerning the establishment of standards for types of pollution not yet covered by the law, the head of the Department of Health and the Environment replied, "I think that there would by many problems if the prefecture tried to do this on its own. We are inclined to wait until the government's experts have developed their ideas, or to parallel the government's progress on this" (Saga Prefecture, 1976). Again, in response to a question of mine about an environment assessment program, the official in charge told me. "I think that local governments must wait and see what the law looks like and then respond to the law." Very few local governments have actually moved beyond the central government of these two issues, but officials in Chiba and Saitama avoided phrases like "wait for the central government." Rather, they referred to the difficulty of the undertaking and emphasized their own efforts.

If the timing and content of Saga's pollution policy have been largely determined by law and common practice, the administration of the policy goes well beyond the requirements of the law. Because Saga is a poor prefecture placing high priority on attracting new industry, I expected pollution policy to be tempered by a concern for economic growth. I found nothing to indicate such compromising and found much to indicate the opposite: pollution control has become a prerequisite for accepting new industry into the area.

Why does such a poor prefecture maintain such a strong pollution

TABLE 4
Pollution-Related Citizen Complaints in Saga Prefecture, 1966–1973

	1966	*1967*	*1968*	*1969*	*1970*	*1971*	*1972*	*1973*
Complaints	49	35	56	49	303	345	339	368

Source: Saga Prefecture, *Environmental White Papers,* 1971 through 1976.

policy? First, the contradiction between pollution control and attracting industry has lessened as the consensus on the need for pollution control has grown stronger. Industry has offered no significant resistance to tougher policies or even to extralegal agreements. Saga officials do not believe that a strong policy puts them at a disadvantage in attracting industry.[1]

A second reason for Saga's strong policy is that farmers and fishermen are the most powerful interest groups in the prefecture and they have been sensitized to the dangers of pollution: farmers and fishermen have often been the first to experience damages from pollutants. Rice farmers in particular must be sensitive to anything that might affect their water supply.

Saga has benefited from the intervention of national forces and is now able to deal with pollution before serious problems develop. The headline of the local newspaper announcing the 1976 edition of Saga's Environmental White Paper summarizes the situation quite well: "Saga Is Still Clean" (*Saga Shinbun,* October 15, 1976). Neither of the other two prefectures can make such a claim.

Chiba and Saitama are industrial prefectures with difficult pollution problems. However, the kind of industry, in each one, and thus the nature of the pollution problem, differs significantly. Chiba, to the east of Tokyo, has a *kombināto* built on land reclaimed from Tokyo Bay. (In crowded Japan, only reclaimed land offers the possibility of consolidating the large tracts necessary for a *kombināto.*) Most of the industry in the prefecture is located on this narrow strip of land, and the concentration of large factories there presents a highly visible air pollution problem. On the other hand, Saitama, to the west of the city, has no coastline and therefore no large industrial parks.

Saitama is the prefecture most affected by urban and industrial sprawl from Tokyo. Industry, though there is a lot of it, is small and scattered throughout the cities nearest Tokyo, and it consists largely of subcontractors for the large factories located around Tokyo Bay. Whereas in Chiba air pollution consists primarily of sulfur oxides from the *kombināto,* in Saitama, a bigger problem is presented by photochemical smog caused by the exhausts of cars and trucks going to and from Tokyo. Water pollution is more visible than air pollution. In both prefectures water pollution comes more from city sewage than from industrial wastes. Chiba's *kombināto* pours its waste water directly into Tokyo Bay. The resulting pollution is less a prefectural than a regional or national problem. Chiba's rivers are small and numerous. Concern about water pollution within the prefecture centers on two large lakes.

Quite the contrary, Saitama contains major rivers forming a network covering the prefecture.

Thus the central pollution problem in Chiba is industrial pollution from the *kombināto,* while pollution in Saitama takes the form of "urban pollution," emissions from small factories located near residential areas. Urban pollution consists as much of noise and odor as of air and water pollution. Although the emissions of many small factories may add up to high levels of pollution in the air and water, those factories more often cause localized problems, the kind of pollution measured more by citizen complaints than by sophisticated monitoring devices.

Urban pollution is the more intractable problem. The legal system for regulating industry fits Chiba's problem—major industrial pollution—more closely than it does Saitama's. Indeed, the efforts of the central government have focused on the pollution problems caused by *kombināto.*Technology, including administrative technology, for controlling industrial air pollution had advanced more rapidly than technology for controlling auto exhausts or water pollution. Chiba, too, has urban pollution. While Chiba's main problem has been the *kombināto,* the northern region nearest Tokyo faces many of the same problems as Saitama. However, pollution policy in Chiba has generally focused first on the *kombināto* region and has been extended to the north afterward, reflecting the difficulty of dealing with urban pollution.

In both Chiba and Saitama, pollution abatement was on the prefectural agenda long before it got onto the national agenda. Saitama's first pollution control ordinance was enacted in 1962 and Chiba's in 1963.[2] In both prefectures popular demand seems to have been the most important factor in bringing recognition of the problem. In Chiba this popular demand was embodied in several active antipollution citizens' movements in the *kombināto* region. With no such visible target, citizens' movements against pollution played a lesser role in Saitama.

Chiba's environmental policy relies heavily on pollution control agreements negotiated with the major factories of the *kombināto.* The use of agreements came naturally to Chiba's government, which had long experience negotiating land sale contracts with the incoming industries. Chiba was well known for taking a high posture toward new industry, driving a better bargain than was common during the late 1950s and 1960s (Tokyo University Social Science Research Group, 1965). The use of agreements was also natural because Chiba's situation parallels Yokohama's just across the bay, and Yokohama was the pioneer in using this tool.

Early pollution control efforts in Chiba primarily meant taking

some responsibility for the side effects of the *kombināto* which the prefecture had planned and built. Though the prefecture continued to develop pollution policies, they continued to be secondary to the larger
goal of industrial expansion, a way of preventing some of the problems
of industrial growth. The shift in priorities, the promotion of pollution
control to primary importance, did not come until 1973, three years
after the central government and the other two prefectures had made
their symbolic shifts. That Chiba failed to change priorities in 1970 was
symbolized by the retention of the phrase, "in harmony with industrial
development" in the preamble of the pollution control ordinance. This
phrase had become the symbolic dividing line between "industrial development with pollution control" and "pollution control even at the
cost of development."

Even with the harmony clause, however, Chiba's 1970 ordinance
must be rated highly, and since the shift of priorities in 1973 Chiba's
policies have progressed rapidly, often leading the central government.
That the change of priorities came late may be attributed to the prefecture's heavy emphasis placed on industrial development and the close
cooperative relationships that had developed between the prefectural
government and the *kombināto* industries. Although Chiba was known
for its firm stand in dealing with incoming industries in the 1950s, it
was also known for its cooperation, even collusion, with big business in
the 1960s and early 1970s (Chiba Prefecture Citizens' Movement Liaison Council, 1973; Ohara and Yokoyama, 1965; Sada, 1975). By 1973,
however, after four major pollution damage suits had been resolved in
favor of those seeking damages (McKean, 1981), business leaders generally came to accept pollution control as a necessary policy, and since
that time cooperation between the prefecture and the *kombināto* has
resulted in stronger, not weaker, environmental policies.

Use of pollution control agreements is not a viable option in Saitama. In the *kombināto* area of Chiba, sixty-three factories account for
98 percent of the sulfur oxides emitted, and the fifty-seven factories
covered by agreements account for most of the other air and water
pollution (Chiba Prefecture unpublished materials, 1976). In Saitama,
agreements with the top fifty or sixty firms would not result in controlling a significant proportion of the pollution emitted because the
firms are too small. Although comparable data are not available for
Saitama, the northern region of Chiba is similar to Saitama and there it
would be necessary to negotiate agreements with over three hundred
firms to control 98 percent of the sulfur oxide emissions (Chiba Prefecture unpublished materials, 1976).

Saitama has had to rely more on formal legal mechanisms, and thus on central legislation, while Chiba has been able to avoid many legal problems by using extralegal mechanisms. Chiba's pollution policy has been made by the prefectural government, Saitama's policy on the other hand, has often had to take the form of making demands on the central government.

The seriousness of Saitama's urban pollution problem is reflected largely in citizen complaints and, although the prefecture does play a larger role in handling these complaints than do the other two prefectures, more of Saitama's pollution policy has been implemented at the municipal level. Saitama's efforts necessarily focus more on planning and coordination. The most visible independent prefectural program is the organization of all levels of government, along with concerned private groups and industry representatives, into three large conferences, one for each of the three river basins.

Because the three prefectures have widely differing problems and signficantly different combinations of policies for dealing with them, they have developed their policies with different relationships to the central government. We now turn to a more detailed analysis of policymaking in the three prefectures.

Pollution Control Policymaking

Setting Environmental Standards. The central government sets environmental standards and intergovernmental relations concerning pollution control take the form of local governments trying to influence central policymaking. Local governments do express opinions and even sponsor scientific research aimed at influencing central decisions, but they generally accept the central government's decisions, bowing to the greater legitimacy of national standards. Central expertise predominates, but prefectures do sometimes exercise their own judgment on this highly technical matter. The clearest examples come from the controversy over nitrogen oxide standards.

The Environmental Agency set the nitrogen oxide standard in 1973 on the basis of slim scientific evidence. Industry spokesmen, including MITI, had argued that the standard was unrealistic from the beginning, but when the World Health Organization recommended a standard half as strict as Japan's, the Environmental Agency found itself in a difficult position. MITI now had a strong case for revising the standard downward, but many local governments had already begun active control programs for nitrogen oxides. To loosen the standards would undercut these ongoing local programs. Local governments were concerned with nitrogen oxides because of the possibility that they lead to photochemical smog, a real and pressing health hazard (OECD, 1975). However, the link between nitrogen oxides and smog was not yet clearly established and the technical case for loosening the standards was the stronger.

The Environmental Agency attempted to resolve these contradictory pressures by accepting weaker standards while at the same time adopting the "no deterioration" principle. Under this principle, areas with low levels of pollution would be required to maintain those levels. Thus, those local programs disigned to prevent expected deterioration would be allowed to continue. However, the new guidelines were too weak. Under the standards adopted, 93.7 percent of the nation's air quality monitoring stations would meet the new environmental standards (*Nihon Keizai Shinbun,* July 11, 1978). Critics called the new policy "no improvement standards."

Those local governments plagued by photochemical smog, therefore, particularly those that had just embarked upon ambitious nitrogen oxide reduction programs, refused to follow the central lead. The four prefectures of the Tokyo region (including both Chiba and Saitama) jointly declared their intention to continue with their programs—that is, to ignore the new environmental standard (ibid., July 30, 1978). Tokyo went further, setting up a prefectural advisory commission to reaffirm the old standards.[3]

Monitoring the Environment. Article 22 of the Air Pollution Control Law states: "The prefectural governor shall monitor and survey the level of air pollution from time to time." Article 15 of the Water Pollution Control Law similarly states: "The prefectural governor shall continuously survey the state of water pollution in the public waters under his jurisdiction." Thus, monitoring the environment is an agency-assigned function, and, technically, the prefectural governor acts simply as an administrator of the central law and under the supervision of the Environmental Agency.[4] In actuality, prefectural officials treat this agency-assigned function precisely the same as their other functions.

Both prefectural and central officials agreed that making environmental monitoring an agency-assigned function makes no difference. A Saitama official told me, "Monitoring takes the form of an agency-assigned function, but if the prefecture does not build the facilities on its own, it simply will not get done. . . . It becomes the prefecture's job." Similarly, an EA official summarized the situation as follows: "If you ask what difference it makes whether a function is an agency-assigned function or a local function, the answer is that it does not make any particular difference." The only local complaint I was able to elicit concerned finance. A Saga official complained, "Monitoring air quality and water quality are both agency-assiged functions. We get subsidies for water quality monitoring but not for air quality monitoring. It does not make sense."

The cases of policymaking I investigated clearly support the conclusions of these officials. I found no evidence of any central government role in decisions taken about air quality monitoring. The situation in water quality monitoring is more complex, but prefectural officials were certainly not acting as central government agents.

The technical aspects of measurement methods are decided by the central government, but these decisions are essentially extensions of those made when environmental standards were set up. The issues involved in monitoring are how many stations to establish where, and whether to establish telemeter systems, and these policies are made by the prefectures. Automatic monitoring stations and telemeter systems (systems for collecting the data from monitoring stations into a central computer) are expensive, and decisions about these facilities must be made through the prefectural budgetary process.

In 1976, Saitama was building up its air quality monitoring system. The Air Quality Division was unable to get money for expanding the capacity of the telemeter computer in the same year they were building several new monitoring stations. They decided to build the stations first and expand computer capacity later. The decision was based on budgetary timing and did not involve the central government at all.

The establishment of Saga's telemeter system clearly illustrates the prefectural nature of policymaking in environmental monitoring. Agricultural Saga has only one large industrial source of air pollution, a thermal electric plant in Karatsu City. This plant alone accounted for 87 percent of the liquid fuel consumed in Saga in 1975 (Saga Prefecture, 1971–76). Beginning in 1971, damage to tangerines attributable to sulfur oxides was discovered in the Karatsu area. Besides negotiating a pollution control agreement with the plant, the prefecture built a telemeter system to provide hourly data on the levels of sulfur oxides in the area. A progressive prefectural assemblyman played a large role in pressing the issue before the prefectural government. One major criticism of agency-assigned functions is that the assembly is excluded from decision making, but this case demonstrates that assemblymen can play key, if informal, roles.

Automatic monitoring stations and telemeter systems are used in measuring air quality. A satisfactory monitoring device has yet to be developed for water pollution. The central government is promoting technological development in this area and the prefectures are waiting for the development to take place. In Chiba and Saitama, however, the waiting is far from passive. Saitama has established an automatic monitoring station, an experimental effort usually left to the central government. Chiba has no automatic stations of its own, but does require those factories with which it has pollution control agreements to install them. Chiba also played an independent role in promoting technological development by sponsoring a "contest" among manufacturers of automatic monitoring devices. Over a hundred manufacturers participated. Although no winners were announced, the "contest" gave manufacturers a chance to test their devices in actual use, and gave both the factories and the prefecture a chance to examine a large number of devices. Here again, the technological nature of pollution policy has not prevented local governments from playing an active role.

Water quality monitoring is also complicated by the fact that both the EA and the Ministry of Construction monitor some waterways directly, the former in an experimental role and the latter as part of its responsibility for water management of the larger rivers. MOC and prefectural officials hold a yearly conference to decide who will monitor what locations. These conferences are apparently without conflict. Prefectural officials expressed satisfaction with the ministry's efforts, though it is known for placing more emphasis on water management than on water quality. The conferences seem to be limited to administrative coordination; the parties take the decisions of the other into account when making their own decisions.

We may conclude that monitoring policies are determined at the prefectural level, despite the fact that this activity is an agency-assigned function.

Setting Emission Standards. The central government sets minimum standards for environmental quality that cover the entire nation. However, since 1970, prefectures have been "allowed" to set tougher standards. In order to achieve uniformity, emission standards must vary according to the concentration of pollution sources, local climate, the size of rivers, and many other local factors. The easiest way to provide for this variation is to delegate authority.

Article 4 of the Air Pollution Control Law states: "If a prefecture recognizes that the existing emission standards with respect to soot, dust, or toxic substances are inadequate to protect public health and the living environment, it may establish by prefectural ordinance, in accordance with Cabinet Order, a stricter emission standard." Article 3 of the Water Pollution Control Law provides a similar delegation of authority and the two Cabinet Orders provide that "when environmental standards have been established, . . . the ordinance shall set permissible emission at levels necessary and sufficient to maintain those environmental standards." Thus, when the central government has set environmental standards, those standards replace prefectural judgment as to when public health or the living environment is threatened.

These prefectural emission regulations are called *uwanose* (literally, "sitting atop") standards. Setting *uwanose* standards is an entity-assigned function; the local government as a whole is assigned the function, not just the chief executive. Since this is not a required activity, the only difference between this entity-assigned voluntary function and a local function is that in the former the authority derives from a specific law. In such cases it is more accurate to speak of delegation of authority than the assignment of functions.

In delegating authority, the central government may, of course, set limits on that authority. In this case, the only limitation is that the emission standards be related to environmental standards. One can imagine this limitation becoming a formula, determined by the central government, for relating emission to environmental standards. This has not happened, in part because of the difficulty of linking emission standards to their environmental results. Setting emission standards requires complex judgments and it is the prefectures that make them. Prefectures enact *uwanose* standards subject only to a reporting requirement and some regulations about the form of the ordinance.

One important exception to the above is that sulfur oxides were omitted from the *uwanose* provision. Because of the relative scarcity of low-sulfur oil, emission standards for sulfur oxides must be coordinated with import policy, or so the central government argues. Though this argument has some basis, most of the larger consumers of oil have been effectively regulated by pollution control agreements without upsetting oil import policies. In any case, sulfur oxides, the major health threat of air pollution, is regulated through an elaborate system of area designations.

The Environmental Agency designates each area (generally in units of municipalities or districts of large cities) as belonging to one of sixteen ranks, each rank corresponding to a specific emission standard. The agency further classifies some areas as fitting into one of three additional ranks of special emission standards, stricter than the normal sixteenth rank, to be applied to new facilities moving into the area. Finally, the EA designates some areas for quota regulation. The final designation requires the prefecture to draw up a plan for the reduction of sulfur oxide emissions.

The Environmental Agency has reserved the authority to link sulfur oxide emission standards to environmental standards. Area designation, by providing the necessary local variations through central regulation, is a clear denial of local autonomy, a centralized alternative to delegating authority. Despite the highly centralized form of sulfur oxide regulation, however, prefectures are not without means to affect the setting of standards within their boundaries.

Prefectures can try to influence the designation process. In 1976 the southern part of Saitama was designated for quota regulation. The case for such a designation was not clear. Although Saitama officials refused to say they had "lobbied" for the designation, the manifest interest shown by prefectural officials was a deciding factor, if not the deciding factor, in the absence of clear evidence. Since a quota regulation plan requires a great deal of work on the part of prefectural officials, their willingness is an important factor in the EA's decision-making process.

Prefectures can also regulate sulfur oxide emissions directly through pollution control agreements. Both Saga and Chiba have imposed quota regulation on larger factories within their respective boundaries. In Saga, the effect of such regulation is not to balance the pollution-absorbing capacity of the environment with the emissions of a concentrated group of factories, as envisioned in the legal provisions for quota regulation. Saga has imposed quota regulation on only four factories in widely separated areas.[5] The effect is rather to close a loophole in the standard style of regulation. The law regulates facilities (particular machines and processes), not factories, so total emissions may be increased by adding facilities. The law also regulated emissions relative to the height of the smokestack (a provision limited to sulfur oxides), and by concentration rather than amount. Thus, a factory could increase emissions by building higher smokestacks or by diluting the pollutant with more air—that is, by building more smokestacks. These options are closed off by quota regulation.

Chiba's agreement-based quota regulation overlaps the legally based regulation. Chiba began renegotiating the agreements to include quota regulation in 1973 and completed the process in December 1975. In November 1974 parts of Chiba were designated for quota regulation by the EA. The designation came as no surprise; quota regulation had been designed with places like Chiba in mind. However, the two systems of regulation conflict.

The key point of conflict concerns the distributional formula: given the same total permissible volume of pollutants, the legal system distributes that total among the factories differently from Chiba's agreement-based system The prefecture petitioned the EA to be allowed to use its own distributional formula. At first the agency was sympathetic, but in the end, it decided it could not treat prefectures differently. The prefecture then had to spend a great deal of time and effort recalculating and drawing up a plan acceptable to the EA.

The legal system has not, however, completely replaced the agreement-based system in Chiba. First, nitrogen oxides are not covered by the legal system, but are covered in the agreement-based system. With respect to suflur oxides, the emission standards for particular factories turn out to be several percentage points tougher under the agreement-based system. The prefecture plans to use the agreement-based system as a cushion. Exceeding the agreement-based figure will trigger a response from the prefecture, but that response can be flexible because it is not determined by law. The cushion helps protect the companies from breaking the law and provides the prefecture with the flexibility to continue to press for greater efforts from the companies.

Being designated an area needing greater regulation of air pollutants caused Chiba some trouble, but overall the designation must be considered a positive contribution to prefectural policy. First, it adds the force of law to quota regulation. Second, it extends the coverage of quota regulation from 57 to 145 factories is the *kombināto* region. Third, newly established factories over a given size will automatically be covered by the law. Fourth, prefectural officials admit that the law's distributional formula has advantages over Chiba's formula. Finally, and most important, the designation extends quota regulation to the northern part of Chiba where agreements are ineffective.

Although the central government's intervention into Chiba's policy-making proved to have positive results, it also entailed costs. In part these costs are the unavoidable consequences of getting ahead of the central government. Similar costs have been imposed on advanced states in the United Stated when the federal government has enacted new laws (Lieber, 1975). However, in this case, one wonders why an exception could not be made, or why the law must set out procedures in such detail. As other examples will illustrate below, the Japanese central government tends to decide as much as possible in the law and central regulations and tends to be unwilling to permit exceptions.

All substances except sulfur oxides are subject to *uwanose* ordinances, and the responsibility for linking emission standards to environmental standards rests with the prefectural government. *Uwanose* ordinances are more important in curbing water pollution than air pollution. In 1975 only six prefectures had ordinances covering air pollution, but all prefectures had ordinances for water pollution (Environmental Agency, 1976). The EA's major role in the establishment of *uwanose* ordinances is to provide prefectures with detailed estimates of what levels of water treatment are technologically feasible for each pollution source. This activity seems a pure case of aiding local government by providing information. One might think that the EA uses this list to prevent prefectures from setting unreasonable standards. The guidelines might have become maximum levels, but have not.

Saga set technologically impossible standards for new industries being established along one particularly polluted river, the Fukushoe River, which had become "essentially the private sewer of a group of paper-pulp factories" (interview in Saga Prefecture, Pollution Control Division, December 14, 1976). The prefecture moved to correct this situation by enacting an *uwanose* ordinance in 1973. The new regulations produced dramatic results: BOD (Biological Oxygen Demand, a generalized measure of pollution levels) dropped from 243 ppm in 1971 to 30 ppm in 1975 (Saga Prefecture, 1971–76). However, this 30 ppm still fails to meet environmental standards. Further improvement must await technological developments or a project to increase the water flow of the river. In the meantime, the prefecture does not want the pollution burden increased by new factories. The use of "unreasonable" standards to prevent further development along a highly polluted river is within the spirit of the law: it is necessary so that water quality can approach existing environmental standards. Chiba, however, has set an "unreasonable" standard that is less clearly linked to environmental standards.

In 1975 Chiba revised its *uwanose* standards. The most controversial part of this new ordinance was the limitation of BOD 10 ppm for the sewage treatment facilities of new housing complexes. Toughening *uwanose* standards was clearly called for, and, with the lack of public sewer systems, housing complexes were a large part of the problem, but this standard has the effect of discouraging new housing complexes by making them more expensive to construct. The 10 ppm standard was set in accordance with a prefectural policy of limiting population growth (see chapter 5). If the prefecture were not trying to limit population growth, or if its Water Quality Division had not taken this policy into account, it is unlikely that such a strict standard would have been adopted.

Chiba's 10 ppm standard represents the kind of coordination common at the prefectural level. The idea was developed within the Water Quality Division without the kind of interagency discussion or leadership that Americans usually associate with coordination. Coordination was effected through a broad statement of policy from the center that was taken into account by local water quality officials. This indirect coordination resulted in an innovative prefectural policy not envisioned in the letter or the spirit of the law.

These two examples demonstrate that the legal requirement that effluent standards must be linked to environmental standards does not limit prefectural discretion. One could interpret the law to mean that *uwanose* standards cannot be enacted unless environmental standards are being exceeded. Officials in the Environmental Agency supported this interpretation. However, acting to prevent water quality from exceeding environmental standards is not excluded by either the letter or the spirit of the law.

In 1977 Saga enacted a new *uwanose* ordinance extending coverage to include the whole prefecture. The rationale was preventive. The improvement in water quality owing to legal effluent standards had leveled off and some rivers near the larger cities had begun to worsen somewhat. With the economy picking up, prefectural officials could predict that water quality would not meet environmental standards in the near future. The case for predicting worsening water quality was not clear-cut, and with the existing state of technology it could not be, The case rested on the judgment of the prefectural govenment.

Levels of effluent standards, and the timing and area covered by *uwanose* standards, are determined at the prefectural level. Most other aspects of regulation are also decided by the prefecture. Effluent regulation applies only to larger factories, but prefectures regularly lower the threshold size. Saga, for example, lowered the threshold from fifty to twenty tons of effluent per day, adding about 160 factories to 220 covered by law and increasing the coverage of industrial effluents from 81 to 89 percent. Prefectures regularly set tougher standards for new plants and larger plants; they add substances to the list of toxic substances; they even alter definitions. Chiba's 1975 ordinance states that expansion of an existing plant beyond a certain threshold will be subject to the standards for new plants, and provides that, when a plant fits multiple categories, the strictest standard shall apply.

The only aspect of effluent regulation that is normally not altered by *uwanose* ordinances is the list of designated facilities—that is, those facilities covered by effluent regulation. A Chiba official summarized the situation this way: "Because the national government has been quite inclusive in designating facilities, we have left the task of expanding the kinds of facilities covered to them. It is a cooperative system in the best sense of the term" (interview in Chiba Prefecture, Water Quality Division, May 10, 1977).

I have not mentioned Saitama in this discussion. Saitama does have an *uwanose* ordinance, but its water pollution problem is much more a matter of city sewage than industrial effluents, so Saitama has chosen to rely more on building public sewer systems than regulating industry. One progressive study group even accuses the prefecture of overemphasizing city sewage and being soft *(amae)* on industrial effluents (Saitama Local Government Problems Research Center, 1976). However, Chiba and Saga could be accused of compensating for their lack of public sewer systems by placing the burden of improving water quality on private enterprise. For present purposes, however, the important point is that the relative weights to be given sewer construction versus industrial regulation is also a matter decided at the prefectural level.

That most decisions on effluent regulation are made by prefectures does not mean, however, that these decisions are influenced solely by internal prefectural factors. For example, one factor promoting the enactment of Saga's 1977 *uwanose* ordinance was the fact that thirty-two other prefectures had already enacted ordinances covering the whole prefecture (*Saga Shinbun*, July 5, 1977). The ordinance was also designed so as not to conflict with the ordinance of neighboring Fukuoka Prefecture, with whom Saga shares a major river. Similarly, one factor in the enactment of Chiba's 1975 ordinance was growing concern over pollution in Tokyo Bay, a concern shared by the region and the nation. National factors influenced prefectural policymaking, but they did not necessarily emanate from the central government.

Uwanose ordinances have created much diversity among the prefectures. Indeed, the situation could well be described by one of the most negative adjectives in the Japanese bureaucrats' lexicon: *bara-bara* (scattered, untidy, without uniformity). Chiba officials suggested that the EA would like to see more uniformity, particularly in the regulations covering the area around Tokyo Bay. The agency is working on a comprehensive quota regulation system for each of the major bays (*Asahi Shinbun*, October 29, 1977, and April 21, 1978). The announcement has already dissuaded Tokyo from developing its own quota regulation system (ibid., January 13, 1977, and January 24, 1978). The case for a regional approach to the pollution of bays and inlets is undeniable, and quota regulation would certainly be a positive contribution to water pollution control in most or all of the prefectures. However, the prefectural role in setting effluent standards could be reduced substantially.

Enforcing Emission Standards. Enforcing emission standards is an agency-assigned function. Article 21 of the Water Pollution Control Law states: "The prefectural governor may, in accordance with a cabinet order, call for a report from a person who discharges effluents . . . or may have his officials enter the specified establishment and inspect the facility or other regulated matter." Article 13 of the Air Pollution Control Law delegates similar authority for air pollution facilities. The main legal enforcement tools have come to be inspections and improvement orders. Both instruments are minutely regulated by central law. However, policies related to the frequency of inspections are left to the prefectures. Moreover, prefectures have developed administrative remedies below the level of improvement orders.

The total number of inspections has been increasing steadily in each of the three prefectures, the rate of increase limited by financial and personnel considerations. Only water pollution inspections in Saga may be said to have reached a satisfactory level. The prefectures often perform inspections within particular industries or areas. Saitama has a policy of inspecting all the facilities in a particular industrial park together, mainly to increase the number of inspections possible with a given number of inspectors. Overall, however, policies relating to the number of inspections do not vary much among the prefectures.

All prefectures use improvement recommendations when improvement is called for, but an order is inapplicable. Saitama also uses a warning for cases that do not warrant a recommendation. Recommendations and warnings are not legal actions but administrative guidance. Usually such guidance is sufficient to bring about the desired improvements, but if an establishment is unresponsive, the prefecture can issue an order or initiate a suit. Administrative guidance is generally preferred to orders and suits, which are used only as a last resort.

To an American, this reluctance to resort to legal sanctions often looks like negligence on the part of the prefecture. An American would be amazed, however, by the degree of compliance, often exceeding the letter of the recommendation, achieved by this administrative guidance. Willingness to take a polluter to court is a sign of a strong commitment in Japan.

A great deal of discretion is available to prefectures in the enforcement of emission standards, but I found no signficant variation among
the three prefectures. Lack of variation may be attributed to the difficulty of taking the "next step" in monitoring compliance. Chiba is one
of the few prefectures to have taken this step.

Chiba has established a "source telemeter" for air pollution that
parallels the environmental telemeter. Automatic monitoring devices
located in the factories are linked to the central computer and give
hourly readouts on the level of emissions. The purpose of the source
telemeter, like that of the environmental telemeter, is to provide immediate notice of emergency situations and to initiate immediate countermeasures. The prefecture can communicate the existence of an emergency situation to all factories involved simultaneously, and monitor
their emission reductions. The source telemeter could also be used to
check compliance continuously, but there is a legal problem.

Legal improvement orders must be based on legally conducted inspections. During 1976–1977, Chiba was still involved in checking the
reliability of the system and central government regulations determining
methods for estimating total emissions under quota regulation had yet to
be set. Though the issue was still in doubt, the prefecture petitioned the
central government to allow the use of the source telemeter and is proceeding on the assumption that they will be able to use it to enforce quota
regulation. A source telemeter represents a quantum leap in compliance
monitoring, and a technology not envisioned in the law. In the past, the
EA has not handled such situations with much flexibility.

Aid to Small Businesses. Both central and local governments offer
low-interest loans to small businesses for pollution control investments.
Aiding small businesses is a local function. Supplementing national aid
programs is also a traditional and accepted activity of local governments. In 1975, thirty-eight of the forty-seven prefectures had independent aid programs, including the three prefectures under investigation
here (Environmental Agency, 1977). Aid programs vary widely, but
the diversity is accepted. What uniformity exists is created by diffusion
among prefectures and the example set by the central government.
Some prefectures, including Chiba and Saitama, have direct grant programs as well as loan programs.

Policymaking in this activity tends to take a more political and less
bureaucratic form. Small business interests are a favorite of local
assemblymen of all parties. Aid programs are also peculiarly local in
character. When describing their policies in the other activities covered

in this chapter, local officials always started with an explanation of the law. When discussing aid programs, officials mentionened the national programs later as another source of aid. One should also note that these programs account for a large part of the prefectural expenditures for pollution control.

One program deserves special mention: Saga's program for controlling livestock pollution. In 1973 Saga instituted a grant program to help farmers build manure treatment facilities. Livestock pollution does not form a large part of Saga's pollution policy in objective terms, but complaints about water and odor pollution were causing problems for farmers.[6] The program was developed within the agricultural administration without direct consultations with the Pollution Control Division. The Livestock Division responded to the needs of farmers and the general prefectural policy of pollution control. This program represents an example of indirect coordination and a case of bottom-up policymaking. The prefecture was not influenced by central actions or the examples of other prefectures. This was as pure a case of local policymaking as I found.

Sewer Construction. Building and maintaining sewer systems is an entity-assigned function, subject to detailed regulation, primarily of the technical engineering aspects of the systems. More important, building sewers is a subsidized activity. Sewers are so expensive that the initiation and pace of construction are determined largely by the grant authorization process. Spurred by concern for water quality, local government demands for grants have far outstripped the supply, despite rapidly growing appropriations. Intergovernmental issues in sewer construction center on finances.

Sewer construction is primarily a municipal-level activity, but prefectures perform two major roles: they draw up detailed plans linking sewer construction to water quality and they build large-scale "basin-wide sewer systems" directly.

Drawing up "comprehensive river basin plans for sewer construction" is an agency-assigned activity. Not only are the plans regulated in detail as to form, but also the final plans require the approval of the minister of construction. Their main purpose is to set priorities. The plans evaluate the areas that need sewer systems to achieve or maintain environmental standards. Prefectures then estimate the cost of construction for all possible combinations of municipalities and choose the best, which are often but not necessarily always the cheapest combinations. These elaborate documents become a basis for grant authorization.

The form of the plans is determined by law and central regulations, but their substance can easily be influenced by prefectural decisions. While many areas of discretion are available, the key decision is choosing the best combinations of municipalities that will share a single sewer system. After financing, the bottleneck involves locating and acquiring a suitable site for a treatment plant. Local governments are much better equipped for this task and the location of the treatment plant affects the rest of the plan in many ways. Other local factors, such as a tradition of animosity between certain cities, affect the plans. Despite detailed regulation, prefectures do the planning. The ministry cannot evaluate the prefectures' decisions effectively because they do not have independent access to the proper information; they can only assure themselves that basic technical requirements have been met.

During the research period (1976–1977), however, the Ministry of Construction could be confident that prefectures generally adhered to the letter and spirit of the law. At that time the law and regulations were not thought of as limitations on prefectural discretion but as the right way to plan, the proper process for prefectural decision making. The discretion available to prefectures was seldom, if ever, used to promote prefectural priorities in conflict with MOC priorities. A consensus still exists on the ministry's priorities.

One potential area of conflict concerns timing. Despite the fact that drawing up the plan is a required function, few prefectures have finished the task. Of the three prefectures under investigation, only Saitama has completed its plan. Chiba has plans for areas with basin systems but not elsewhere. Saga has yet to complete a plan largely because there are no suitable sites for a basin system in the prefecture. A comprehensive plan is practically required to get a basin system approved, but beyond that the MOC seems to have little leverage. Prefectures draw up plans as part of the grant authorization process, not because doing so is a required agency-assigned function.

The law defines a river basin system as one that includes two or more municipalities. Actually, not all sewer systems that fit this definition are classified as basin systems because that classification brings with it a higher grant ratio. The central government pays two-thirds of the cost of municipal systems but three-quarters for basin systems. Basin plans must be approved by the MOC, but the final say rests with the Ministry of Finance (MOF). Basin systems are quite attractive to municipalities and the ministry was worried that the proliferation of such plans would place a strain on the budget. It therefore established minimum size requirements.

The demand for basin sewer systems far exceeds supply. If politics, either electoral or bureaucratic, plays a role in Japanese intergovernmental relations, it should play a role here. Although I expected these grants to be used to reward some prefectures and punish others, when I asked if prefectures had to compete for basin systems, officials emphasized objective factors in granting funds.

Chiba officials told me, "If a plan meets minimum requirements, and if the prefecture believes that a basin system is necessary, then I think the ministry will approve it." Another reported "It is not the case that winners in a competition get grants and losers do not. Rather, the places with the greatest need, from a national point of view, are started first" (interview in Chiba Prefecture, Department of Urban Affairs, First Sewer Division, Planning Section, July 27, 1977).

National-level officials, however, painted a different picture. A MOC official told me, "what priorities? It cannot be done. There are just too many plans. If there were a particularly unique plan, or if it fell into four or five priority categories, then we could pay attention to those plans, . . . but they all fall into some priority category. In the end, it amounts to nothing." The same official, however, also told me, "We do not cut plans when the requests are sincere" (interview in MOC, Sewer Planning Division, May 14, 1977).

These contradictory pictures of the grant process can be explained in large part by different perspectives. National officials are frustrated by their inability to run the grant process smoothly, based on objective factors alone. They use objective factors, but those factors do not bring the number of acceptable plans down to the size of the budget. Thereafter, the only indicator of "need" available to them is the number and intensity of local petitions. Prefectural officials spend a great deal of time and energy preparing and presenting their case in objective terms. The central decision-making process seems somewhat mysterious to them, but good plans, sincerely offered, are approved.

The best evidence on the grant process came from Saitama's experience in getting a new basin system approved. Saitama has been very active in promoting sewer construction. The prefecture has five basin plans, including one of the country's largest. It has used the MOC's planning process to encourage cooperation among municipalities even when the resulting projects fall below the size requirements for a basin system. Most of the municipalities in Saitama participate in either a basin plan or a regional plan, as they call their smaller cooperative projects. These regional plans are part of a prefectural program and receive no special consideration from the central government. In 1977 the Tone River Regional Sewer System Plan was enlarged and came to meet the requirements for a basin system. Saitama requested and received approval for its fifth basin plan.

Approval of the Tone River plan should have been difficult to obtain. If the Finance Ministry wants plans to be as large as possible, this plan barely met the minimum. The timing of the request, after the national five-year plan for sewer contruction had already started, was not auspicious. If balance among prefectures were considered, Saitama could not argue that it had not got its share. If ministries use grants to discipline prefectures that deviate from ministry policies, the MOC should have had some desire to discipline Saitama. It does not approve of Saitama's policy of limiting population growth and is not particularly happy with Saitama's housing policy. (See chapter 5.) If the LDP uses grants to discipline prefectures that elect opposition party governors, Saitama's governor, who belongs to the Socialist party, should have had trouble. Yet, when I asked Saitama officials if there had been any problems getting the plan approved, the reply was, "Not particularly. On the other hand, the prefectural Finance Division was negative about the plan at first" (interview in Saitama Prefecture, Department of Housing and Urban Affairs, Sewer Division, July 27, 1977). The prefecture did mobilize its Dietmen to help petition for approval, but the key hurdle was the prefectural budgetary process.

The volume of sewer construction within a prefecture is determined by the prefecture. Sincere requests are not refused, and petitioning is a demonstration of sincerity. The ministry must have some mechanism for matching expenditures to its budget, but grant approval is not that mechanism. The necessary cutting seems to take place during the detailed negotiations over the timing of payments and the pace of construction. The effect is similar to that of an across-the-board percentage cut. All sewer construction projects are behind schedule and I could find no evidence of some projects being given priority. Thus, the volume of construction within a prefecture is affected by the overall availability of grant money, but a prefecture's share of the grant money is determined primarily by prefectual priorities.

Conclusions

Pollution control policymaking had, by 1976–1977 shifted from the political to the bureaucratic arena. Controversy had died down and a new consensus had emerged on the necessity of a strong policy. Nevertheless, the basic characteristics of the previous period remained.

Neither the authority hypothesis nor the principle of least interest had much explanatory power. Influence was best explained by the policy substance hypothesis: it was still true that the party pushing for stronger environmental policies tended to win because they were considered both better policy and better politics.

I observed three major disjunctures between authority and influence in this area. First, agency-assigned functions are treated as local functions. Local officials simply do not make the distinctions that law professors spend so much time arguing about. The minister's authority to oversee local implementation of agency-assigned functions has no practical consequences for day-to-day administration. The central government has more authority over agency-assigned functions than over local functions, but no more influence.

Second, in setting effluent standards for water pollution, central authority and constraints on local authority did not prove important. The law contains many provisions that could give the central government influence or that could constrain local policymaking. Neither of these things has happened. The provision for *uwanose* standards is now the operative section of the law. Perhaps because some local governments were involved in setting effluent standards before the central government intervened, the law has not structured policymaking as thoroughly as one might expect in a bureaucratic state.

Third, the Environmental Agency retains the authority to set emission standards for SO_2, but locally negotiated pollution control agreements generally supersede the EA's standards. Setting emission standards for SO_2 is the most centralized process in pollution control. Local variation is to be provided for by central designation. Yet, in practice, locally negotiated extralegal agreements determine the effective standards for most industrial sources.

The law does make a difference; it structures the whole policymaking process. All local policy must fit into the legal framework. Thus, when the *uwanose* provisions were enacted, all the local governments had already enacted emission standards changed them to conform to the *uwanose* format. Every major revision of the law has meant that local governments must adjust their ordinances. Usually the changes are more a matter of form than of substance; their purpose is to maintain administrative uniformity. This commitment to administrative uniformity also produces inflexibility in the face of local variation unless exceptions are provided for in the law. Chiba's quota regulation of air pollution is a case in point. Maintaining administrative uniformity is a policy and it does affect local policy. Moreover, the agenda effect of national policymaking should not be underestimated. Every piece of central legislation places that topic onto all local agendas and sets off a wave of (often minor) local policymaking. Nevertheless, the substance of policy is primarily determined at the local level. The central government influences the timing of local policy more than the substance. It can bring the problem to the attention of local governments but cannot control what the local governments do. Central laws establish the framework of policy, but within that framework local governments set the parameters of the policy.

The main effect of the uniform administrative framework is to make communications and comparison easier. The names and definitions of policy parameters are virtually uniform throughout Japan. Local governments that get ahead of national policy often suffer from the central government's insistence on administrative uniformity, but that uniformity makes the whole system of intergovernmental policymaking run more efficiently. The tradeoff is between efficiency on the one hand, and local policy innovation and experimentation on the other.

Pollution policymaking has shifted from the political to the bureaucratic arena without an increase in the degree to which authority produces influence. The explanation for this surprising result seems to be that in 1976–1977 policymakers still perceived overwhelming popular support for stronger pollution control policies. This also explains why the principle of least interest failed to explain the patterns of influence I found. Policymaking had shifted to the bureaucratic arena but the bureaucrats assumed that this shift was contingent on continuing progress in pollution control. With good reason, they assumed that any backtracking or any sign of lessened commmitment might reactivate public opinion and the political policymakers. Thus, in an argument between doing more and doing less, the former option was given the benefit of the doubt.

My findings on Japan's pollution control policies give some limited support to the three remaining hypotheses. The information hypothesis provides insight into several specific cases of policymaking, but does not explain the overall distribution of influence, because information remained relatively evenly distributed. While the total amount of information in the system had increased immensely by 1976–1977, central and local governments maintained a rough parity. On the one hand, local governments had gained a great deal of expertise. Chiba Prefecture, for example, volunteered to do the environmental assessment for the Tokyo Bay Highway if the EA did not feel up to it. Citizens' movements had also become more sophisticated, taking their own measurements of air and water quality. On the other hand, the development of sophisticated monitoring devices had made knowledge of local conditions available to the central government. The EA's promotion of regional quota regulation plans, which would centralize the setting of emission standards, would have been impossible without the detailed data produced by systematic monitoring. Both expertise and knowledge of local conditions had become widely diffused throughout the system. In terms of hypothesis testing, the case of pollution control does not provide us with a test of the information hypothesis because there is no variance in the independent variable.

The salience of electoral politics and elected politicians had clearly declined, but continued to dominate one area: aid to small businesses. The type of politics had changed from the partisan redistributive politics of the 1960s to a nonpartisan distributive competition for the votes of well-identified groups, a politics similar to that involved in the case of the medium-sized stores noted above. Nevertheless, political decision making dominated bureaucratic considerations. Moreover, this type of politics produced the most purely local of any local policymaking I found in my research. Saga's program for control of livestock odor pollution stands out in this regard.

Finally, financial factors were not particularly relevant except in sewer construction. Sewers are an important part of pollution control policy but sewer construction is the Public Works Department's contribution to pollution control. The personnel involved are different and they deal with the Ministry of Construction, not the EA. Sewer construction also entails a major grant program, unlike any other part of pollution control policy. Policymaking in this area has more in common with that in housing construction than with the rest of pollution control. I shall therefore postpone the discussion of sewer construction until the next chapter.

5

Housing Policy

*T*HE COUNTRIES that participated in World War II faced a tremendous growth in housing demand after the war. Japan faced particularly heavy demand stemming not only from the wartime destruction of housing, but also from the repatriation of thousands of Japanese nationals from the prewar colonies. The government estimated a shortage of 4.2 million houses (Hayakawa and Wada, 1973), and the first housing policies to be enacted after the war were emergency measures designed to provide some shelter for everyone. Around 1950 the crisis had abated enough so that Japan could begin establishing a permanent housing policy. The first major act created the Housing Finance Bank (HFB, *Jūtaku Kinyū Kōko*), and in 1951 the Public Housing Law (*Kōei Jūtaku-Hō,* literally, "publicly managed housing") was enacted. This law provided for subsidies to local governments to build low-rent housing for low-income families.

As the Japanese economy began to pick up during the Korean War, rapid urbanization gave rise to acute housing shortages in the larger cities. The government's response was to create the Japan Housing Corporation (JHC, *Nihon Jūtaku Kōdan*), a public corporation, to build large-scale housing projects in urban areas. Then, in 1966, housing policy was given a new coherence by the Housing Construction Planning Law, which mandated five-year plans. Local governments were also active in housing construction. Besides public housing, most prefectures and large cities built housing through semiprivate housing associations. In 1965 the government expanded the role of these associations by enacting the Local Housing Supply Corporation (LHSC, *Chihō Jūtaku Kyōkyū Kōsha*) Law. Local governments converted their associations into LHSCs. These corporations are funded both through the

HFB and local government, and are meant to respond to peculiar local housing needs.

The basic structure of housing policy was set by 1966. The structure forms a hierarchy providing aid for each income level. Public housing is divided into "type two" for the lowest income groups and "type one" for those somewhat better off. For those whose incomes exceed the limits for public housing, JHC rental housing is available. The JHC also builds condominium housing for slightly higher income groups. LHSC housing caters to essentially the same income groups as JHC housing, but is substituted for JHC housing in more rural areas where the JHC does little construction. LHSC housing may also help fill any gap left between public and JHC rental housing. Finally, the HFB offers loans to those who can afford to build their own homes. There are also many smaller housing programs catering to special groups.

Together with a booming private sector, publicly financed housing did a fair job of keeping up with demand.[1] The percentage of families needing housing dropped from 20 percent in 1963 to 15 percent in 1968 and to less than 9 percent in 1973 (Yamaoka and Kyōsu, 1976: 29).[2] In 1965 the number of houses exceeded the number of families for the first time since the war and the government began to shift attention away from quantity toward quality (Koizumi, 1971).[3] The goal of the first five-year plan (1966–1970) was summarized in the slogan: "a house for every family"; the slogan of the second plan was "a room for every person"; the third—and current—five-year plan focuses on detailed minimum housing standards.

Despite significant progress, not all went according to plan. In particular, housing built directly by government agencies (public, JHC, and LHSC housing) failed to meet plan targets (see table 5). In the middle of the second plan the Arab oil embargo caused Japan's economy to falter. Inflation, particularly inflation in land prices, made housing construction much more difficult. Land price inflation, combined with several other factors, produced a new kind of problem, the "empty house" problem.

Japan has long been a difficult place to find sites for large projects of any kind. Land tends to be divided into complex patterns of small plots and land prices have risen faster than prices in general (Hanayama, 1972 and 1973). Small owners often do not wish to sell because land is such an excellent investment. The post–oil crisis inflation accelerated land price inflation to emergency proportions. Another factor making it difficult to find suitable sites was the growing scarcity of easily developed sites near urban centers. Though this scarcity seems to be more

TABLE 5
Japan's Five-Year Housing Construction Plans

	First Plan (1966–70)		Second Plan (1971–75)		Third Plan (1976–80)
	Target	Actual %	Target	Actual %	Target
Public	520	92.1	678	74.0	495
Housing Finance Bank	1,080	100.7	1,376	121.5	1,900
Japan Housing Corporation	350	95.7	460	62.4	310
Other	480	138.3	945	70.9	620
Total Public	2,700	95.0	3,838	81.4	3,500
Private	4,000	104.4	5,738	89.5	5,100
Total	6,700	100.6	9,576	86.3	8,600

Sources: first plan, Ministry of Construction materials; second plan, Construction White Paper, 1976, p. 30; third plan, Construction White Paper, 1976, p. 134.

Notes: Figures are in thousands of housing units. Figures for the third plan include estimates for the later years. LHSC housing is included in HFB housing.

relative than absolute, housing projects, particularly JHC projects, began around the mid-1960s to be built further from urban centers. The JHC also began to build larger projects, partly in response to demand for more housing, but also to provide a large enough population to attract the necessary services, stores, and so on. The increased size of projects, however, intensified other problems.

A housing project means incoming population, and the local government must provide these new residents with a large variety of services. When the housing project is large, or when the rate of population growth is high and continuous, the cost of providing these services can become a heavy burden on the local budget. In particular, local governments have difficulty locating and buying sites for schools, day-care centers, and other public facilities. During the 1960s the costs of population growth became painfully obvious to many local officials and was the subject of academic debate.

Table 6 provides estimates on the costs of population growth. In rapidly growing municipalities each new resident costs the local gov-

TABLE 6
Estimates of Per Capita Revenues and Expenditures for New versus Existing Residents in Rapidly Growing Municipalities, 1971

	Rapid Growth Municipalities			Other Municipalities
	Overall	New Population	Existing	
Revenues	$27.40	$34.60	$25.60	$27.10
Taxes	11.10	9.55	11.50	7.00
LDT[a]	2.10	3.70	1.75	6.35
Grants	3.15	4.40	2.80	3.20
Borrowing	4.00	10.95	2.25	2.70
Expenditures	26.55	38.90	23.45	26.25
Construction[b]	10.80	23.75	7.60	9.55
Balance	+0.85	−4.30	+2.15	+0.85

Source: Adapted from Tatsuta Kiyoshi, "Jinkō Kyūzō Shichōson no Zaisei" ("The Finances of Rapid Population Growth Municipalities"), in Henkaku ni Taiō suru Chihō Zaisei (Local Finances Responding to Change), ed. Tsunematsu Seiji (Gakuyō Shobō, 1974), p. 131.

Note: Figures are in dollars per capita, figured at 200 yen to the dollar.

a. LDT refers to the local distribution tax, a form of revenue sharing.

b. Construction here is regular construction, i.e., excluding disaster reconstruction and so on. Rapid growth municipalities refers to those cities, towns and villages that have been experiencing at least 10 percent rise in population over the last five years.

ernment an average of $4.30. The old population subsidizes the new. The differences in services received by the new and old populations is difficult to estimate accurately, but is clear even to the casual observer. Everything in the housing project is new while everything in the rest of the city is old and probably in need of repair. These visible differences, plus socioeconomic differences between the two groups of residents, provide fertile ground for political conflict. The local government is caught in the middle and has insufficient funds to keep up with the demand for basic services.

The problem is not new, but awareness of it has been growing. In the late 1960s local governments began to deny cooperation to developers and make demands on them. Some cities instituted policies of limiting population growth and many enacted guidelines for housing developments. These guidelines typically required the developer to provide land for, or bear part of the cost of, public facilities made necessary by the development, particularly schools (Kuze, 1973; Masago, 1975; Ueda, 1973; Ikeda, 1977). American local governments faced similar problems and developed similar policies in the 1960s and 1970s (Rosenbaum, 1978; Frieden, 1979; White, 1981).

These local policies affected the JHC most directly, but prefecturally built public housing, LHSC housing, and large private developments were also subject to the same demands. The effect of these policies was to raise the cost of construction and make it even more difficult to find sites close to urban centers. Since rents for publicly financed housing are based on construction costs, rents also jumped (see table 7).

While housing is becoming more difficult and expensive to build in Japan, housing demand has been changing. Whereas the number of

TABLE 7
Rising Rents in Publicly Built Housing, 1970–1974

	Public Housing			
	Type 1	Type 2	JHC	LHSC
1970	$34.64	$24.58	$88.50	$64.90
1971	37.76	26.49	102.00	66.98
1972	40.80	28.72	208.00	88.50
1973	51.26	35.29	112.00	91.50
1974	—	—	140.50	126.08

Source: Adapted from Yamaoka and Kyōsu, Kore kara no Jūtaku Seisaku (Housing Policy from Now On) (Jūtaku Shimpōsha, 1976), p. 199.

Notes: Figures are in dollars, figured at 200 yen to the dollar. These are monthly rents.

families needing housing—an objective indicator—has been falling, dissatisfaction with present housing—a subjective indicator—has remained high. Many complain about the small size of most Japanese houses. Public agencies have been slow to respond to demands for more spacious housing.[4] As a result of changing housing demand, rising rents, and increasing distance from urban centers, public housing agencies began to experience difficulty in renting or selling their houses. The JHC was hardest hit, but other types of publicly built housing were not exempt. The popular phrase, "too expensive, too far, too small" *(takai, tōi, semai)* has been applied to all of them.

Although both governmental and media attention has focused on the empty house problem, it is primarily a big-city phenomenon. Yet it may be considered part of a larger change in the environment of housing policymaking: the diversification of housing demand from both potential occupants and local governments. In some real but as yet ill-understood sense, the quantity problem has been solved and has been replaced by several kinds of quality problems. The government can no longer build almost any type of house almost anywhere and expect people to flock to their doors. More important, from the viewpoint of intergovernmental relations, the central government can no longer make policy on the assumption that housing needs are similar throughout the country (Shiroya, 1977; Sumita, 1977).

This chapter will examine prefectural housing policies by focusing on two issues. First, how is the number of units of each type of housing to be built in a prefecture determined? Under this "quantity" heading, I will discuss the development and implementation of five-year plans and prefectural policies toward JHC, LHSC, and public housing. Second, I will focus on aspects of public housing management: specifically, who gets into public housing and how rents are determined. These questions omit several important aspects of housing policy, particularly housing finance and land use regulation. I chose to focus on how the number of units is determined, who gets into them, and what rents will be charged, primarily because these matters are formally decided by prefectures. Housing finance is primarily a central government activity and land use guidelines are mainly enacted by cities.

The Three Prefectures

Saga is an agricultural prefecture. Although it had been losing population, more recently it has just been holding its own. Saga's population is not highly mobile and prefectural officials perceive housing demand as overwhelmingly oriented toward owner-occupied dwellings. Tosu City, and to a lesser extent Saga City, are exceptions to this generalization, but the market for rental housing is limited primarily to those who cannot afford to buy. Housing policy therefore focuses on public housing for those who cannot buy and condominium housing built by the LHSC for those who can.

Saga is a relatively easy place to build houses. Land prices, though rising, are still among the lowest in the nation, and land is available even around the larger cities. Although the prefecture is taking precautions against urban sprawl, in most areas cities are more interested in attracting and holding population, and housing is a way to attract people. In the old coal-mining areas there are districts of dense, low-quality housing that need to be cleared, but this problem is as close as Saga comes to facing a "housing crisis."

Saitama falls on the opposite extreme of the continuum, facing the problems associated with having the highest population growth rate in the country. Chiba is second. Both prefectures border on Tokyo and Tokyo's population has expanded in an arc around Tokyo Bay, starting in Kanagawa and proceeding through Saitama to Chiba. In both prefectures, population has grown most rapidly along the commuter rail lines leading to central Tokyo, but in Chiba the pattern is broken up somewhat by the presence of the *kombināto* as an independent magnet for population growth. In Saitama nothing breaks the pattern and population growth is almost exclusively a function of commuting time to Tokyo.

Both prefectures are blessed and cursed with large areas of easily developed flat land and both have had high rates of land price inflation. Both have been afflicted with urban sprawl and are dotted with high-rise apartment complexes. Both contain cities that are essentially "bed towns" for Tokyo commuters. A significant number of Saitama's in-migrants have been young people, originally from a rural area, who came to Tokyo seeking employment and moved to Saitama upon getting married. These people tend to remain oriented toward Tokyo, at least until their children reach school age, and are popularly known as "Saitama's Tokyoites."[5] Chiba's northern area faces similar problems, but in-migrants further south are more likely to have come directly from rural areas, drawn by the opportunities produced by the *kombināto*.

Apart from the *kombināto*, differences in problems faced by the two prefectures often stem from differences in timing and degree. Saitama was overwhelmed with population growth before much of a policy response could be made. For example, Saitama has the largest number of cities of any prefecture in Japan. Before plans could be made to amalgamate towns and villages into reasonably sized cities, they had become cities by virtue of population. Because Saitama's population growth has consisted largely of young married couples, the growth will continue in the future even if in-migration were to come to a halt.

Chiba benefited somewhat from the experience of Saitama and of Kanagawa before that. Chiba's policymakers were able to foresee the coming of Tokyo's population wave and to prepare for it more than either Kanagawa or Saitama. Chiba is building three "new towns" to accommodate population growth in a planned and orderly fashion (Chiba Prefecture, Land Division, 1976). Unfortunately, the 1973 oil crisis intervened and the construction of these new towns is not proceeding smoothly (*Chiba Nippo,* May 26, 1977). These new towns have, however, shaped Chiba's housing policy both by providing planned projects that can absorb some population growth and by committing the prefecture to enough population growth to fill the new towns.

Both Chiba and Saitama embarked upon population limitation policies in 1972. In Saitama one of the first acts of the newly elected progressive governor was to create a broadly based project team to study the problems of rapid population growth (Ushimi, 1973 and 1977; Tsunoi, 1975). In 1973 Governor Hata took the single most important step in implementing the population limitation policy: he announced that city planning districts would be frozen indefinitely. Japanese city planning is based upon establishing "urbanization districts" in which development is encouraged and "urbanization adjustment districts" in which growth is controlled. In the 1960s and early 1970s many developers, including the JHC and LHSCs, bought land in adjustment districts on the assumption that they could get development or that the area would be reclassified. The announcement of a freeze on reclassification had the effect of ending this speculation and holding down land prices.

Both Saitama and Chiba enacted tough guidelines on what kind of projects would be granted permits in adjustment districts. Chiba announced a freeze on large-scale projects in 1972 and scaled down the planned size of the new towns. Both prefectures joined with Kanagawa to reduce population growth due to JHC housing construction (Oshimoto, 1968). Saitama and Kanagawa issued a plea to private developers to give priority to people already living in the prefecture and Saitama reports significant levels of compliance. All three prefectures held down their five-year construction plans.

Despite these and other similarities in the two prefectures' population limitation policies, there are some signficant differences. First, Saitama uses a stronger term for its policy,[6] and gives the policy greater publicity. As noted above, Chiba is committed to some population growth in the new towns. Second, although the list of reasons for pursuing the policy are virtually identical, emphases do differ. Whereas Chiba places the primary emphasis on an insufficient water supply, Saitama emphasizes the financial problems caused by population growth. Though these may only be differences in public postures, they do seem to be related to ideological differences. Chiba takes a relatively low posture and emphasizes "hard" statistical facts. Both the Ministry of Construction and the JHC are receptive to the water shortage argument. Saitama's arguments are more fundamental critiques of the system and the arguments seem more directed toward the citizenry than the central ministries.

Having described population limitation policies, I should note that the effectiveness of these policies is in doubt. First, local governments point to their lack of tools for controlling private developers. For example, Ushimi (1973) presents estimates that only a quarter of the private housing projects in Saitama are subject to city planning permits. Other projects were too small to fall under the regulative provisions. Local governments are seeking more authority over these "minidevelopments."

The Ministry of Construction and the JHC argue that population limitation policies are ineffective and even harmful. They argue that if one holds down population pressure by restricting large developments, it is merely diverted into small, unplanned private developments that contribute to urban sprawl. Thus the MOC argues that local governments should not restrict large-scale developments and local governments argue that the ministry should give them the authority to control small-scale developments.

Having presented an overview of Japanese housing problems and policies, I now turn to a more detailed examination of policymaking in the prefectures.

Housing Construction

Five-Year Plans. When asked about planning for housing construction, Japanese officials at any level of government will begin with an explanation something like the following. First, the government makes a detailed estimate of housing needs based upon the national housing survey. Combining these estimates of needs with the general policy line (such as "a house for every family"), the Construction Ministry draws up a national plan, which the cabinet approves. It then breaks down the plan into twelve bloc plans. Using the bloc plans, and in consultation with other prefectures in the bloc, each prefecture draws up its own five-year plan, which they report to the MOC. Planning is thus depicted as a rational, top-down process. This picture is correct but incomplete.

First, there is a significant flow of information and ideas from the bottom upward. At each stage of the process, prefectures present data and opinions to the MOC, providing the data upon which the national plan is based.[7] Providing data sounds harmless, but the "data" provided are actually draft prefectural plans; they are labeled and thought of as such. The planning process, as distinct from the data-gathering and analysis process, may be said to start with these prefectural drafts. The process of drawing up a national plan may be characterized as adding up the numbers in the prefectural drafts and making some adjustments.

Characterizing the planning process as following either a top-down or a bottom-up pattern is inadequate. Both are incomplete descriptions of a complex process that starts almost two years before the cabinet makes its formal decision. The process—in the case of the most recent plan—started with "explanation" meetings in October 1974, in which MOC officials explained the proper procedures and general policies governing housing construction planning. Prefecture-by-prefecture hearings followed in June and July 1975 and again in September when the prefectural draft was due. During the period from June through December, hearings and negotiations were held both formally and informally. The MOC actually had its first draft ready in August, before the prefectures presented their drafts. Both the MOC draft and the prefectural drafts were based on sound information about the thinking of the other parties; by the time they were drawn up, they all contained elements of both MOC and prefectural thinking. These drafts represented the end of the decision-making process, though many formalities remained before cabinet approval in March 1976.

The process is carried out largely through face-to-face hearings. Whatever documents are used in the early stages are informal and soon discarded. Also, prefectural drafts are usually thrown out, so it proved impossible to follow the process from the beginning. I did, however, find some cases of intergovernmental conflict that help illuminate the process.

Both Chiba and Saitama were able to keep their estimates of total needed construction low, in line with their population limitation policies. A Saitama official described the process:

The government has its own estimates of Saitama's future population. Saitama has its estimates based on our population limitation policy. Differences naturally arose, but we managed to get our figures through. The government presented their figures and Saitama stressed population limitation. We started with 493,000 and it went through without change. (Interview in Saitama Prefecture, Housing Division, April 7, 1977)

Data (draft) presentation is an agency-assigned function and, as such, detailed procedures for estimating housing needs are drawn up by the MOC. Despite this uniformity of procedures, prefectures do have significant discretion in estimating needs and were able to use the planning process to pursue policies that the MOC considers undesirable.

Another bit of information comes from the formal prefectural opinions on the final plan. These opinions are a formality with no effect on the outcome. Nevertheless, twenty-four prefectures chose to express some dissatisfaction. Of these, fifteen stressed financial problems and twelve complained that the MOC had lowered their plan targets, with three prefectures making both complaints (unpublished MOC materials). Even though the MOC was unable to get the Kantō bloc (which includes Chiba and Saitama) to raise their plan targets, it was able to lower targets for at least four blocs. One of these blocs was Kyūshū, which includes Saga, and I was able to find data on both prefectural and MOC drafts (see table 8).

The Ministry of Construction wanted the prefectures to build more public housing and its estimates of private construction were much higher than those of the two prefectures. The ministry cut both HFB

TABLE 8
Prefectural and MOC Drafts for the Third Five-Year Plan, Kyūshū Bloc

	Prefectural Total	MOC Draft	Difference
Public	72,800	73,000	+200
Housing Finance Bank	250,100	235,000	−15,100
Japan Housing Corporation	28,900	24,000	−4,900
Other	54,400	45,000	−9,400
Private	494,600	566,000	+71,400
Total	900,800	943,000	+42,400

Source: Saga Prefecture, Construction Division, Dai-san-ki Jūtaku Kensetsu Go-ka-nen Keikaku: Sankō Shiryō (The Third Housing Construction Five-year Plan: Reference Materials) (June 1976), p. 4.

Notes: Figures are in housing units.

and JHC housing targets. Saga officials believe that the ministry generally underestimates the demand for HFB loans in Kyūshū because income levels are lower there than the national average. They think past
experience is a better indicator. For their part, ministry officials think
that rural prefectures tend to rely too much on past performance and
fail to take the government's deconcentration policies sufficiently into
account. They also believe that prefectural officials prefer to keep the
proportion of publicly financed housing high by deflating private-sector
targets and inflating HFB targets.

As these conflicting views indicate, the planning process is not completely rational and contains a substantial dose of politics. HFB and
private sector targets are less plan targets than forecasts. Except for
public housing, there is no need for prefectural totals to add up to the
ministry's bloc totals. The differences in the drafts are not necessarily
resolved. As a Saga official explained, "MOC does not say we have to
follow the plan exactly. It is, after all, a five-year plan and one must
make adjustments year to year. We figure plus or minus 10 to 15
percent. Thus, even if we do not bring our totals up to MOC's figures,
they will accept it" (interview in Saga Prefecture, Department of Planning and Finance, Land Policy Division, July 13, 1977). The only
figures that must add up are those for public housing because they
involve a direct subsidy from the central to the prefectural governments. With this exception (discussed below), prefectural plans are prefectural, and central plans are central. Each party takes the other's planning into account, but such coordination that exists occurs primarily
through the exchange of information.

The flexibility of the planning process is well illustrated by Saitama's revision of the plan midway through the second five-year plan.
As part of the newly elected governor's program, a mid-term prefectural plan was proclaimed, including revised targets for rental housing.
According to law, such changes must be reported to the Construction
Ministry. Saitama offered to submit a revised plan, but the MOC refused. A MOC official explained that it was not necessary because of
the large element of forecasting in the plan. The provision for revising
the plan has never been used. Saitama officials admitted that their revision was mainly a matter of revising forecasts, not a change in policy.

Housing plans do provide important information to both private and
public developers. The information includes both forecasts and the intentions of both central and prefectural governments. The plans are not,
however, hard and fast plans of action that determine housing construction. As Japanese officials are wont to put it, the plans are "flexible."

The most important conclusions about intergovernmental policy-making that can be drawn from this discussion are that information flows both upward and downward, and that prefectural plans are based on prefectural priorities. These conclusions must be qualified by two important caveats, however. First, the third plan, from which all my examples are taken, could be atypical. Local government unwillingness to build more housing became an important factor only after the second plan was in effect. All my informants agreed that the atmosphere of local assertiveness was much greater during the third planning process:

> In the first and second plans MOC's higher level plans were very strong and there was a lot of MOC changing of numbers. But for the third plan, the contentions of local governments became significantly stronger. A large gap developed between MOC's bloc plans and the numbers that the prefectures had in mind. But MOC did not try to force the issue. (Interview in Saitama Prefecture, Housing Division, April 7, 1977)

The difference between the second and third plans seems to be that "negative power" had passed from the central to local governments by the time of the third plan. The Ministry of Construction cannot force local governments to build or plan more, and local governments cannot force the ministry to plan or pay for more. The party that is willing to cut is in the more advantageous position. The principle of least interest applies nicely.

The second qualification concerns prefectural priorities. Prefectures have not taken issue with the basic goals of the plans. All prefectures base their calculations on MOC procedures and national goals. The differences that arise concern basic policy less than perspective. Even population limitation policies serve the basic goal of housing planning: the reduction and eventual elimination of substandard housing. Chiba and Saitama merely take this goal to apply to their own citizens first. Under a situation of rapid population growth, housing construction does not necessarily reduce the number of substandard houses. The new housing unit may not be occupied by a person moving from substandard housing within the prefecture but by an in-migrant. Even if a substandard unit were vacated, an in-migrant might well find it more attractive than a nicer house in a more distant location. Chiba and Saitama find it difficult to build enough housing to relieve the pressure on substandard housing. The only way to relieve the pressure is to slow down population growth.

If population limitation policies serve the prefectures' housing goals, these local policies make it more difficult to achieve the same goals nationally, assuming continued migration to the Tokyo metropolitan area. Subnational governments represent their currently resident population. The national government represents both residents of a locality and those people who might wish to move into the area. When this mobile population threatens the local quality of life, central and local governments can come to represent conflicting constituencies.

The Japan Housing Corporation. The JHC bore the brunt of both the empty house problem and local population limitation policies. In the 1960s, the JHC seemed a powerful institution with lots of money to throw around. In the 1970s, however, it appeared to be the easiest target for population limitation policies and subject to the whims of local governments.

The JHC is subject to local influence both as a matter of policy and as a matter of power. It is required by law to consult with local governments before constructing a housing project. It is also committed to sound city planing and orderly urban development and is therefore open to local demands phrased in these terms. The central mission of the JHC is, however, to build houses. If a local government wants to attach conditions to a project, the JHC has little choice but to comply. Theoretically it could build in some other jurisdiction, but this possibility virtually disappeared in the 1970s. The JHC's weakness is demonstrated by its acquiescence, within the limits of the law, to local guidelines.

The JHC does not build in Saga except for a few company housing projects (see table 9). Saga officials say the JHC is inflexible and unwilling to build according to local needs. The JHC refuses to lower

TABLE 9
The JHC in Prefectural and National Five-Year Plans

	First Plan (1966–70)		Second Plan (1970–75)		Third Plan (1976–80)
	Target	Actual %	Target	Actual %	Target
Saga	250	12.8	0	—	100
Chiba	46,600	105.1	67,000	67.7	50,000
Saitama	51,900	61.5	68,000	54.3	38,000
National	380,000	95.7	460,000	61.7	310,000

Sources: Materials provided by the prefectures and the Ministry of Construction.
Note: Figures are in housing units.

standards, and therefore prices, to fit Saga's housing market. Saga and the JHC have agreed to ignore each other, but both of the other two prefectures have come into sharp conflict with the JHC.

The 1970s saw increasing demands made upon the JHC, particularly from the three prefectures around Tokyo. In 1971 both Chiba and Saitama demanded consultation before land purchases, and by the end of 1972 the three prefectures (including Kanagawa) had managed to get the JHC to admit prefectural citizens on a priority basis to 80 percent of the new housing projects and to provide 20 percent of the development sites for prefectural public housing.

The prefecture's original demands were priority for its citizens in all JHC housing, including not only new but also other open units. The JHC managed to deny local citizens priority in 20 percent of the new units and in all of the openings in old projects and therefore maintained its national mission. The limitation of priority to new projects was significant because these are the projects that are subject to the empty house problem. Open units in older projects are more desirable because they are cheaper (rents are seldom raised), and are usually nearer metropolitan areas. Despite their small size, these units are very popular. The JHC likes to use them to provide housing for people already in JHC housing who are forced to move. Despite these concessions to the JHC, the agreements represented a clear victory for the prefectures. They succeeded in blunting the population-inducing aspects of JHC housing projects and forced the JHC to aid them in satisfying prefectural demands.[8]

Chiba Prefecture's relationship with the JHC is unique because it negotiates written agreements with the JHC for each five-year plan. The practice actually began in 1965 before the first five-year plan. The purpose was to get the JHC's cooperation with prefectural housing projects, to obtain earlier consultation on its projects, to reduce the financial burdens on muncipalities, and to shift its emphasis from rental to condominium housing.

Chiba has essentially coopted the JHC into helping build the prefecture's new towns. The JHC is happy to build in locally plannned projects. The shift from rental to condominium housing is less clearly a part of the corporation's national mission, though it would seem to be consistent with the LDP's policies.[9] In any case, Chiba's demands were heeded and the percentage of rental housing dropped from 96 percent between 1955 and 1965 to 70 percent between 1966 and 1970, and again to 65 percent between 1971 and 1975.

When asked about JHC resistance to their demands, prefectural officials responded that it was negligible. While there is a difference in perspective, the corporation does take local demands into account. And they can hardly stop building in the prefecture. This national institution has, to some degree, been captured by local interests. Moreover, this conclusion is not limited to the third five-year plan. Chiba significantly influenced JHC policies even during the period of high demand for JHC housing. Public corporations would seem a centralized alternative to directly subsidizing local governments. In this case, however, local governments may have little authority over the JHC, but they have a great deal of influence. What may have been lost is flexibility and responsiveness. A more decentralized system may have been able to respond to the empty house problem sooner and more effectively.

Locally Financed Housing. When Local Housing Supply Corporations were created out of local building associations in 1965, local governments gained flexibility and received HFB financing. LHSCs are authorized to perform a long list of functions. The central government essentially created a flexible tool for local housing policy. An intergovernmental conflict has arisen, however, over the formula for determining the maximum rent LHSCs can charge on rental housing.

Under the present formula, LHSCs lose money on rental housing and most simply refuse to build it. The Construction Ministry's position is that it is the prefectures' responsibility to subsidize the rents if they wish, and some do. Of the three prefectures studied here, however, only Chiba's LHSC has built rental housing and it has built very little. Chiba and Saitama depend on the JHC to build the rental housing that is necessary. In Saga there is little demand for any rental housing more expensive than public housing. Chiba uses its LHSC to build its new towns.

Both Chiba and Saitama have loan programs that help their citizens purchase their own houses. These programs are not regulated by law; they are the housing counterpart of the loan programs for small businesses for buying pollution control equipment.

Public Housing. Since the plan targets for public housing represent a promise of central grant money, prefectural targets must add up to national targets and the planning process involves greater central control. Formally, the targets for public housing are set separately by the MOC. The target represents a promise of grants, but the actual grant decision is made yearly during the budget process. The promise is reliable enough that local governments can plan ahead and buy the necessary land, but the yearly process adds flexibility. If some prefectures fall behind, other can pick up the slack. After the oil crisis, many urban prefectures found themselves unable to meet their targets and twenty-nine prefectures (including Saga) were able to build more than planned. Rural prefectures were not, however, able to take up all the slack; only 76 percent of the plan target was achieved nationally.

Up until the oil crisis, local government demand for public housing grants exceeded central government supply. After the oil crisis, the Ministry of Construction had surplus funds to allocate. During the third planning process, it was asking prefectures to do more. Even in rural Kyūshū bloc, it wanted to build 200 more units than did the prefectures (see table 8). In these circumstances, the number of public housing units built depends, first of all, on the ability of the prefecture to find suitable sites, and second, on the prefecture's willingess to allocate funds to public housing. The availability of grants is no longer the limiting factor, unless one considers the possibility of substantially improving the terms of the grants. This possibility is precisely what the urban prefectures are demanding. The focus of intergovernmental policymaking has shifted from the local arena, where people ask: "What can we get for our prefecture?" to the national arena, where the question is: "How should the grant system be changed?"

One such national-level conflict concerns "excess burdening" *(chōka futan)*. This problem extends to the whole grant system and involves the method of calculating the size of the grant. The government establishes a grant ratio: half for type one and two-thirds for type two public housing. The government does not pay half of the actual costs, however. Instead, it pays half of the "standard cost." The central government does not want to pay for any extras the local government might wish to provide. But just what facilities should be considered extras is a matter of dispute. In particular, the formula for standard costs is not adjusted often enough to keep ahead of inflation. Reduction of excess burdening is a prime goal of the National Governors' Conference, as well of each individual prefecture.

The Ministry of Construction has been relatively responsive to demands for more complete estimates of standard costs. Table 10 presents estimates of excess burdening for Chiba and Saga. Yearly figures can be misleading because the amount of excess burdening depends on whether the prefecture is starting most of its projects or finishing them. The closer to completion a project is, the greater the excess burdening because finishing touches are not covered as thoroughly in the standard cost formula. The basic pattern is clear, however: actual costs jumped after the 1973 oil crisis and standard costs fell behind. Since that time, however, the MOC has revised the formula until, at present, prefectural officials agree that excess burdening is no longer a signficant problem in public housing.

Local governments have proved effective lobbyists in getting the Ministry of Construction to reduce excess burdening, though they have not been as successful with other ministries. Local governments have also had more trouble getting a fundamental revision of the grant system. While they have had little success in changing the law, they have used considerable ingenuity in adding to their stock of public housing outside the legal framework.

Both Chiba and Saitama have ordinances providing for "special" public housing. Saitama was host to the National Japan Games in 1967 and the JHC built some housing for the athletes. When the games were over, Saitama bought some of the housing and converted it into public housing. Although this is not a continuing program and involves a limited number of units (844), the program is completely independent of the central government.

TABLE 10
Estimates of "Excess Burdening" in Public Housing Construction in Chiba Prefecture

	Type 1			Type 2		
	Standard	*Actual*	*%*	*Standard*	*Actual*	*%*
1966	994	1170	85.0	969	1084	89.4
1967	1122	1298	86.4	1056	1254	84.2
1968	1190	1381	86.2	1107	1317	84.0
1969	1272	1533	83.0	1160	1469	79.0
1970	1446	1621	89.2	1352	1629	83.0
1971	1607	1885	85.3	—	—	—
1972	1842	1989	92.6	1697	1971	86.1
1973	3034	4226	71.8	2959	3809	77.6
1974	4276	4798	89.1	4231	4509	93.9
1975	4846	5030	96.3	4466	4729	93.8

Sources: Chiba Prefecture, Housing Division, *Chibaken no Jūtaku, 1976 (Chiba Prefecture's Housing, 1976)*, p. 37.

Note: Figures are average construction costs per housing unit in thousands of yen. Because the exchange rates between the dollar and the yen has varied widely over this period, the figures have not been converted to dollars. All figures are for housing of similar structure, what might be called "middle-rise" (four or five stories). Thus, Chiba did build type 2 housing in 1971, but not of this structural type.

Chiba's special public housing program is less independent of the central government, but demonstrates great ingenuity. In 1969 the prefecture began offering to rent land from municipalities and to build prefectural public housing on it. For muncipalities that have land but cannot afford to build their own public housing, this program offers a way to provide their citizens with public housing while receiving rental fees from otherwise idle land. The prefecture gives municipal residents priority for 90 precent of the new units (Ishii, 1973). The program was quite successful in the first few years, reaching a peak of 396 units in 1971. The program has slowed since that time, as suitable sites owned by muncipalities have been used up. The program had limited potential but it was an innovative way of providing over one thousand units of public housing that would probably not have been built otherwise.

Managing Public Housing

Entrance into Public Housing. Determing who shall live in public housing is of crucial importance to potential occupants. Those that get in will pay much less for much better accommodations than those who qualify but do not get in. The gap is particularly wide in urban areas.

The first determinant of entrance is the MOC's maximum income requirements. The ministry makes the decision, but input from local governments plays a significant role. Local governments generally favor higher income limitations, partly because they are aware of particular families who cannot get in (some of whom are younger local government employees). Local governments are active in pressing for revising income limitations upward in response to inflation. In the 1977 revision, local governments were especially active in promoting special consideration for the handicapped, the aged, and fatherless households, and these provisions were enacted. The decision is, however, national and no local variation is allowed.

Normally there are more qualified appliants than openings. Although cases of unfilled public housing can be found, low rents continue to attract applicants even in relatively remote areas.[10] The MOC regulates the selection process in principle but not in detail. The law requires that the procedure be set in an ordinance, that the prefecture investigate the needs of applicants, that the applicants meet national requirements, and the process be public. National requirements include the exclusion of single persons and the requirement that applicants have a genuine need for housing, as well as the income limitation. Of these, the only effective limitations on prefectural decision making are the income limitation and the exclusion of single persons. The other restrictions are too vague to be effective (Watanabe, 1975; *Toshi Mondai*, August 1973 and August 1975).

The overwhelming majority of prefectures use a lottery, supplemented by consideration for special cases. Both Saga and Chiba fall into this category. Saga, for example, tries to use openings in older projects for special cases, and such cases are often brought to the administration's attention by assembly members.

The main attraction of a lottery system is the ease of administration. Two other methods have been widely discussed: a point system whereby need is estimated by formula, and a registration system in which a waiting list is drawn up (Watanabe, 1975). As of 1975, seven prefectures had implemented a point system, either alone or in conjunction with a lottery (MOC, General Affairs Division, unpublished materials, 1975). In that year both the MOC's permanent advisory commission and a Saitama project team concluded that a registration system would be preferable (Yamaoka and Kyōsu, 1976; Ushimi, 1977). Thereupon, Saitama began to implement Japan's first registration system.

Registration has the advantages of reducing uncertainty for applicants and allowing the prefecture to give preference to families in greater need, local residents, or persons with skills needed in the area. Registration also has implications beyond its usefulness as a selection system. In particular, construction planning can be based on more accurate estimates of both need and demand. Registration applications have already helped the prefecture plan the location of public housing. More precise figures will also mean that Saitama's estimates of the need for public housing will be hard for the MOC to refute. The system has the potential of creating a truly bottom-up planning process. Many problems remain, however, before this potential can be realized.

One troublesome legal problem stands in the way of effective implementation of the registration system. Saitama checks the income of applicants at the time of registration, but the law says that the family must meet the requirements at the time of taking occupancy. The prefecture must check again and, if income has risen beyond the limitation, the applicant is no longer qualified. The possibility of being refused entry after being properly registered weakens one of the primary advantages of the system: applicants no longer have to wait in suspense as lottery tickets are drawn. The Ministry of Construction does not seem particularly responsive to this problem: "Naturally, we will expect them to obey the law" (interview in MOC, General Affairs Division, April 19, 1977).

Registration has been implemented only in public housing. Extending it to other publicly financed housing will depend upon the success of the system as judged by other prefectures, the MOC, and the JHC. The difficulty of implementing and administering the program remains a major drawback. No matter what the final outcome, Saitama is providing the Japanese political system with a large-scale policy experiment.

Ejecting People from Public Housing. A high proportion of entrants into public housing are young families. Because Japanese employment practices create a high correlation between age and income, poor families tend to be young but their income tends to rise over time. Thus, many families receiving the heavy subsidy of public housing are actually quite well off, while other families are waiting for an opening. The injustice involved has been cause for national concern, symbolized by press accounts of expensive foreign cars parked in public housing parking lots (*Sankei Shinbun,* 1976).

The central government responded to these problems in 1959 with a system for charging higher rents to families whose income exceeds set limits, and by making it the duty of higher-income families, to find other housing. Neither of these policies has had much effect. Rents were still much lower than for other comparable housing and the legal duty to look for other housing was too vague to be implemented. In 1969 local governments were given the authority to ask high-income families to leave. This authority, though still vague, was important because of the strong position of renters under Japanese law (Koizumi, 1973; Kotaka, 1973).

Local governments seldom exercise this authority to ask high-income families to leave public housing. They recognize that even relatively well-off families have great difficulty locating, affording, and getting into other suitable housing. They also tend to feel that income limits are too low and that a revision of income limitations would mean that many families drop out of the high-income category. On the prefectural level, only Tokyo has been active in prohibiting high-income families from abusing the system. At the other extreme, Kanagawa did not even put the "high-income family" provision into its ordinance until 1976, seven years after it had the authority to do so. Prefectures do use other, less authoritative, means of reducing the number of high-income families in public housing. Some provide separate lotteries for such families who wish to enter JHC or LHSC housing or to get an HFB loan.

The Ministry of Construction has been in the position of pushing local governments to do more toward reducing the number of high-income families in public housing. The limited response from local governments illustrates the limits of administrative guidance.

Setting Rents for Public Housing. Maximum rents for all publicly financed housing are determined by MOC formulas based on cost of construction. For public housing, central grants are subtracted from construction costs to produce lower rents. Local governments cannot charge more than the maximum, but they can add subsidies of their own to further reduce rents. And rents on new public housing have gotten too high. The post–oil crisis inflation has been translated directly into higher rents. Most of those involved agree that the system for setting rents should be changed from a construction cost basis to a percentage of income basis. Until such a system is worked out, however, local governments must deal with the problem of high rents on their own.

All three of the prefectures studied here have taken steps to reduce rents. Saga has no continuing program but did reduce rents by up to 20 percent in 1974 and 1975. Chiba excludes the price of land from rent calculations. Saitama has taken two significant steps to rationalize rents. First, officials pool the calculations for construction costs, combining all the projects completed in a single year, adjusting for such factors as location. Second, Saitama has adopted a system of sliding rents. Rent the first year of occupancy is a percentage of the income limit, 15 percent for type two and 16 percent for type one housing.[11] In the second year of occupancy, and for a maximum of five years thereafter, rents are raised a minimum of 5,000 yen (approximately $25) each year until the legal limit is reached. The rationale for the system is that individual incomes generally rise over time, and that raising rents is difficult. Saitama's public housing occupants get only a temporary reprieve, but the system has much to recommend it and even this temporary reprieve costs the prefecture over half a million dollars a year.

Prefectures have independent programs to lower rents, but they would prefer a revision of the grant system to make prefectural rent subsidies unnecessary. They are petitioning the central government to this effect.

Setting rents also involves raising rents on older public housing units. Local authority—indeed, responsibility—for raising rents is clearly stated in the law. However, few local governments have taken advantage of this provision. Raising rents is politically unpalatable. The lessons of the 1957 JHC rent strike and the recent problems the JHC has had trying to raise rents have not been lost on local governments (Kamada, 1973; *Asahi Shinbun,* August 18, 1977, and October 13, 1978). The result is an extreme imbalance among rents based on the year of construction. This imbalance is made worse by the fact that older projects tend to be located in more convenient areas. Thus, occupants of older projects, who tend to be more affluent, pay less for more convenient housing. Tenancy in an older project has become a privilege to be cherished. Everyone recognizes the problem, but no one wants to take the responsibility for raising rents. In particular, no one wants to go first.

The ice was broken when the Ministry of Construction issued a circular in August 1975 and began a campaign of administrative guidance. Local governments could then shift some of the responsibility onto the ministry, telling the occupants of public housing that they were being pressured by the central government. The problem of who should go first was resolved through bloc conferences; several prefectures within a bloc would agree to raise rents simultaneously. Political responsibility could be further diffused by pointing out that all the neighboring prefectures were doing it.

Of the three prefectures under investigation here, only Saga effected rent revision during 1976–1977. Saga raised rents simultaneously with three other prefectures in the Kyūshū bloc. The prefecture feared protest, but opposition was defused by the prefecture's willingness to hold explanation meetings as often as necessary and by its promise to invest virtually all of the increased revenue into repairs and improvements.

Chiba had revised rents in 1969, but because of the post–oil crisis inflation, the need for further reform was great. Despite the obvious need and pressure from its Finance Division, Chiba has no plans to move ahead on this issue. The prefecture is now emphasizing welfare policies, and raising rents does not fit this general policy.

During 1976–1977, Saitama was reluctantly planning to raise rents. It has since done so, but included only increases for management and maintenance, excluding other factors, thus holding the increase down to an average of 54 percent (*Nihon Keizai Shinbun,* January 31, 1978).

The rent revision case again illustrates the limits of administrative guidance. A MOC official explained, "If the conditions for acceptance of administrative guidance are not present, nothing happens. If local finances were not in trouble, I do not think they would have revised rents" (interview in MOC, Housing Planning Division, April 12, 1977).

Conclusions

This chapter is divided into two main sections, housing construction and housing management, and the conclusions must also be so divided. The factors that proved important for explaining influence over construction projects were not the ones that proved important for explaining influence over administrative tasks. I reached this same impasse in the previous chapter: sewer construction did not fit with the rest of pollution control policy. The first set of conclusions presented here will, therefore, apply to construction projects, including both housing and sewer construction. The second set of conclusions will apply to managing public housing.

Construction Projects. The weakest hypothesis for explaining influence over construction projects is the electoral politics hypothesis. No significant partisan differences have developed on either housing or sewer construction. Unlike the case of Britain, for example, the parties do not compete with promises to build more houses, do not argue about rental versus owner-occupied housing, nor do they fight over public versus private construction (Mitchell, 1974; Heady, 1978; Dale, 1980; McLeay, 1984). These issues have not become left-right election issues in Japan. Neither has pork-barrel politics been important in these fields. I found no evidence that prefectures with more political clout at the national level got more housing or sewers than less favored prefectures. Saitama's latest basin sewer system is a case in point. Such political factors may play a role at some other level—Lower House electoral districts or municipalities—or may be important in other fields—roads, railways, and airports would seem likely places to look—but I found no evidence of political or policy discrimination in the distribution of housing or sewer construction. Japan is more like France than Italy: the way to mobilize central resources is through the bureaucracy, not the party system (Tarrow, 1977).

The policy substance hypothesis explained little about construction projects. There were few substantive disagreements among levels of government. Even in the one case of a major disagreement—local population limitation policies—there was no consensus on which policy was technically correct. In fact, both central and local governments were right from their own perspectives, prefectures taking the part of their own citizens and the national government taking the broader view. The policy substance hypothesis did help explain one weakness of the JHC. Local demands phrased in the proper jargon and fitting the current housing orthodoxy were hard for the JHC to reject. Thus, Chiba was able to coopt the JHC into helping build Chiba's new towns.

I find mixed results for the two traditional hypotheses concerning the distribution of authority and of finances. The mix of positive and negative findings is, however, beginning to form a pattern. General formulations of proportionality do not work. Influence over a policy is not directly proportional either to one's authority over it or to one's financial contribution to it. On the other hand, legal requirements and financial factors can have significant effects at a more micro level. Little pieces of authority can be used in surprising ways. Seemingly unimportant regulations can inhibit local policy innovation, while grant formulas may contain unintended incentives. Some slack resources are necessary for innovative policymaking.

I find no support for the idea that, regarding construction projects, influence is proportional to authority. Reading the law gives one the strong impression that housing and sewer construction are determined by rational top—down processes; yet that is clearly not the case. My findings are thus very similar to Garlichs' and Hull's (1978) findings on highway construction in the Federal Republic of Germany. It would seem that sophisticated techniques of rational planning are not effective in controlling construction programs. Planning does have an effect, and, indeed, produces a good deal of coordination. However, the effective part of the plans were the slogans that put ideas on all agendas simultaneously, and the important process was the intensive exchange of information that let each actor in the system know the intentions of the other actors. Each government could base its actions on accurate expectations. At least with respect to construction programs, we can hypothesize that all planning is indicative even when it has much more ambitious goals.

The authority that proved effective in influencing construction projects consisted of seemingly minor delegations. Chiba and Saitama enforced their population limitation policies primarily through designating city planning districts and giving development permits. Both of these activities are agency-assigned functions. The intent of the law is to assign tasks to the prefecture, not to delegate authority. Nevertheless, these assigned tasks carried with them enough authority to make significant differences in the way housing construction was carried out within the prefectures. This finding is very similar to Milch's (1974) observations on housing policy in France. It would seem that the implementation of construction projects necessarily gives subnational governments influence over those policies.

The findings on the distribution of finances hypothesis are similarly mixed. Influence is not proportional to financial contribution. The best evidence is the weakness of the JHC, an institution with plenty of money but few other resources. Neither public housing nor sewer construction is tightly controlled through the national budgetary process. Prefectures got basin sewer systems approved when the central government's financial constraints seemed tight. Again, these findings coincide with those of Garlichs and Hull (1978) in Germany.

The financial factors that proved important, like the authority factors, were on a more micro level. The overburdening *(chōka futan)* phenomenon caused local governments significant problems but seems to have been an unintended consequence of rapid inflation. The factors discouraging LHSCs from building rental housing seem to indicate a more purposeful central policy. Neither overburdening nor the disincentives for rental housing involve large sums of money relative to the cost of the projects. Both affect the local budgetary process at the margins by raising the per-unit cost. From the local perspective, the big-money decisions, the proportion of the cost to be borne by each level of government, and the grant formula, are constants. These factors are predictable and cause no budgetary or policy problems. Problems are caused by the unpredictable changes at the margin because such changes absorb what otherwise would have been discretionary funds.

Slack resources are hard to measure, but they are important. With no slack resources, a prefecture would have to respond to the incentives of the grant system. Slack resources allow the local government to choose and to innovate. LHSCs can build rental housing when its deemed necessary if the prefecture has some discretionary funds available. Prefectures can use the system creatively, using only small amounts of slack resources. Chiba and Saitama both had special public housing programs that demonstrate this point. The two financial factors that affect local autonomy most are predictability of funding and slack resources.

The two hypotheses that best explain the distribution of influence over construction projects are the information hypothesis and the principle of least interest.

The effective information variable is the distribution of expertise among various levels of government. The distribution of detailed knowledge of local conditions does not vary significantly. Local knowledge gives local officials the advantage unless counterbalanced by centralized expertise. Because expertise is concentrated in sewer construction but not in housing construction, central officials exercise more control over the former.

Detailed local knowledge is more important and more concentrated at the local level in construction programs than in other kinds of programs. In order to build something, one must buy land—one of the most complex actions a government can take (Feldman and Milch, 1982). The accumulation of laws on property rights and land use in modern nations is a maze. Local officials are much better equipped to negotiate this maze. Air and water quality can be measured scientifically and summarized statistically, but finding an appropriate parcel of land requires information unavailable in a computerized format. The local advantage in construction projects is hard to overcome. Neither the centralization of authority in a sophisticated planning process nor the concentration of financial resources in an agency like the JHC can overcome the concentration of relevant information at the local level.

Finally, the principle of least interest works well for predicting relative influence over the planning process. During the first two five-year plans, demand exceeded supply; the MOC was the least interested party and thus exercised more influence. During the third plan, supply exceeded demand, local governments became the least interested parties and their influence grew. This hypothesis also works well for predicting influence over particular projects. In the 1960s, the JHC had many places to build and built according to its own priorities. In the 1970s, land became scarcer and local governments more reluctant to accept housing, so the JHC had to build according to local priorities.

The key reason why the principle of least interest works so well in construction projects seems to be the high cost of delay. A construction project is complex; many tasks must be performed simultaneously by many different actors. If one actor does not cooperate, it soon affects the entire project. And there are substantial costs associated with delay, holding costs for the land, and so on. Therefore, actors who are willing to wait can force the others to meet their demands.

Managing Public Housing. The hypotheses that explain the distribution of influence in housing construction fail to explain it in housing management. The principle of least interest does not apply because there are no particular penalties for delay. Policy can be made slowly because the ongoing system will continue to function. Neither does the information hypothesis prove helpful here. Detailed local knowledge is necessary for making exceptions for people in special circumstances, but local officials can make these decisions without disturbing the regulations that make decisions routine. Expertise plays only a small role. The tasks are relatively simple and local officials are just as familiar with the theories of housing managment as are central officials. Finally, the policy substance hypothesis does not apply because there were no serious policy disputes in housing management policy.

The authority hypothesis works well in some cases, but its one major failure provides an interesting insight into intergovernmental relations in Japan. The authority to raise rents on public housing is clearly delegated to local governments, yet the only effective way of raising rents was for the Ministry of Construction to orchestrate a campaign of administrative guidance in an atmosphere of local financial strain. The authority to perform politically unpalatable tasks is to be avoided. Local governments had the authority but no influence. This discrepancy was caused not by the successful attempt of central officials to extend their influence, but rather by local officials' success in avoiding responsibility for raising rents. Most intergovernmental conflicts may arise from competition over who should influence policy, but sometimes the goal is to avoid responsibility.

Authority did prove important in several cases, particularly in dealing with the problems of implementing Saitama's registration system for applicants desiring public housing. This was a case of enforcing rules in circumstances that had not been envisioned when the rules were written. A reasonable rule, that entrants should meet the requirements at the time of taking occupancy, became problematic under the new system. The MOC may have been using this rule as a weapon to undermine Saitama's innovative policies, but it may also have been a simple case of bureaucratic inflexibility. Little pieces of authority can be used to influence seemingly unrelated policies, but authority also represents a kind of policy inertia that must be overcome with any innovation.

The financial hypothesis also proved useful regarding slack resources. Although influence over management policies is not proportional to financial contributions, slack resources are important for most local innovations. The clearest examples are policies that affect rents. The various policies aimed at keeping rents low were calculated carefully and negotiated with the prefecture's Finance Division. Pressure from prefectural Finance Division was also an important factor promoting rent reform. Although it was affected less directly than rent policies, Saitama's registration system cost a signficant amount to implement and such costs are one barrier to its diffusion.

The most important factor in explaining housing management policy is politics. In fact, the effects of authority and finances cannot be understood without knowledge of the political background of policy-making. The basic political fact is that the residents of public housing react strongly to any policy change that affects them. More general electoral considerations sometimes play a role, as when the governors of Chiba and Saitama avoided raising rents because it did not fit the image they were trying to project. However, the most important political fact is that the governments do not want to arouse an organized protest by residents. Raising rents on public housing is controversial in any system (see Mitchell, 1974, re Britain), but the Japanese political system seems more responsive to small, intense groups than are other democratic systems.[12] The problem of relatively affluent people living in public housing and the ridiculously low rents charged for older public housing units could be used to arouse a welfare backlash, and the media has on occasion publicized the problem of "welfare Cadillacs" (*Sankei Shinbun,* 1976). The political system remains sensitive to the interests of public housing residents even when their legal and moral position is weak.

The politics hypothesis explains why raising rents and ejecting unqualified residents is so hard. Only central bureaucrats can promote these policies and they are the most politically insulated actors in the system. The politics hypothesis also explains the strangest phenomenon revealed by my research: the first prefectures to raise rents under MOC guidance were those with the least need, those where the imbalance between old and new rents, and the amounts of money involved, were smallest. Needs, defined either financially or in terms of distance from the accepted ideal, were overwhelmed by politics. It is easier to raise rents a little than a lot, and easier to regain a balance among rents when that does not require raising some rents a lot more than others. The greater the need for a reform, the greater the political difficulty of enacting and implementing it. The latter fact turns out to be more important than the former.

6

High School Education Policy

*E*DUCATION POLICY MAKING presents a different case. Whereas pollution and housing policy are dominated by assigned functions, education is the most often cited example of a "naturally" local function. The principle of local responsibility pervades discussions of education policy and has some significant effects on intergovernmental relations. More important, education policymaking is highly politicized, in several senses of that term.

First, education policy is the object of direct and intense concern of parents and that concern finds continuous organizational expression in the PTA. The PTA is the attentive public in education policy, a role played by citizens' movements in pollution control policy and residents in housing management policy. The PTA, however, represents a larger potential voting bloc, parents, and is more continuously attentive to the issues than are the publics in the other two areas.

Second, a permanent, organized opposition exists in education policy: the teachers' unions (Duke, 1973; Thurston, 1973). On the national level, the polarization is so great that the unions can be trusted to oppose virtually any move made by the Ministry of Education (MOE). The situation in the prefectures varies widely, but the poles of disagreement are represented in each prefecture and the presence of a large attentive public gives the weaker pole a potential for creating controversy.

Finally, education policy is politicized in the partisan sense. Teachers' unions support the left and their positions are reflected in the policies of the left. Regarding pollution control and housing management, partisan positions are much less clear.

This political polarization is based on the firm foundation of divergent educational philosophies. Whereas in pollution control and hous-

117

ing there is a broad consensus concerning the kinds of policies that represent progress, in education it is precisely the direction of policy that is in dispute. Whereas pollution and housing are basically "valence" issues, education is a "position" issue (Schneider, 1980). Everyone agrees that there should be less pollution and more housing, but people disagree over whether better education could be obtained by having a more egalitarian educational system or a freer, more competitive system.

Although many disputes between teachers' unions and the Ministry of Education involve pay, prestige, and academic freedom, a continuing theme in their conflict is the choice between free competition and equality. The union emphasize equality and deplore any kind of "tracking" of better students into special classes or schools. The conservatives, represented by the ministry, emphasize freedom, competition, and the pursuit of "excellence."[1] This theme is also part of the debate over comprehensive schools in Europe (Levin, 1978; Heidenheimer, 1974), and racial integration in the United States (Heidenheimer and Parkinson, 1975).

Despite a broad consensus on the desirability of keeping politics out of education, and despite the organizational separation of local boards of education from the rest of local administration, education is the kind of issue that produces political conflict. Controversy is particularly common in policies concerning high schools in Japan (Rohlen, 1976, 1977, 1980, 1983) and elsewhere (see Merrit and Leonardi, 1981, re Italy; Peterson, 1971 and Jennings, 1977, re Britain; and Van de Graff, 1967, re Germany).

In Japan, the American occupation imposed a 6–3–3 system: six years of primary education, three years of middle school, and three years of high school, but the final three years were not made compulsory. Thus, high schools stand between the noncompetitive, equal education offered in primary and middle schools on the one hand, and the highly competitive college entrance exams on the other (Cummings, 1980, 1976). Leftists think that high schools should be more like compulsory education, open to all. Conservatives tend to see high schools as the first stage in a winnowing process that will produce an elite.

The actual competitiveness of high schools depends on many different factors, but three variables stand out: (1) the number of high schools, particularly the number of public high schools relative to the number of private schools; (2) the number of general as opposed to vocational high schools; and (3) the rules governing entrance into general high schools. All three of these variables are determined primarily at the prefectural level, with remarkably little interference from the Education Ministry. These three topics will serve to organize the rest of this chapter.

Building Public High Schools

Public high schools are built and run by the prefectures. The central government operates a few and larger cities often run one or two, but these are exceptions to the rule. The responsibility for high schools lies with the prefecture. A prefecture might be able to obtain some cooperation from its cities, but it cannot expect much help from the MOE.

The Education Ministry operates several grant programs aimed a promoting certain aspects of education, particularly vocational education and sports. It gives grants for renovating dangerous structures in schools and helps pay teachers' salaries, but it does not provide basic support for either the construction or operation of high schools. The only way a prefecture can reduce the burden of building and running high schools is to depend on private schools.

Nationally, about 30 percent of all high school students are in private high schools, but this ratio varies widely by prefecture. In part, this variation is explained by urbanization: more urban prefectures tend to have more private schools dating from the prewar period, and starting a private school is less of a risk in an urban area. However, an important part of this variation must be explained by the prefectures' response to the baby boom of the early 1960s (Ushiogi, 1974, 1975; Pempel, 1973). Particularly since the increased number of students was known to be a temporary phenomenon, some prefectures chose to let private high schools meet the demand.

The decision to let the proportion of private high schools rise has important consequences for students and parents, for despite the existence of a few highly ranked private schools, going to a private school normally means paying a great deal more for a significantly inferior education. (See table 11.) Public high schools are both better and cheaper. It is, therefore, extremely important to get into a public high school, and the greater a perfecture's reliance on private schools, the greater the competition for admission to its public schools.

The second wave of the baby boom began to reach high school age around 1973 and is now working its way through the system. This wave differs from the first in that it is concentrated in those prefectures that have been experiencing rapid population growth. Some rural prefectures now even face the prospect of excess facilities as their high school population drops. Measured in terms of percent growth in high school population, Saitama faces the biggest problem in the nation and Chiba runs second. A rising proportion of middle school graduates going on to high school, reflecting the rising demand for both high school and college education, adds to the demand for new schools. The breadth and intensity of this demand makes it virtually a political necessity to maintain at least the status quo in opportunities, for a high school education. Both Saitama's and Chiba's governors have made education generally, and high school construction specifically, a keynote of their administrations.

Table 12 summarizes the construction plans of the two prefectures and illustrates their differing definitions of the status quo. The estimates of middle school graduates in 1980 are simply the number of fourth graders in 1975, a method of estimation that ignores in-migrants and therefore holds the forecasts down. Estimates of the precentage of students advancing to high school is a matter of judgment and Saitama's guess is somewhat higher than Chiba's. Setting the proportion of students to be admitted to public high schools is a matter of policy.

Chiba plans to better its status quo by 10 percent. Chiba officials decided that it could not attract enough new private high schools, and thus determined to take up the slack with public schools. Saitama officials took the average of the previous three years to arrive at their estimate of 65 percent of high school students in private schools. They realize that attracting enough new private high schools will be difficult,

TABLE 11

Expenditures Per Student in Public and Private High Schools: An Estimate from Aichi Prefecture, 1971

	Parents' Expense	Prefectural Expense	Total
Public[a]	$7.32	$80.50	$87.82
Private	30.75	4.42	35.17

Source: Mori Tadashi, "Aichi-ken no Kyōiku" ("Aichi Prefecture's Education"), in Kempō to Chihō Seiji (The Construction and Local Politics), ed. The Aichi Constitutional Conference (Fūbōsha, 1973), p. 56.

Note: Figures are in U.S. dollars calculated at 200 yen to the dollar.

a. Public here refers to prefectural high schools only.

but judge it less difficult than building more public schools. Actually, these figures represent political and administrative judgments about the maximum number of schools the prefecture could construct under budgetary and other constaints as much as estimates of need.

Both prefectures are stretching their resources to respond to public demand and to keep their respective governors' campaign promises. Both have raised the maximum size of schools, Chiba from ten to twelve classes and Saitama from nine to ten.[2] Both have had to add on to existing schools to avoid the cost and difficulty of finding suitable sites for new schools. Chiba has also begun planning a new "high school complex" of three or four schools located together and sharing some of the same facilities. This controversial undertaking was begun in part to take advantage of a site already owned by the prefecture (*Chiba Nippo*, February 2, May 9, and August 1, 1977; *Nihon Keizai Shinbun*, May 24, 1978). Both prefectures have used considerable ingenuity in finding cost-reducing construction methods and designs (*Asahi Shinbun*, February 25, 1976; *Nihon Keizai Shinbun*, April 14, 1977, and March 17, 1978). Finally, both prefectures have lobbied the MOE to get grant money to help overcome this temporary bulge in high school students.

Saitama's Governor Hata was a leader in this movement to get a grant program. Saitama's teachers' unions were the most active in the

TABLE 12
High School Construction Plans in Chiba and Saitama Prefectures

	Chiba	*Saitama*
Middle School Graduates		
1975	48,549	53,613
1980	69,673	77,900
Increase	21,124	24,300
Percent Advancing to High School		
1975	90.7	92.3
1980	94.3	95.0
Public High School Capacity		
1975	65.0	63.7
1980	75.0	65.0
New Construction by 1980	35 schools	37 schools

Source: Materials provided by the respective prefectures.

country in collecting signatures on a petition to the Education Ministry. Seventy percent of all the signatures collected nationwide were collected in Saitama. The National Governors' Conference picked up the issue by publishing a report that 687 schools would have to be built by 1980 and "proving" that local finances were too weak to finance this construction alone (*Asahi Shinbun,* January 9, 1977; *Naigai Kyōiku,* January 18, 1977).

The breakthrough came in the 1976 national budget. Up until that time, the MOE had played absolutely no role in high school construction policy. Indeed, the ministry officials had studiously avoided the issue. They did not offer any suggestions about the desirable ratio of public and private schools or even provide forecasts of the percentage of students likely to go on to high school. The success of the lobbying effort, both in the mass media and in the Diet, forced a reluctant ministry to accept the principle of a temporary grant system.[3] The grant program forced the MOE to deal with the issue of high school construction. The ministry chose, under some pressure from the LDP, to minimize the government's commitment (*Asahi Shinbun,* December 9, 1975). The program pays one-third of the construction costs, excluding land purchases, up to the total amount budgeted. Three other conditions are added to minimize the goverment's intervention into this policy area.

First, only facilities that were needed to maintain the percentage of students advancing to high school in 1975, or needed to bring the prefecture's advancement rate up to the national average, are subsidized. Any decision to raise this percent is left a prefectural responsibility. It is also important to note that 100 percent advancement is a progressive slogan.

Second, the government subtracts any empty seats in existing schools. Regional imbalances within a prefecture could cause empty seats in one area while there is a shortage in another. Administratively, this policy is a refusal to pay for uneeded facilities. It is also the case, however, that regional imbalances are more likely to occur in prefectures with small, strict school districts—those preferred by progressives.

Finally, proper financial effort is required. This means that prefectures must raise their tuition rates to the standard set in the formula for computing the distribution tax. Low tuition is again a progressive slogan.

All three of these grant conditions are administratively rational, but also have a definite conservative coloration. Administrative rationality often produces conservative results, but the active participation of the LDP's education committee probably added to the conservative tilt of Japan's educational policy.

The grant programs have not had a conservative effect in either Chiba or Saitama. (Saga does not qualify for this program.) At present neither prefecture could reasonably expect to increase the advancement rate significantly. In both prefectures, school districts are large and open enough to prevent regional imbalances. Finally, both prefectures would have probably raised their tuition rates without the incentive of the grant program. Raising tuition is the obvious way to increase revenues. Revenues are being shifted to high school construction from other departments and those departments demand financial effort as vigorously as the Ministry of Education. Finally, MOHA has been waging a separate campaign of administrative guidance to raise tuition rates (*Nihon Keizai Shinbun,* January 20, 1978).

The grant program did have one significant effect on Saitama's policy. Saitama had been following a policy of slow-paced construction, starting a new school with six classes and waiting three years before adding two to four more classes. The normal pattern, and that followed by Chiba, is to open six classes the first year, eight the second, and ten the third. Saitama officials believe that their slower pace allows the school faculty, staff, and students to develop working relationships before they are asked to handle an increased load. The grant program, however, subsidizes only new construction defined as the amount completed within three years of opening the school. The three-year cutoff point was based on common practice (and a line had to be drawn somewhere), but Saitama will have to abandon its slow-paced construction policy in order to maximize grant revenues. This result was accidental. Because central policy must be made on the assumption of some uniformity, it produces uniformity in unintended ways.

The Education Ministry's grant formula is aimed at minimizing controversy. Education officials feared that the grant formula would become a focus for debate, each prefecture arguing for a different "rational" formula based on its own self-interest. In order to prevent a debate and insulate the grant distribution process from politics, the ministry kept the grant formula secret for the first year of the program's operation. By using a strict formula and by avoiding controversy, the ministry limited its own discretion in order to discourage influence attempts.

The subsidy for new high schools is a clear case of local government influence in the national arena. Local governments managed to change national policy. There were costs involved in inviting the central government into this issue area, but the benefits clearly outweighed those costs.

Vocational High Schools and Diversification

Progressives are fond of quoting the "three principles of high school education" established under the American occupation: coeducation, comprehensive schools, and one school per district. None of these principles has been fully implemented in Japan, but the least successful has been comprehensive schooling. The ideal envisions a single school offering both general and vocational classes. In Japan general and vocational courses are administered separately even when they are located in the same school. The entrance examinations for each course are separate and changing courses is virtually impossible.

The most important classification of high school students is by "course" *(gakka)*. Courses are classified into general, industrial, commercial, agricultural, fishery, home economics, and "other." Within each vocational course, more specific "subcourses" may be set up and have their own entrance examinations. For example, an industrial high school course might offer subcourses in machinery, electrical, electronics, and chemicals.

Only those students in general courses have a significant chance of getting into college. Given the importance of college in Japanese society, students go to a vocational high school only if they cannot pass the entrance examination for a general high school. Moreover, vocational courses are ranked industrial, commercial, and agricultural, from top to bottom. As the proportion of students going to college has risen, getting into a general high school has become more important. As part of the same trend toward higher levels of education, most students and parents feel that a high school diploma is necessary. Thus, an increasing number of students in vocational courses are there only to get a diploma and have no interest in the subject matter. Not surprisingly, these students have low morale and high rates of delinquency.

The dominant and inescapable fact facing high school education policymakers since the 1960s has been the growing number and proportion of students going to high school. In 1966, the MOE's permanent advisory commission conceived the problem as one of growing diversity among high school students. No longer could high school be considered elite education. They recommended that high schools be diversified to match the varied interests and abilities of students and the complex needs of the economy. Their concrete recommendation was that new subcourses be created in all courses. In its new Study Guidelines, the MOE increased the listed number of subcourses by twelve (see table 13). These twelve were only meant as a general guide, and the

TABLE 13
Number of Subcourses by Course in Japanese High Schools, 1966–1975

	Recommended			Actual						
	1960	1970	1976	1966	1970	1971	1972	1973	1974	1975
Agriculture	9	10	7	51	53	59	64	66	69	67
Industrial	17	21	12	131	139	133	141	140	134	128
Commercial	1	7	4	12	20	22	20	21	20	20
Fishery	7	6	3	13	13	13	12	14	14	14
Home Economics	4	5	4	10	11	14	14	15	14	15
Other	—	—	—	8	15	15	21	20	19	20
Total	38	50	31	225	252	257	273	277	271	265

Source: Adapted from *Sangyō Kyōiku* (June 1976), pp. 44–46, 19.

Notes: Subcourses are defined by name, not content, so the possibility of double-counting because of slightly different names in two prefectures does exist. However, uniformity in names is remarkably high and I doubt that double-counting adds more than three or four to the increase since 1966.

creation of other new subcourses as also encouraged. The response was impressive: an increase of twenty-five in the three years following the ministry's revision of the guidelines and fifty-two at the movement's peak in 1973. The response was far from uniform, however. Some prefectures, notably Toyama, responded wholeheartedly (Kita Nihon Shinbun Local Government Group, 1975; Ishiguro, 1975). Others, notably Kyoto, opposed the whole idea.

In all prefectures, the issue of diversification activated opposition from the teachers' unions. Progressives see diversification as a means of pigeonholing students according to test scores, of maintaining an elite track by drawing off the students with lower grades into dead-end vocational courses that serve the interests of big business. They also argue that specialized subcourses fail to prepare students for a changing world. The aspects of diversification that drew the most fire were the linking of night schools to specific industrial establishments, the creation of an elite math-science subcourse within the general course,[4] and the plan to raise the proportion of vocational to general courses.

Although the three prefectures studied here do not represent the extremes of prefectural responses, they do contain significant variation. Chiba diversified its high school courses, with the exception of industrial courses. Saitama diversified very little, with the exception of commercial courses. Saga did not diversify, except for adding a data management subcourse. Chiba followed the ministry's lead and the national trend. In Saitama the teachers' unions were more successful in stopping diversification, but failed in commercial high schools because the new subcourses were established in new schools. When a new subcourse is established in an existing school, the teachers' union is organized, on the scene, and has many avenues of participation. They have none of these advantages when the subcourse is established in a new school. In Saga the teachers' unions have traditionally been strong; the prefecture was not building many new schools.

When asked if the Ministry of Education might cause any kind of trouble for them because they were not following its diversification policy, officials in Saga and Saitama denied the possibility. The ministry did back its policy by raising the effective grant ratios for vocational high schools, but had no mechanism to punish those who did not follow the policy. Diversification was just a slogan. The primary effect of the policy was to provide conservatives with the rationale, legitimation, and occasion for changing prefectural education policies. The ministry's policy was automatically placed on every prefecture's agenda, but a prefecture's response to this central initiative depended on prefectural-level factors, particularly the local balance between the teachers' unions and the conservatives.

The Proportion of Vocational and General Schools. Apart from the creation of new subcourses, diversification also meant increasing the number of vocational schools relative to general high schools. Toyama's diversification program planned a ratio of seven vocational to three general ones (Ishiguro, 1975). Popular demand, however, is for general courses. Even in Toyama, the prefecture had to abandon the principle of restricting access to general high schools.

The ratio of general to vocational schools depends first on the degree of urbanization in a prefecture. Less urbanized areas have more vocational schools. However, all three prefectures studied here are moving toward higher ratios of general schools. Chiba and Saitama are building many new schools and they follow demand by building only general high schools. In this policy area, Saga has the more difficult problem: the prefecture must respond to demands for more general courses, yet there is little need to build new schools.

Saga's problem is summarized in table 14. Despite the fact that Saga is an agricultural prefecture, the number of applicants to high school agricultural courses has fallen off drastically and the number applying to general courses has risen correspondingly. In order to reduce this gap between supply and demand, the prefecture has built some general high schools, one in 1974 and two more for 1977. Although the relevant age group has not been growing, rising rates of advancement to high school has created the demand for these new schools. Population movement has also caused regional imbalances best solved by new construction. The other half of the problem is more difficult: reducing the oversupply of agricultural schools.

Saga officials consider it mandatory that Saga's high schools turn out enough agricultural graduates to replace retiring farmers. Under this criterion, the prefecture estimates that only about 700 of the 1,000 agricultural high school seats are needed. Even if this reduction were accomplished, however, 6–8 percent of the high school seats would be agricultural, while only 3 percent of the students want to go to agricultural school. This deviation of planned ratios from estimated demand is justified by the economic rationale that there must be enough graduates to keep the farms operating, but financial and political reasons also play a role.

It would have been financially difficult for Saga to build many more general high schools by 1981. It also would be politically difficult to do

TABLE 14
Course Preferences and Seats in Saga Prefecture High Schools, 1974
(in percent)

	General	Agricultural	Industrial	Commercial	Home Economics
Seats	49.5	10.3	16.5	17.7	6.0
Preferences					
Student	59.2	3.1	15.9	16.2	5.6
Parent	61.7	2.5	15.4	14.6	5.8
Recommendation	55	6–8	15–17	15–17	5–7

Source: Saga Prefecture High School Education Promotion Commission, *Report*, October 22, 1974, pp. 32–33.

Notes: Preferences are from a survey based on a 15 percent random sample. Recommendation refers to the targets set for 1981 in the commission report.

anything that might appear to deny the importance of agriculture. Each high school has an alumni organization that can be counted upon to defend the old school. Because of the centrality of agriculture in Saga's politics, the only way to reduce the number of agricultural high school students is to demonstrate an even greater commitment to agricultural education. The prefecture is accomplishing this by planning to replace some old agricultural high schools with fewer but better new ones.

In this process of planning the desirable ratio of general to vocational high schools, the Education Ministry is silent.

New Directions. Table 13 indicates that the growth in the number of subcourses reversed itself in 1973 and thereafter began to fall. The arguments of the leftists were beginning to take their toll, particularly the less ideological arguments about a high school graduate's ability to adjust to a changing job market. Many vocational high school students were not interested in the subject matter and were not getting jobs in fields related to their training. Diversification was not working. More importantly, the popular demand for more general education was hard to ignore. Thus, in 1976, the Ministry of Education officially abandoned the policy of diversification, recommending a return to more basic subcourses (*Sangyō Kyōiku,* June, 1976). The advisory commission report goes on to suggest ways in which the popularity of vocational education could be restored.

The problem is most pressing in Saga. Table 15 shows the decline in the proportion of agricultural high school students getting jobs related to agriculture. In an agricultural prefecture, the fact that only 20 percent of the graduates actually take up farming causes distress. The prefecture's response is to raise the standards of agricultural high schools by upgrading the facilities. This response is suggested in the ministry's advisory commission report, but MOE intervention does not seem to have been an important factor. MOE support for upgrading facilities at vocational high schools was helpful but had little effect on Saga's policymaking.

In Chiba and Saitama, vocational education forms a much less visible part of education policy and the MOE report helped stimulate prefectural policymaking. In Saitama, the prefecture issued a request to local universities to increase the number of students admitted into vocational departments from vocational high schools, to agricultural departments to take more agricultural high school graduates, and so on (*Saitama Shinbun,* March 8, 1977). The basic reasoning behind this move was that a higher probability of getting into college will raise the popu-

TABLE 15

The Decline in Relevance of Agricultural High Schools in Saga Prefecture, 1969–1976
(in percent)

	1969	1970	1971	1972	1973	1974	1975	1976
Graduates going into farming	39.4	26.2	19.3	18.2	14.4	13.5	12.7	14.2
Graduates from farmer training courses going into farming	52.7	35.3	26.1	25.1	21.9	19.7	18.2	19.2
Percentage of above going into agriculture-related jobs	—	51.1	43.7	36.6	39.5	38.2	40.2	37.8

Sources: Report of the Saga Prefectural High School Education Promotion Commission, October 27, 1974, pp. 42, 47, 110; supplemented for 1975 and 1976 by prefectural materials.

Note: "Farmer training courses" refers to courses like agricultural or livestock that aim at producing farmers and excludes related courses like food processing, landscaping and so on.

larity of vocational high schools. This policy is recommended in the MOE report and the timing of the policy was clearly influenced by the report.

Chiba's advisory commission suggested a recommendation system for entry into agricultural and physical education courses (*Chiba Nippo,* January 22 and March 30, 1977). The rationale behind this policy was that students who enter a course on the recommendation of their middle school teachers will be those who are really interested in that vocation. The possibility of entry by recommendation, avoiding the normal "exam hell" competition, may also make more middle school students consider a vocational education. Again, this policy is suggested in the MOE report and the timing was influenced by the ministry's action.

If the timing of recent vocational education policies in Saitama and Chiba have been largely determined by MOE actions, the content of those policies has not. At most, the ministry presented a list of suggested policies from which the prefectures made selections. A national advisory commission report puts the topic on all prefectural agendas simultaneously, but whether the prefecture acts and what policy it adopts depend more on prefectural-level factors.

Although the Education Ministry played a large role in putting vocational education on prefectural agendas, some prefectures played a large role in putting the topic on the ministry's agenda. Prefectural disenchantment with the diversification policy was one reason the ministry abandoned the policy. The number of subcourses began dropping three years before the MOE report. Moreover, some prefectures took the lead in searching for innovative solutions. For example, Aichi began experimenting with entrance by recommendation in 1974 (Aichi Prefecture, Board of Education, 1973). From one angle, this interactive process of intergovernmental policymaking looks like the prefectures serving as the implementers for the MOE policies. Prefectural complaints are thus a form of feedback. From another angle, however, the process looks more like the ministry serving as the legitimator of any emerging consensus that occurs mainly at the prefectural level and the disseminator of innovative ideas created and tested at the prefectural level. Both images capture parts of the reality.

Entrance into General High Schools

The U.S. occupation established the principle that there should be one high school per school district. The American ideal was a local high school where all of an area's qualified students may go. In the early 1950s all prefectures established something approaching this system. The Kantō region (including Chiba and Saitama) was a partial exception because the occupation officials in charge of this region were less enthusiastic enforcers of this principle. The maintenance of single-school districts was soon made difficult by the baby boom and rising rates of high school advancement. Differing rates of population growth led to unequal access to high school education. Building new schools meant redrawing district boundaries, boundaries that would hardly reflect an existing community spirit. Finally, parents began to ignore district lines, finding ways to get their children into school districts with many openings or into "better" schools. Parents were wont to ask, "If my child is smart enough, why shouldn't he go to the best high school?"

In the face of these problems and pressures, some prefectures began to loosen school district regulations. These policies took three basic forms. First, districts were enlarged. Aichi led the way in 1956 by dividing the whole prefecture into only two districts (Motoyama, 1957). Second, some prefectures adopted rules allowing a certain percentage of a school's enrollment to come from outside the school district. A third approach was to allow students living close to the border to cross it. Some prefectures established "adjustment districts" from which students could choose from among two or more districts. Others simply allowed students to choose from among their district and all neighboring districts. A passive policy of not revising school district lines when new schools were built also resulted in larger school districts.

When students are given the freedom to choose from among many schools, a ranking develops. The high school with the best record of getting their graduates into Tokyo University and other elite universities becomes the "best" school. The distinction between public and private schools, and within public schools between general and vocational courses, produces competition. The ranking of public general high schools produces a much more pervasive kind of competition because it divides the students into smaller groups, thus putting more students on the borderline between success and failure.

The ranking mechanism is a self-fulfilling prophecy: a high school's record of getting its graduates into good universities develops into a consensus on each school's rank; more students take the examinations for the "good" schools, trying to increase their probability of getting into a good university; "good" high schools are therefore able to select from among the best students; with better students, more of their graduates pass the examinations into elite universities, proving the consensus correct. The process would produce a ranking even if the starting point was one of complete equality among schools. In fact, the starting point was a set of prewar schools that had already been ranked. Newly constructed schools start and stay at the bottom of the list.

The self-fulfilling prophecy is fueled by the belief that one's life chances are largely determined by one's education and parents feel that it is therefore worth almost any sacrifice to get their child into a better school. Given the freedom to choose among schools, this mechanism can create clearly excessive competition. Progressive writers have no trouble finding heart-rending stories of failures at fifteen, the loss of friends in the final year of middle school, the tension and single-minded concentration on only those subjects included on entrance examinations (Motoyama, 1957; Zenkoku Shinro Shidō Kenkyūkai, 1974; Kita Nihon Shinbun Local Government Group, 1975). More concrete indications of excessive competition include the widespread use of prefecture-wide practice tests prepared by private companies, given six to ten times in the third year of middle school, and the fact that nationally 38 percent of middle school students attend tutoring classes after school (MOE, Ministerial Secretariat, 1977).

The private enterprise tests are used by middle school teachers to "advise" students on what high school to try for. The private tester in Saitama lists "safe" scores for each high school and they range from 172 (out of 200), 143 and 137 for the top high schools, to 61 and 48 for the bottom of the twenty-two schools (Saitama Prefecture High School Teachers' Union, 1974: 7). Given these estimates and the results of surveys taken by the prefecture and published in the newspapers showing the number of students who plan to take the examination for each school, students plan their strategy. Should they try for the best school they might get into, or play safe with the second-best? The ratio of applicants to openings drops to almost unity for the top schools and competition centers on second-rank schools.

The ranking mechanism works inexorably but not precisely. The result is a pyramid, not a list. The lower the ranking the greater the number of ties. Moreover, there tends to be considerable overlap in student test scores in even the top few schools.[5] Part of this overlap is due to differing strategies among students and to miscalculation. The degree of overlap, however, indicates that some students are choosing strategies on grounds other than maximization of a curriculum vitae. There may also be a limit to the number of schools that can be ranked. A Saitama official claimed that only ten of the eighty schools are actually rankable; if students do not try for one of these ten, they choose the school closest to home, minimizing commuting time (interview in Saitama Prefecture, Department of Education, Planning and Research Division, May 11, 1977). These qualifications, however, concern the precision of the ranking mechanism and do not weaken the conclusions about its dominance or its effects.

There are many ways to try to mitigate the effects of ranking. One way is to reduce the weight given to the entrance examination and increase the weight given the student's middle school record. In theory, this practice should reduce the pressure on the students to do well on a single examination. Actually, the effect has been to spread competition over all three years of middle schools, because one bad term, even one bad test, could ruin one's chances to get into a good university (Saitō, 1968). Prefectures have also reduced the number of subjects tested to lighten the students' burden. The result has been that studentes ignore the subjects not on the test and work even harder on the remaining subjects.

It is not the form of the test that places the students under pressure but the stakes involved in passing or failing. Prefectures also try to reduce the differences among schools by shifting teachers periodically and making the facilities of all schools precisely equal. The effect on ranking is negligible. The dominant difference between good and bad schools is the students. Schools that get good students will have more pass the examinations to elite universities and thus will get better students.

The only effective way to reduce ranking and its effects is to reduce freedom of choice by keeping school districts small and avoiding exceptions. In densely populated Japan, however, single-school districts are very difficult to maintain. Normally, several schools will be located within easy commuting distance of each other. Thus, several prefectures have developed "comprehensive entrance systems" designed to substitute for single-school districts.

A comprehensive entrance system first groups several schools together. Examinations are given for the whole group, not for single schools. Those who pass the examination are assigned to schools on criteria designed to equalize the test scores of students in each school. No two comprehensive systems are alike, but common bases for assignment include commuting time, test scores, and the student's preference (Hyōdo, 1976). Comprehensive systems work, but arouse controversy because they restrict freedom in a direct and tangible way.

At the beginning of this section, I noted that there was a movement toward greater freedom of choice in the late 1950s. Table 16 illustrates these trends. The number of prefectures maintaining single-school districts dropped rapidly until only Kyoto, home of the only progressive governor to survive throughout this period, remains. The number of prefectures with only very large districts increased until 1973. Similarly, the number of prefectures with comprehensive entry systems increased dramatically in 1973. The general pattern is clear: a trend toward more freedom from the late 1950s continued until 1968 or 1969 and then was reversed in 1973. This reversal would have been significantly greater if moves to reduce freedom had not been aborted in several prefectures because of a lack of popular consensus (Matsui, 1976).

More important than the trends, however, is the fact that in the midst of strong trends, some prefectures move in the opposite direction. In 1956 when eleven prefectures were broadening freedom of choice, Hiroshima instituted a comprehensive entrance system. In 1973

TABLE 16
Trends in School Entrance, 1954–1981

	Prefectures with single-school districts only	Prefectures with six or more per district only	Prefectures with comprehensive entry systems
1954	13	0	7
1955	12	0	7
1956	7	0	7
1957	8	4	7
1960	5	5	7
1961	4	5	7
1962	3	6	7
1963	3	7	7
1964	3	9	7
1965	2	10	9
1967	1	12	—
1969	1	13	8
1971	1	13	8
1973	1	9	12
1975	1	9	15
1977	1	9	15
1979	1	9	14
1981	1	9	15

Sources: Compiled from the MOE, Primary and Secondary Education Bureau, *Kōritsu Kōtō Gakkō Nyūgakusha Senbatsu Jisshi Jōkyō ni Kansuru Chōsa Hōkokusho* (*Report on the Survey Concerning Public High School Entrance System*), 1954 to 1981.

when six prefectures were moving to restrict freedom and several more were attempting to do so, Fukushima reduced the number of districts from sixteen to eight. In almost every year there were prefectures moving in both directions. This phenomenon is unimaginable in housing policy or pollution abatement, and I suspect that one would be hard pressed to find any other example in Japan. Even in the other parts of education policy there is a general consensus on direction. Why is high school entrance policy different? Let us examine the problem more closely by looking at the three prefectures.

Saga. Saga has not altered its school districts since they were established after the war. Nor has Saga loosened school districts in other ways. On the other hand, new districts have not been created when new schools were built. The result is seven single-school districts, one district with two schools, one with three, and one with five. Within the two larger districts ranking does occur, but not enough to cause serious problems. While an apparent drop in the achievement levels of Saga high school students is being discussed by policymakers, such discussion has not yet been made public. Some blame the lack of competition, and a movement is afoot to divide the prefecture into four or five districts of three to five schools each. From the end of the war through 1976, however, officials avoided conflict by not making policy.

Saitama. Like Saga, Saitama has yet to redraw district lines, but unlike Saga, it never had single-school districts to start with. Moreover, in 1956 Saitama began permitting students to apply to the schools in neighboring districts. This simple provision had the effect of increasing freedom of choice enormously. The minimum number of choices a Saitama middle school student has is 14 high schools; students in the most populous area have 79; and the average middle school graduate has 61.6 choices. The peak, or most preferred, high school is located in Saitama's first district and 93 percent of all middle school graduates may apply. In other words, the peak high school can choose from among a pool of over 90 percent of the middle school graduates in the prefecture. Thus Saitama's high school entry system is wide open, and the results are a clear ranking of high schools and intense competition among students. The peak high school accounted for 85 of Saitama's 128 entrants into Tokyo University in 1977 and 1978, compared to 16 for the next best school (*Shūkan Asahi,* April 1, 1977, and May 31, 1978).

In August 1973, the governor charged the standing educational advisory commission to consider high school entrance. The commission was weighted toward the conservatives and only about 20 percent of the members supported smaller districts at the beginning of the debate.[6] The debate, however, changed many minds. The Saitama Teachers' Union argues that the progressive position was simply the right one and that anyone who examined the problem seriously could come to the same conclusion:

> If you face the problem head on, I think the result will always be the same. However, under the conservative administration, the School Board did not take up these problems head on. The great advantage of a progressive administration is that it makes these problems that have been around for a long time the center of debate. If the proposing side does not propose, if they bring up other problems, no matter how much noise we make, that is the end of it. Once the problem was taken up, even though the opponents outnumbered us eight to two, two years of debate brought this result, the fourteen district proposal. (Interview in the Saitama Prefecture High School Teachers' Union, June 9, 1977)

One may doubt whether the progressive position is always so convincing, but, in the wide-open system then in force in Saitama, the progressive case was strong.

The interim report of August 1974 recommended revision to about fifteen "middle-sized" districts of from two to six schools each (*Saitama Shinbun,* August 9, 1974; Saitama Prefecture, Bureau of Education, Guidance Division, 1976 and 1977).[7] The Bureau of Education drew up a proposal with fourteen districts with from three to seven schools each (*Saitama Shinbun,* September 10, 1974). The proposal contained no exceptions, but as a transitional phase, for the first year only, the prefecture was divided into four blocs. A student could apply to any school within the bloc and any school in a neighboring district outside the bloc. Even with these exceptions, the bloc proposal represented a significant restriction of freedom. The average middle school graduate would have had 29.0 choices, down from 61.6, and 55.6 percent could apply to the peak school, down from 92.9 percent. Under the ultimate fourteen-district plan, the average middle school graduate would have had only 6.25 choices.

Despite the relative looseness of the bloc plan, opposition began developing even before the plan was published. Even though it had representatives on the commission, the Middle School Principals' Association asked for a delay and the PTA Liaison Council came out in opposition, resolving to take forceful action unless the implementation of the plan were delayed. A few days later, the LDP's prefectural assemblymen voted to oppose the plan and drew up a list of exceptions that should be included if the plan were to be effected. Three of the five suggestions would have increased the number of students that could apply to the peak school.

The school board argued that the bloc system was almost no change at all, that adjustments could be made during the year under the bloc plan, that the plan had widespread support, and finally even offered to include some exceptions, but the tide was against them. On September 25, the board concluded that they could not implement the plan because "at the present time we lack the understanding of not only other education groups, but the citizens as well, and to continue would only increase the confusion" (*Saitama Shinbun,* September 27, 1974). The JSP, silent throughout the debate, finally came out in favor of working with the existing eight districts. The final blow came when, on October 9, the assembly's education committee voted unanimously for a resolution to abandon the fourteen-district plan and to work with the existing eight districts.[8]

Why did the plan have to be scrapped? First, simply because opposition developed. Japanese government is vulnerable to small relatively intense interest groups. The idea of enforcing the plan in spite of the opposition was never considered. A Bureau of Education official blamed the newspapers for leaking the story before everyone had been consulted and for not giving sufficient coverage to the interim bloc plan. This explanation rests on the assumption that consensus building in education is a fragile process, but it does not explain that fragility. A Teachers' Union official thought that the conservatives on the commission were convinced by rational argument and evidence, but that once the consensus broke down, conservative organizations reverted to their ideological positions. This explanation also assumes that a consensus on education reform is fragile.

The fragility of consensus in education policy is based on a grassroots phenomenon. There is a genuine popular demand that something be done about excessively competitive education, but whenever a concrete plan is proposed, those directly affected oppose it intensely. Japanese call this a gap between the collective argument *(sōron)* and the individual argument *(kakuron).* Put in its worst light, the position amounts to: "We should restrict freedom of choice to reduce competition, but *my children* should be able to go where they wish." Unless the collective argument is well organized, the individual argument will dominate because of the intensity of parental interest. Similar events in Osaka (Aoki, 1976), Nagano (Yamagishi, 1973; Matsui, 1976), and Hyogo prefectures (Takizawa, 1977) support this interpretation (see also Cummings and Ishido, 1976).

Saitama's Board of Education and the commission continued to work on reducing the size of school districts and have come up with a new plan. This time every precaution has been taken to gain a firm consensus before making concrete proposals. The new proposal involves far less regrouping of municipalities, is clearly based on the existing eight districts, and involves less restriction of choice. Under this plan the average middle school graduate will have 35.2 choices and 56.2 percent of students can apply to the peak school. While this plan represents a major improvement, the number of choices is still so high that one doubts wheter it will make much difference. Whether competition is reduced or not, the political distance moved, as evidenced by the effort required, was substantial.

Chiba. Like Saitama, Chiba has never had single-school districts, but unlike either of the other two prefectures, Chiba has revised its school districts several times. Starting with eighteen districts, Chiba reduced the number to nine, increased it to eleven, returned to nine, and again went to eleven—all before this study began. The system in effect during the study (1977) dates from 1974.

With three more school districts and fewer exceptions than Saitama, Chiba offers its students a significantly smaller choice of high schools. The major exception provides that middle school graduates may apply to a high school in another district if their municipality borders on that district. The definition of "neighboring" is thus much narrower than Saitama's. Although several other specific exceptions have been added, the result is an overall average of 19.3 choices per middle school graduate and an average of 24.8 choices in the most populous areas. Although Chiba does have a clear peak school, with 76 of Chiba's 143 Toyko University entrants in 1977 and 1978 compared to 20 for the next best school, its reputation as the best school is not as marked as that of the leading high school in Saitama; sixteen Chiba high schools had at least one entrant into Tokyo University in these two years compared to only seven in Saitama (*Shūkan Asahi,* April 1, 1977, and May 30, 1978). Chiba's entrance system is significantly less open than Saitama's, but the problems associated with excessive competition are still present. If there is a threshold level of freedom, 19.3 choices per student is clearly above it.

In 1970 Chiba instituted a comprehensive entrance system in three of its school districts. In no districts did the comprehensive grouping contain all the schools in the district, but they did contain the elite schools. The five schools participating in the first district, the six in the second, and the three in the third each became a single choice for the purpose of entrance examinations. Chiba's comprehensive system aimed to reduce the ranking of schools but also to do so while respecting individual preferences as much as possible. The top-scoring 20 percent (raised to 30 percent in the second year of operation) were allowed to go to the school of their choice.[9] Individual preference was also given priority in assigning students to schools. Even though the system aimed to minimize the restrictions on freedom of choice, it did result in a significant leveling, as shown in table 17. Another result was political controversy.

In 1975 Chiba's incumbent governor retired to run for the House of Councillors. The LDP chose the vice-governor to run for the vacated post. The opposition parties managed to unite behind a single candidate for the first time in Chiba's history. The candidate had been the superintendent of schools who had supervised the implementation of the comprehensive system.[10] The LDP had supported the comprehensive system, but now began to attack it. The switch was due in part to the personal convictions of the party's gubernatorial candidate, but was also influenced by tactical considerations. The progressive candidate was

TABLE 17
The Effects of Chiba's Comprehensive System: First School District

Overall Grade Scores	Average Scores on Entrance Exam		Number of Entrants into Tokyo University	
	Before	After	Before	After
A	444	397	35	41
B	391	367	0	2
C	373	373	0	1
D	350	373	0	1
E	329	366	0	1

Sources: Average scores are from the Chiba Prefecture League for Democratic Education, *Yutaka na Kōkō Kyōiku wo!* (*Toward a Full High School Education!*), and the Tokyo University entrants are calculated from *Shūkan Asahi*, Tokyo University entrants are calculated from *Shūkan Asahi*, April 1, 1977, pp. 22–25, and May 31, 1978, pp. 21–23.

Note: The schools are not necessarily identified by the same letter in the average score and entrant rows.

clearly identified with this controversial policy. The policy affected only the more urbanized areas of the prefecture where a progressive could be expected to run well. The comprehensive entrance issue could help negate the progressive advantage in the urban areas. The strategy seems to have worked, for the LDP candidate won by a surprisingly large margin (*Chiba Nippo*, April 14, 1975).

The new governor instructed the education advisory commission to reconsider the comprehensive entry system. Upon reconsideration, the commission decided that the system should be abolished (*Asahi Shinbun*, July 18, 1976; Sasaki, 1976). Although many reasons were cited, the bottom line was clearly "lack of consensus." It is not clear how much this lack of consensus extended to the grass roots, but the Board of Education did a survey showing that pluralities of middle school students, high school students, teachers, and parents opposed the system. The final commission report was published with a dissenting minority opinion, a rare phenomenon in Japan indicating a high degree of conflict. This series of events left everyone quite embarrassed. They myth of rational, nonpolitical, consensual decision making had been exploded in public.

Chiba's Board of Education continued to consider reform and in 1977 proposed a new system of districts. Although officials denied any connection between the end of the comprehensive system and the reduction of school districts, the latter was substituted for the former. The key provisions of the proposed system are the division of the old third district and tightening up on exceptions (*Chiba Nippo*, April 30 and May 1, 1977). The comprehensive system had meant a reduction in the average number of choices per middle school graduate from 19.8 to 14.7 (from 24.8 to 17.9 in the area directly affected). The reduction of school districts will result in a figure of 15.9 (19.7 in the directly affected area). Thus, the new school districts were to be only slightly more free than the old comprehensive system had been.

The Role of the Ministry of Education

When asked about their role in high school education policy, MOE officials emphasize the degree to which authority is granted to the prefectures. The ministry's authoritative roles are limited to setting standards and drawing up study guidelines. The MOE does take a biennial survey of prefectural practices in high school entrance and distributes that information back to the prefectures, but it takes no active role. In sum,

The MOE does not take the lead. . . . We only provide information. This is pretty passive, but I do not think there is any other way. It would be difficult for MOE to say all high schools must conduct examinations in this way. The prefectures would not follow and there is a power that will oppose anything the MOE proposes, you know, the Japan Teachers' Union. They would say that any problems with the entrance system are MOE's fault. That is just the world we live in. (Interview in MOE, High School Education Division, June 22, 1977)

As this statement indicates, the basic reason that the Ministry of Education does not take a more active role in high school education pollicy is fear of the political repercussions of active intervention. Where controversy is less heated, as in building new high schools, or where popular concern is less intense, as in vocational education, the ministry plays a more active role. When a consensus can be reached, it can legitimize that consensus to great effect, but the ministry is largely limited to an agenda-setting role.

Conclusions

As I have emphasized throughout this chapter, political factors dominate intergovernmental policymaking in Japanese education. Nevertheless, with one exception, all of the hypotheses have something to contribute as explanations for the distribution of influence. The exception is the principle of least interest.

In chapter 5 we found that the principle of least interest worked well in construction projects, but it does not work for high school construction. In part this difference is due to the overwhelming public demand for high schools. Prefectures cannot stop building because they lack the cooperation of the central government; they must continue to build in any circumstances. As in pollution control policy, influence accrues to those institutions that respond to clear public demands.

Another important difference between high school construction and housing and sewer construction is that high school construction is not a central program. Before 1976, the central government was not involved at all. I expect that one would have found the principle of least interest operating between prefectures and cities before 1976, but there was no intergovernmental policymaking between the central government and the prefectures. Even after the MOE became involved in subsidizing high school construction, it avoided making policy. That the principle of least interest works so well in other construction programs suggests that the MOE could have demanded a great deal for its small financial contribution, but for political reasons it chose to minimize its own influence.

Information played a very small role in education policymaking. In an ideologically polarized issue, the expertise of one side is not accepted by the other. Expertise without its gloss of objectivity has little power. Similarly, in Britain, Neve (1977) found that the local education officer has more influence in less politicized issues and in less policitized local governments.

Neither is knowledge of local conditions particularly relevant. The information that did play a role was simply information about policies in other prefectures. The ministry disseminated information almost passively, muting its own preferences. Nevertheless, information influenced prefectural policymaking. The agenda-setting function of information cannot be ignored. The agenda effect was clearest in the case of vocational high schools, but was also present in the diffusion of policies toward school districts, comprehensive entrances systems, and so on. The MOE's efforts at disseminating information promote diffusion and help maintain a modicum of uniformity in prefectural policies.

The policy substance hypothesis fails for similar reasons. When there is no consensus on what direction represents progress, there can be no technically superior policy. Nevertheless, policy substance proved effective in one rather remarkable instance: the conservatives on Saitama's education advisory committee were convinced, on the merits of the case, that school districts had to be made smaller. Their conversion did not last long, as their ideological predispositions reasserted themselves, but that they were convinced at all, even briefly, lends support to the policy substance hypothesis. The issue at stake can make a significant difference even in a polarized situation.

Findings for the authority hypothesis fit the patterns found in earlier chapters. The situation is similar to that of raising rents in public housing: officials find it more important to avoid responsibility than to gain influence. In the housing case, the MOC finally had to assume responsibility even though it had no authority. In high school education, however, the MOE successfully used the principle of prefectural responsibility to avoid making policy. The basic difference between the two cases is that the Ministry of Construction is better insulated from political pressures than is the Ministry of Education. Ideological polarization and the existence of the powerful opposition in the teachers' unions keep the MOE in the middle of a political thicket. Consensus decision making does not work in education, and the issue is forced on the actor most capable of taking political responsibility for a nonconsensual decision, the governor.

We have noted above that the authority that proves important tends to be seemingly minor provisions; that finding is confirmed by this case. Even though the Education Ministry tried to avoid involvement in high school education policies and tried to minimize the effects of its intervention, the grant program had significant effects on prefectural policies. A completely neutral program proved impossible. The main effect of the grant program was pressure towards uniformity. Central programs have to assume uniformity and the assumption tends to be self-fulfilling. As in previous chapters, the main effects of central authority have been inadvertent. There is no evidence to suggest that the MOE wanted Saitama to abandon its policy of slow-paced construction, yet that was the biggest single change in prefectural policy produced by the grant program in the three prefectures under examination.

Findings on the financial hypothesis discussed in connection with pollution control are also replicated in this chapter. Proportionality can again be rejected: influence in education policymaking is not proportional to financial contribution. In fact, the subsidy for building high schools was a case of local governments raiding the treasury to pay for local projects, not the more typical case of the central government trying to bribe local governments to participate in a national program. The ministry's influence did increase after the grant program was enacted, but the amount of the financial commitment had nothing to do with the amount of influence gained. If the political situation were different and the MOE had tried to maximize its influence, it could have done so without paying a larger share of the costs. Conversely, given the political situation, an increased financial contribution would not increase the MOE's influence.

Finances played a major role in determining prefectural educational policies, but again the relevant variable was slack resources. The number of high schools planned was carefully matched to financial capacity. Both Chiba and Saitama stretched that capacity but were limited by it. The only innovations were those that saved money.

Politics was dominant. Two facts form the political context of education policymaking. The first is its polarization and politicization from top to bottom. Education policy must be made cautiously, because a misstep can lead to political controversy. Demands must be met; general high schools must be built; Saga must maintain its agricultural high schools. The balance of conservative and progressive forces at the prefectural level makes significant differences in the degree of diversification and in entrance policies. Because policymaking is more political and less bureaucratic, there is little uniformity among prefectural policies. Prefectural policy differences have accumulated over time to the degree that the quality of the diversity is different from that in other policy areas. Inertia leads to increasing variation. There are fewer well-defined dimensions along which policy varies. It would be difficult to design a national policy because very little can be assumed about prefectural policies.

The second political fact that makes education policymaking different is that amending high school entrance policies offers politically a no-win prospect. Any change in entrance policies will create a disadvantage for someone and the disadvantaged are likely to protest. Because of ideological polarization, the authorities have trouble convincing the disadvantaged of the rationality, necessity, and legitimacy of the policy. The disadvantaged can always find powerful allies to oppose the policy. The best political strategy is to avoid responsibility in this area. This result is similar to the issue of rents in public housing but the cause is different. In the rent issue, the technically correct policy was politically unpalatable. In high school entrance, no policy is technically correct and any policy is likely to be politically costly. Without a consensus on general directions, it is hard to aggregate interests. In Britain the breakdown in consensus caused by the issue of comprehensivization made interest aggregation more difficult and increased the role of local policymaking (Jennings, 1977). The British and Japanese cases taken together suggest the hypothesis that, when interest aggregation is difficult, central control will also be difficult.

7

Conclusions

*W*E ARE now in a position to evaluate each of the hypotheses concerning the distribution of influence in Japanese intergovernmental relations. Each of the hypotheses has been confirmed both here and in previous research. These are not directly competing hypotheses and our purpose is not to reject all but one. Rather, the problem is to specify the conditions under which each hypothesis applies.

The Authority Hypothesis. We can reject the simplest form of the authority hypothesis: influence is not proportional to authority. In Japan, as elsewhere, it is easy to find cases in which authority and influence diverge markedly, actors with no authority exercising great influence and actors with great authority exercising virtually no influence. In fact, in the case of pollution control policy, we found authority being awarded to those actors who had exercised influence. This finding is the key to reinterpreting the role of authority in intergovernmental policymaking.

Relations among various levels of government are based on a political bargain. The distribution of authority delineates the outlines of the bargain at any given time. The distribution of authority is the result of the bargaining process, not a major determinant of the overall bargain. Thus, the authority hypothesis does not apply when the intergovernmental bargain is being renegotiated, as was the case in Japan in the late 1960s and early 1970s. More generally, the more controversial the issue and the greater the role of political actors as opposed to bureaucratic ones, the less relevant the authority hypothesis. Authority is most important in relatively low-visibility areas dominated by bureaucratic decision making.

146

One of the most surprising findings of this research is that the important pieces of authority are seemingly minor provisions in the law. Grand phrases assigning general responsibilities are seldom effective. The law assigns responsibility for high school construction and for raising rents on public housing to prefectures, but neither the Education Ministry nor the Construction Ministry was able to use these legal provisions to avoid taking responsibility. The law was no more than a starting point, the provisions of a previous bargain now under renegotiation. The effective provisions of the law would be difficult to guess from reading the law. Reading the law on housing planning would lead one to believe that it is a purely top-down process, but the seemingly minor provision for prefectural submission of data proves more important than it looks. Similar findings for highway planning and even constitutional revision in Germany confirm this generalization (Garlichs and Hull, 1978).

We are faced with a paradox: small bits of authority produce influence, but large chunks do not. The role of politics resolves the paradox. Large pieces of authority tend to be brought up in relatively controversial and politicized cases in which authority is not an important resource. In political arenas the intergovernmental bargain is being renegotiated. Instead of authority producing influence, influence in political bargaining is formalized in a revised distribution of authority. Small grants of authority prove more effective because they are useful in those arenas in which authority is a major resource: low-visibility administrative policymaking.

In administrative arenas, authority proves important in two different ways. First, local governments can use little grants of authority in ways never intended by the authors of the law.[1] This process was described by Banfield (1961) in the United States and Milch (1974) in France. The best Japanese examples are pollution control agreements, land use guidelines, and the population limitation policies of the three prefectures surrounding Tokyo.

In bureaucratic arenas, the political bargain is a given and authority represents inertia. Whenever a local government tries to innovate, some little provision of the law is likely to cause a problem. The procedures for inspecting polluting facilities caused problems for Chiba's source telemeter system; the provision that entrants into public housing meet the requirements at the time of occupancy caused problems for Saitama's registration system; and the three-year definition of "new" high school construction forced Saitama to abandon its practice of slow-paced construction. In each of these cases, the effect was unintentional.

The law had not anticipated the innovations and accidentally hindered them. The local policies were in accord with the spirit of the law but violated the letter of the law. This problem is probably anavoidable, but could be handled with greater flexibility than is the norm in Japan.

We can derive two revised hypotheses from this discussion. First, we find that small grants of authority can be used in ways not intended in the law. The form of this hypothesis is not very helpful. It predicts only that one may be surprised. Just which bits of authority should prove important may be inherently unpredictable. Second, we may hypothesize that the more detailed the legal framework of intergovernmental relations in a policy area, the harder it will be for local governments to innovate. If the law represents policy inertia, the more policy features that are already decided in the law, the more likely a local innovation will run into some legal barrier.

The Financial Hypothesis. We can reject the simplest form of the financial hypothesis: influence is not proportional to financial contribution. In intergovernmental relations, he who pays the piper does not necessarily call the tune. Even more than the distribution of authority, the distribution of financial responsibility for particular projects is a static aspect of the intergovernmental bargain. The overall financial bargain, the percentage to be paid by each level of government, may be important in getting the program started, but has little effect on how the program is administered. The important financial factors are marginal costs and slack resources, and the complexities of intergovernmental finance make it hard to estimate either factor.

As we found with authority, the important financial factors are often seemingly minor ones. It is costs at the margin that count. The marginal costs that affect intergovernmental finance are not those used in economic theory, not the cost of producing one more unit. In the case of overburdening, it was changes in cost per unit that caused the trouble. The grant program for high school construction was not very lucrative but was welcomed because it reduced the local governments' cost per unit. I doubt that cost per unit will prove important in all cases, but these findings do suggest that the financial factors that prove important will be those that disturb the local budgeting process at the margin. To the degree that the environment of local budgeting is stable and the parameters are known, local officials make autonomous decisions within a framework established by the central government. Local officials complain most bitterly when the parameters of intergovernmental finance are changed at the margin.

The second financial factor that proved important was slack resources, money that can be shifted among programs or to new programs as needed. Flexible resources allow innovative policymaking and free the local government from many of the central government's fiscal incentives. They have proven important in many different studies of innovation (Mohr, 1969) but also notoriously difficult to measure. In the cases examined here, the key factor was simply the size of the budget: prefectures with larger budgets had more slack and were therefore better able to implement their own priorities. In any budget a certain portion must be left relatively uncommitted and reallocable in order to provide the minimum flexibility required by an unpredictable environment. In larger budgets this percentage is a larger absolute figure and it is the absolute amount that is important in the types of cases examined here. If a prefecture has twenty construction projects under way, it can shift funds among them and do innovative things simply by using the money that would otherwise be in the bank waiting for one project to reach the next stage. Chiba and Saitama both had special public housing programs that illustrate this point. Saitama's policy of slow-paced high school construction is another case in point. Prefectures constructing one or two projects do not have this kind of flexibility.

Again, I do not expect the size of the budget to be the best measure of slack in all cases, but it is a factor often overlooked. In any case, the financial factors that proved important in explaining the distribution of influence were marginal costs and slack, not the proportion of the project paid for. We can therefore propose two revised hypothesis: local governments with more slack resources will have more capacity to innovate, and central policies that affect local budgeting at the margin will be more likely to result in central influence and to inhibit local innovation.

The Information Hypothesis. Two aspects of information were found to be important: technical expertise, generally favoring the central government, and knowledge of local conditions, generally favoring local governments. Both types of information are necessary for making and implementing policy. Only when both are evenly distributed does the information hypothesis fail to explain significant aspects of the distribution of influence.

Central governments tend to have an advantage in technical expertise: they tend to have better-educated personnel, better and more staff resources, and access to the best research facilities in the nation. However, this advantage is more relevant in some policy areas than others.

Some policy areas are simply more technical. Expertise also tends to be diffused, so that the central advantage tends to decline over time. For example, I do not expect the central government's advantage in expertise on sewer construction to last long. As local governments gain experience building sewers, they will have less need to depend on central guidelines and advice.

The central government tends to have the advantage in expertise, but the primary determinants of expertise are experience and attention to problems: those governments that have been concerned about and involved in a policy area longer will have greater expertise. Pollution control, as a new and highly technical issue, would seem to have been destined for centralized policymaking. However, some local governments had been involved longer in pollution abatement and had paid more attention to environmental problems. The result was that these local governments had more expertise than the central government. A similar phenomenon occurred in the United States, with Los Angeles and California having greater knowhow in pollution control than the federal government (Krier and Ursin, 1978).

We must also note that political controversy can attentuate the effectiveness of expertise. Expertise is not just technical knowledge; it also includes the legitimacy that goes with objectivity. To be effective, expertise must be apolitical. In highly politicized situations, expertise loses its claim to objectivity. Early pollution activists refused to believe the testimony of industrial and government experts. This mistrust helped negate the normal central advantage in expertise, while activists and local government developed their own countervailing skills. Similarly, some aspects of high school education policy are so ideologically polarized that objectivity is impossible. Information is evaluated by its source (our side or theirs) and by its conclusions (supporting our side or theirs). Like authority, expertise tends to be more effective in low-visibility bureaucratic decision making than in controversial political contexts.

The distribution of knowledge of local conditions tends to favor local governments but also varies by policy area. On some issues, the key information needed for effective implementation can be readily packaged in a statistical form available to anyone. Pollution-monitoring devices churn out data that can be evaluated as easily by a bureaucrat who has never visited the area as by a long-time resident. On the other hand, locating and acquiring a suitable construction site requires such detailed and idiosyncratic knowledge that a central official could not spend the time and energy to do it effectively. Knowledge of local conditions can always add something to a strictly statistical approach, but the need for such knowledge varies.

The variance in need for local knowledge is partly a function of the problem and the degree to which satisfactory measures have been developed. Variance is also caused by program design. A program can be designed to use only statistical information or to allow flexibility for individual cases. The more strictly bureaucratic the program, the easier it is to centralize decision making.

Our original information hypothesis needs little revision: the institution that controls the information necessary for effective policymaking and implementation will have influence. We can, however, refine the hypothesis by stating the conditions of low-visibility bureaucratic policymaking and by noting that the need for expertise or knowledge of local conditions varies according to policy area.

The Policy Substance Hypothesis. Despite the popular refrain, "It's all politics," the debate over the substance of the policy has a significant effect on the outcome and on the distribution of influence. It is not all politics. No one would suggest that policymaking is a purely objective rational process. In fact, it cannot be. Nevertheless, the merits of the case do make a difference. The position backed by the stronger technical arguments has a definite advantage. The only cases in which the policy substance hypothesis had no effect were those in which there were no substantive disagreements among the levels of government.

Examples of the power of technical arguments are easy to find. Perhaps the most impressive case was Saitama's education advisory commission overcoming ideological polarization through two years of discussion. The agreement did not last long; ideology reasserted itself; but the merits of the case had an effect even in this polarized environment. Other, more lasting examples of technical arguments having a significant effect include Chiba coopting the JHC into helping build its new towns because new towns were consistent with the JHC's mission, and all the examples of "illegal" ordinances that were later legalized by amending the law.

The policy substance hypothesis needs little revision, only qualification: the effect of technical arguments will be greater in low-visibility bureaucratic policymaking.

The Principle of Least Interest. The generalization that the party least interested in a joint venture has the greatest control over its outcome proved a remarkably effective hypothesis under certain conditions.

First, it must be a bureaucratic issue of low visibility. There must be no
relevant actors except the parties to the joint project. As soon as a third
party—which in intergovernmental relations is most often the public—
becomes involved, incentives get too complex for this simply hypothesis. Second, there must be pressure to keep working on the project. The
costs of delay must be high. These costs can be administrative as well as
financial. Some programs keep on functioning when ignored, while
others require the active attention of both parties. The principle of least
interest applies only to the latter.

The principle of least interest does not apply to changes in the
management of programs because the program continues to function
under standard operating procedures. It applies best to grant programs
for construction projects. The costs of delay are high and the active
attention of all actors is required. This is one of the clearest findings of
this study and it is supported by several studies done in other countries
(Garlichs and Hull, 1978; Hartley, 1971; Milch, 1974; Sbragia, 1974).

We should note that the relevant factor is disinterest, not obstruc-
tion. Any intergovernmental program can be sabotaged by either party,
but sabotage will be met with counterforce and become controversial.
Once the issue becomes controversial, the principle of least interest no
longer applies. Again, the least interest hypothesis requires little revision, only specification of the domain to which it applies.

The Politics Hypothesis. The most important single factor is politics,
the least studied. Each of the other hypotheses applied primarily to
noncontroversial bureaucratic matters. As political policymakers get involved, the other hypotheses become less relevant; when the issue gets
political, politics dominate.

A good deal of confusion has come from the assumption that intergovernmental relations are essentially bureaucratic. We have studied
low-visibility bureaucratic policymaking and extrapolated the results
into areas of political policymaking. Officals involved in intergovernmental policy making are mightily concerned with authority and bits of
authority prove remarkably effective weapons. Therefore, one might
assume that the overall distribution of authority under the law, or the
constitution, should make a lot of difference in the distribution of influence in any given system. The inference is incorrect, however, because
authority is not a particularly effective weapon in political arenas. Local
officials worry about money constantly and complain bitterly about
how grant programs are administered. Therefore, one might assume
that the proportion of the program paid for by the central government

and, more generally, the proportion of taxes collected by the central government are good indicators of centralization. Again, this supposition is incorrect because the overall terms of financial sharing are determined in different, more political, arenas.

My findings clearly indicate the importance of politics, but how does intergovernmental politics, as opposed to intergovernmental administration, work? I began by trying to apply existing typologies to my findings. Lowi's (1972) model of distributive politics fits perfectly and explains a good deal about intergovernmental politics. Local governments act as interest groups trying to get benefits from the central government. Although they are actually competing against each other for pieces of a limited pie, they act as if each request were independent of all others, just as Lowi describes the process for private-sector interest groups. Local governments also play distributive politics with local interest groups. In this arena local governments are the distributors of governmental largesse, not the benefactors.

The distributive politics model fit intergovernmental politics like a glove, but I could find no other helpful typology. The key difference between distributive and other kinds of intergovernmental politics is that in distributive politics local governments are essentially unitary actors. In other types of politics, they are divided. In these cases, the primary fault lines that divide local governments are partisan, so I shall label this type of intergovernmental politics "partisan politics." To make the typology symmetric, one should distinguish between national and local partisan politics, but I found no cases in the latter category. Although there may be important local issues at some times in some places, I found none in Japan. Local parties and factions either fight over issues that divide them at the national level or over personnel decisions like who shall be chairman of the assembly. The only purely local policies I found were distributive.

We are now left with three types of intergovernmental politics. First, we can distinguish distributive from partisan politics. Then we can further divide distributive politics into local and national levels. The theoretical possibility of local partisan politics must be noted, but will not be discussed because I found no examples of it in Japan.

This typology applies to politics about policy, but as I analyzed my cases I became increasingly aware of a kind of politics that has nothing to do with policy. A great deal of political maneuvering and political conflict takes place over who shall take the credit or blame for some government action. The policy stays the same, no matter who wins. If the conflict is inconclusive, as it often seems to be, policymaking may be delayed. Strange, technically irrational clauses may creep into the bill, but policy is irrelevant to the conflicts. The politics of responsibility occurs in both distributive and issue politics; politicians want to take credit for a new school but avoid blame for rising tuition, for example. The politics of responsibility is a separate dimension that must be discussed separately.

National Distributive Politics. My findings concerning local governments in their role as interest groups seeking benefits from the central government are paradoxical. On the one hand, Japanese politicians seem to believe that distributive politics is the way to win elections. Issues are less important than public works. On the other hand, I observed no variance in the distribution of central largesse. I found no evidence that prefectures with progressive governors were less effective playing the game of distributive politics. Neither did I discover any evidence that prefectures that deviate from the ministerial policy line lose funds because of it. Indeed, I found impressive evidence that local governments can confront the central government without fear of reprisal. The one exception is the Ministry of Home Affairs. If this ministry thinks a prefecture is fiscally irresponsible, it can and will cut the prefecture's requests for authority to borrow. Ex-Prime Minister Tanaka's district is probably a second exception, but the evidence is far from clear (Hirose, 1981). The system is well symbolized by the yearly budget negotiations. Thousands of supplicants descend on Tokyo to lobby for their favorite projects, but the effect is minimal.

My finding that there is little variance in the distribution of governmental benefits is surprising. Common sense tells us that, when in power, one ought to reward one's friends and punish one's enemies, but research seems to support the contention that such discrimination is rare (Arnold, 1979; Mladenka, 1980; Tarrow, 1977). In Japan this finding can be explained by the LDP's electoral interests: it is in the interest of the LDP to keep the distribution of central benefits fairly equal and to obscure any variation that does exist. Each and every LDP candidate wants to be able to claim that his connections were the key to getting more benefits for the district. If the winners and losers in the distribution process were clearly identified, only the winners would reap the electoral rewards. As a way of getting more votes, keeping inequalities hidden and trying to take credit for every benefit received by anyone is vastly superior to merely rewarding friends and punishing enemies. Moreover, since every district has some elected officials from the LDP, punishing a prefecture for electing a progressive governor, for example, would also punish the LDP Dietmen from the prefecture. The strategy of rewarding friends and punishing enemies is hard to implement.

Although the distribution of central benefits is not perfectly equal, nor it is based solely on bureaucratic rationality, its few inequalities may be obscured for political purposes. My research design was not large enough to find and explain the variances in the distributive process. A more sophisticated study involving more prefectures over a longer period would be necessary to control for potentially confounding variables (Arnold, 1979). Nevertheless, I can make one generalization: bureaucratic processes are more important than political processes in the allocation of central benefits in japan.

Local Distributive Politics. When interest groups are organized at the local or prefectural level, a different kind of distributive politics occurs. The local government becomes the distributor, instead of the receiver, of governmental largesse. The normal beneficiaries are small businesses, not only in Japan but also in Britain and Germany (Johnson and Cochrane, 1981). Prefectural banks have close ties to prefectural governments through such financial decisions as where the prefecture will keep its deposits. Particular industries are often concentrated in particular prefectures. In Saga, agriculture is primary. In Chiba the interests of the *kombināto* cannot be ignored. Hiroshima City took a keen interest in the fate of the Tōyō Kōgyō, manufacturer of Mazda cars, when it was in trouble (Pascale and Rohlen, 1983). On a smaller scale, local budgets are littered with token subsidies to small interest groups (Noguchi et al., 1978).

In issues involving local interest groups, local governments will dominate and the central government will avoid involvement when it can. The basic principle is political courtesy. Just as in the U.S. Congress no one is asked to vote against his or her district, so central officials avoid putting local officials in the position of having to do something that would hurt their reelection chances. These are the truly natural functions of local government. The only purely local policies I found involved local interest groups: aid to small businesses for pollution control equipment, and especially Saga's program to curb livestock pollution. Even when such programs grow to national proportions, as in the case of the medium-sized stores, the politics is local and the central government is relatively passive.

Partisan Politics. Local governments are more likely to get involved in partisan politics when they are controlled by the party out of power at the national level. The opposition parties normally control some local governments, but in the early 1970s the opposition controlled most of Japan's major cities and several prefectures (MacDougall, 1980). A similar situation existed in France (Kesselman, 1970; Schain, 1979) and Italy (Chubb, 1980; Seidelman, 1981), where conservative central governments faced many cities controlled by the left. In Germany in the 1970s the Social Democrats won the federal elections but the Christian Democrats won most of the state elections, and in the German system this gave the right control of the upper house (Smith, 1982: 158ff). When such disjunctures occur, intergovernmental relations get more political.

Parties can use local governments to help fight national-level battles. This phenomenon explains local policies that have very little to do with local government: resolutions on issues of foreign policy or the Korean registration case described in chapter 3. Opposition-controlled local governments also resist national policies, with varying degrees of seriousness, in order to make a political statement. Resistance to the diversification of high school education is a good Japanese example. Many examples from British housing policy have been documented (Hartley, 1971; Mitchell, 1974). Labour-controlled local governments also resisted Conservative expenditure cuts in a manner reminiscent of Governor Minobe's "financial war" with the central government (Gyford, and James, 1983). Local governments can also become an important intraparty battleground. The Asukata administration in Yokohama served both to showcase the Socialist party's ability to govern, and to demonstrate the electoral appeal of the mayor's brand of progressive politics to his rivals within the party. A similar but more serious battle occurred within the German Social Democratic party (Braunthal, 1984).

Local governments can be used for partisan purposes, but they also have interests of their own and central-local cleavages can develop that cut across party lines. The pollution control issue started as a left-right issue in which the left just happened to be dominant in local governments. However, a central-local cleavage soon developed in which local officials were more likely and central officials less likely to support strong policies, whether they were conservative or progressive. Gyford and James (1983) document similar cases of central-local cleavages cutting across partisan ones in Britain.

The hypothesis that can be drawn from the study of pollution control in Japan is that, under conditions of persistent public demand, those institutions that respond effectively to that demand will gain influence. If the institutions involved are political parties, this generalization makes good sense: the party that responds gets more votes. The competition between central and local governments can also have an electoral impact, albeit a less direct one than that between two parties. It is probably easier to appeal to the voters' areal loyalties and interests than to abstract class loyalties and interests (Peterson and Kantor, 1977). We can also use the analogy of U.S. presidential-congressional relations again. Issues between the president and Congress often cut across partisan lines and the institution most responsive to public demands tends to gain influence (Huntington, 1965).

The Politics of Responsibility. Finally, there is a form of intergovernmental politics that is not concerned with what is to be done but rather with who is to take the political credit or blame. Competition over political credit is easier because it is easier to share. A great many politicians can line up at a ribbon-cutting ceremony or co-sponsor a bill. Opportunities for taking credit for governmental actions is primarily a function of formal office. Thus, a politician is rational to seek relatively powerless jobs like serving as chairman of the prefectural assembly or to become the minister of education even though he has no particular policy preferences in education. These offices not only make him appear more important to his constituents, they also give him more opportunities to attend ribbon-cutting ceremonies.

Political blame is harder to deal with. Someone must take the responsibility for those decisions deemed necessary but which will probably lose votes. These are "hot potato" issues which are pushed around from institution to institution until someone "bites the bullet."

The politics of responsibility is an integral part of the democratic process but it is also the kind of politics that gives politics a bad name. When the word "politics" is used as an expletive, it often refers to endless wrangling over "petty" personnel problems. The jockeying to avoid responsibility for necessary actions, the inability to take a controversial stand, makes politicians look like big children playing with big matches. The question of who takes responsibility for politically sensitive issues and under what circumstances should be treated as an important problem of democratic theory. My findings on this question are somewhat counterintuitive: the weak are better able to avoid responsibility than the strong. More precisely, the institution most capable of making the decision will take responsibility for necessary but unpopular policies.

When a problem arises that must be dealt with but is politically a no-win situation, who makes the decision? My first hypothesis was that the institution least able to avoid responsibility would make the decision. Thus, in the case of rent revision, local governments successfully avoided responsibility and proved more influential than the Ministry of Commerce, but in the case of amending high school entrance policies, the Ministry of Education proved itself more powerful by forcing the prefectures to decide. However, upon reflection I rejected this hypothesis. The vacillation and confusion displayed by local governments in rent revision and the MOE on the issue of high school admissions does not look like strength, nor does it look like successful dissimulation. It is, in fact, weakness.

The key to this puzzle is the fact that avoiding decision making is easy. It is virtually impossible for one governmental institution to force another to make a decision no matter how greatly advantaged it may be in resources. In fact, to force a particular decision is tantamount to making the decision and taking responsibility for it. Both the weak and the powerful try to avoid hard decisions but, as everyone delays and demurs, everyone also gets more and more anxious that something be done. A strange kind of bargaining ensues in which all parties urge action on all others. In this type of bargaining, weakness is a strength: one cannot be asked to do what he cannot do. The party that finally steps forward is the one most capable of taking the political heat. The way to avoid blame is weakness, either technical or political incapacity, not strength, some sort of political power.

Like the principle of least interest, the generalization "Weakness can be a bargaining strength" is a powerful predictor of how decisions will be made in certain circumstances. Weakness is a bargaining strength when all parties involved agree on what must be done and on the urgent necessity of action. One important real-world example of these conditions is that in which technical considerations unambiguously point in one direction and political considerations point just as clearly in the opposite direction.

Responsibility for hard decisions can be assumed in two very different ways. Bureaucrats take responsibility based on their insulation from politics. Their expertise protects them because it is a claim to special knowledge, and to objectivity and political neutrality. Politicians take responsibility based on the popular mandate they have received or hope to receive. They are insulated from the specific demands of the groups directly involved by the claim of majority support.

The institution most capable of taking responsibility for hot potato issues varies according to the type of issue. First, the degree of politicization will affect the probability of a bureaucratic or a political institution assuming responsibility. Controversy pushes the issue toward the politicians' court. Technical complexity pushes it toward bureaucratic arenas. Second, the degree of interest aggregation affects the probability of central or local response. I have argued that the organization of demands for stronger pollution control in citizens' movements in Japan was one reason that local governments were more responsive to the problem. The development of the pollution issue in Australia (Roddewig, 1978) and the issue of school comprehensivization in Britain support this hypothesis (Peterson, 1971; Jennings, 1977). On the other hand, the nationally organized pollution groups in the United States were stronger to begin with and got more effective over time, and the federal government was more active than other central governments (Jones, 1975; Solesbury, 1976).

Which institutions are most capable of taking responsibility for politically unpopular decisions also varies by country. In Japan the central ministries are the most insulated bureaucratic actors, but in Britain (Scarrow, 1971) and Sweden (Anton, 1975) the local bureaucracy may be even more protected. The political institution most capable of taking this type of responsibility in Japan is the prefectural governor or city mayor. Although some prime ministers have taken responsibility on occasion, the Liberal Democratic party has certainly not bitten the bullet very often. Political responsibility of this type is perhaps rarer in Japan than elsewhere. Japanese politicians feel particularly comfortable with consensual issues. Because we have so few cases and because of the confounding effects of the type of issue involved, it is hard to generalize. Nevertheless, in the 1960s and 1970s the official who most often took political responsibility was the governor or the mayor. The local "presidential systems" focuses political attention more effectively than the national parliamentary system.

My findings, the revised hypotheses, are summarized as follows:

I. When decisions are made by bureaucrats on noncontroversial issues:
   A. These generalizations apply to all cases:
      1. Small bits of authority can be used in ways not intended in the law.
      2. The more detailed the formal distribution of authority, the harder local innovation will be to carry out.
      3. Local governments with slack resources will have greater capacity to innovate and to avoid slavishly following the fiscal incentives of central grant programs.
      4. Central policies that affect local budgeting at the margin will be more likely to result in central influence and more likely to inhibit local innovation.

B. In noncontroversial areas that require expertise:
   1. The institution with the greater expertise will have greater influence, *ceteris paribus*.
   2. The central government tends to have the advantage in expertise, *ceteris paribus*.
   3. An institution's expertise depends primarily on the amount of its experience in and attention paid to the policy area.
C. In policy areas that require knowledge of local conditions:
   1. The institution with the greater knowledge of local conditions will have more influence, *ceteris paribus*.
   2. Local governments tend to have an advantage in knowledge of local conditions, *ceteris paribus*.
   3. The degree to which central officials have access to knowledge of local conditions depends on the degree to which the requisite knowledge has been summarized in a statistical form.
D. In cases of substantive disagreement among levels of government, the party with the stronger technical argument will have more influence, *ceteris paribus*.
E. In joint projects in which the costs of delay are great, the party least interested in the project will have more influence over it, *ceteris paribus*.

II. When political actors get involved in policymaking:
A. Under conditions of politicization in which there is a persistent public demand:
   1. Those institutions that respond to the public demand will have more influence.
   2. The institutions involved need not be levels of government. The probability of such a political competition taking place among levels of government is enhanced when local governments are controlled by the national-level opposition parties.
B. In distributive politics with local governments as supplicants to the national government, the variance in benefits received by local governments will be low and the central governments will try to obscure the variance that does exist.
C. In distributive politics with local governments as the distributor of benefits to local interest groups:
   1. The central government will avoid involvement.
   2. Local innovation will be common.
D. On issues in which policymakers agree on the technically correct policy but perceive that same policy to be politically costly:

1. The institution most capable of making the decision will take political responsibility for it. Weakness is a bargaining strength.
2. The more effectively interests have been aggregated, the more likely the central government will be to take responsibility. The converse holds for local governments.
3. The more controversial the issue, the more likely political institutions will be to take responsibility. The converse holds for bureaucratic institutions.

Implications

The distribution of influence among levels of government can vary in three different domains: at the international level, at the national level, and among policy areas. My findings have implications for each. The comparative approach to intergovernmental relations is ultimately designed to compare countries, but studies of variation in local autonomy across policy areas and across local governments have one great advantage: studies that can be conducted in one country are much easier to carry out. Considerations of efficiency suggest that one-country studies be used to develop the hypotheses to be tested in comparative studies.

We know that some countries give their local governments more autonomy than others. How can we study the differences among countries? On the basis of this analysis of Japan, we can reject two approaches: comparing constitutional and legal provisions for local governments, and comparing the percentage of taxes or expenditures by the central government. Two other approaches, however, are very promising. First, since local autonomy varies among subnational governments and across policy areas, one should compare similar local governments as they deal with specific policy areas (Webman, 1977, 1981; Johnson and Cochrane, 1981; Ashford, 1982). Second, since the primary finding of this study is that political actors can make a huge difference in intergovernmental policymaking, we need more studies of intergovernmental politics (Tarrow, 1977; Gyford and James, 1983). One relatively easy study would be to compare local governments as they operate in the national arena—local governments as interest groups. More important, but more difficult, would be to study the relationships among elected officials at different levels.

My findings have more direct implications for variations in autonomy within nations, and my basic conclusion is that larger local governments tend to be more autonomous than smaller ones. Larger local governments tend to have more financial slack, better access to expertise, and, most important, greater political resources. In national distributive politics, larger local governments have the advantage both directly because they can command the attention of central officials by themselves, and indirectly because the leaders of national organizations of local officials tend to come from larger local governments. Larger local governments also tend to have more competitive politics which leads to greater innovativeness. A local unit's large size and the competitiveness of its politics also make its local elections more important to national electoral competition.

Smaller local governments have no advantage over larger ones in any of the variables associated with autonomy except perhaps knowledge of local conditions, and even here large local governments continue to have the advantage over the central government. The only other factor that favors small local governments is their low visibility. Central officials spend little time or attention on particular local governments, especially small ones. They only way that a small local government can maintain autonomy is to do little. To puruse active policies is to invite the central government's attention, money, expertise, and politics into the local arena, and thus local officials lose control over local policymaking. In chapter 1 I noted a syndrome of inactivity common to very small local governments. We can now explain why this happens.

Larger local governments tend to be more autonomous, other things being equal, but this finding should not be interpreted as a recommendation for enlarging local governments. First, local autonomy is not an unalloyed good. Maximum local autonomy would be independence and secession from the nation, not something normally recommended by political scientists. Second, autonomy is not the only goal served by local governments. One must also consider local democracy (Sharpe, 1970, 1978). Though the evidence is not clear, smaller local governments seem to be more democratic (Dahl, 1967). That larger local governments tend to be more autonomous does not mean that they are "better" local governments for their citizens.

Finally, my findings have implications for variation among the kinds of policy under discussion. The degree to which the distribution of authority has been decided in detail (partly a function of the age of the policy area), the degree to which expertise and knowledge of local conditions is required, and, most important, the degree to which an issue has become politicized, all affect the distribution of influence over any given policy. Studies of variation across policy areas can produce comparative hypotheses: one factor contributing to the centralization of power in France has been the central government's overwhelming advantage in expertise. This type of study could also become important in another area of research, policy studies. Several of the factors affecting local autonomy can be altered by program design, particularly the degree of detail in the law and the degree to which expertise or knowledge of local conditions is required. One may hypothesize that designing a program for centralization would produce greater efficiency, but also greater rigidity. On the other hand, designing the program for local autonomy would produce greater flexibility and local innovation at some cost to efficiency and uniformity.

Japanese Intergovernmental Relations

The preceding conclusions are meant to be applied to intergovernmental policymaking in all industrial democracies. We now turn to conclusions about the Japanese intergovernmental system.

The most obvious question concerns the degree of centralization in Japan. Elsewhere I have argued that there is a great deal more local autonomy in Japan than the literature would lead us to believe (Reed, 1982). In comparative terms, we can say that Japan is more centralized than the United States or Canada, but less centralized than France. Japan falls somewhere in the middle range with Britain and Germany. Given the fact that autonomy varies among various parts of a nation and among policies, however, one can doubt the usefulness of such broad generalizations. It is probably more useful to ask whether Japanese local governments are autonomous enough.

My final evaluation of Japanese local government is positive. That local governments were able to respond to the otherwise unmet needs and demands of the 1960s proves to me that Japanese local governments are autonomous enough. The Japanese intergovernmental system may not be ideal, but it is good enough to enhance the input and ouput functions of the polity. Local governments add a positive increment of democracy and of policy performance to the Japanese political system. Although this is a positive assessment, a more detailed evaluation is also necessary. Why does the system work well? Where does it work badly? To use Sharpe's (1970) terms, local governments should be both efficient and democratic.

Efficiency. Japan's intergovernmental system must be given high marks for policy performance. Local governments certainly do a good job of implementing national programs. However, effective implementation requires both uniformity and variety. Some variation is necessary to meet the different needs of different areas; on the other hand, there would be no national policy at all if too much variation were allowed. Japanese local governments do provide the uniformity necessary for effective policies, but they are less successful in providing necessary variation.

I found many cases of the central government's intransigence in the face of any deviation from uniformity. The central ministries tend to react negatively to any new policy from local governments. Even if they approve of the policy, they think it should not be enacted by local governments. If it is a good policy it should be enacted by the central government and applied uniformly. When a local innovation is within the spirit of the law but violates some particular letter of the law, the central ministries tend to enforce the letter of the law. Chiba's quota regulation of air pollution, their source telemeter to enforce pollution controls, and Saitama's registration system for public housing are all examples.

As an American, I kept asking myself: what could it hurt to allow the prefectures to keep their policies as long as they were in the spirit of the law? Upon reflection, however, I found a reasonable argument for enforcing such uniformity of detail. The most important fact about policymaking is that one starts from where one is. A tremendous inertia is built into any policy and this inertia is located in the seemingly insignificant details. Those little decisions that cannot be avoided but could have been decided either way, and have little or no effect on policy outcomes, are important for intergovernmental relations. If all the little details are the same throughout the country, or vary only along a few well-defined dimensions, central policymaking is much easier because central officials can assume a single starting point. If there are many different local starting points, it is hard to design policy changes.

Chiba's quota regulation system is a good example. If the Environmental Agency had allowed Chiba to use its formula, the spirit of the law would have been preseved. However, when it came time to amend the law, the amendments would either have to make special provision for Chiba or they would have to be phrased broadly enough to cover both formulas. Phrasing a law broadly makes it harder to enforce. Grant programs in the United States must be written in broad terms to cover multiple state and local starting points and are therefore harder to implement (Derthick, 1970, 1975). Central Japanese policymakers are normally able to write clearer, more easily implemented laws for local governments because they do not have to consider so many exceptions. Moreover, the principle of inertia also means that uniformity, once established, tends to persist and the same is true of diversity. There is no uniformity in high school entrance policies and therefore the Ministry of Education had trouble designing a grant program. The regulation of water pollution has reached a relatively advanced stage of diversity because *uwanose* provisions have been used so vigorously. I am sure the EA would like to reestablish uniformity, but it is proving difficult. Derthick's (1970) study of the effect of federal grants on one state program over time illustrates the difficulty of creating uniformity out of diversity.

It is impossible to estimate whether the costs of imposing uniformity are outweighed by the benefits of having similar starting points. It is important to note, however, that in a system that preserves uniformity, local policymakers pay the cost, and central policymakers reap the benefits. Chiba paid a real price in time, effort, and client good will to add the central quota regulations system to its own in order to make the EA's job easier in the future. In a system of diversity, central officials pay the price and local officials reap the benefits. Central officials are forced to deal with diversity, so that local officials can decide minor details that make no difference in the effectiveness of the policy. A system of uniformity has a strong built-in bias against local innovation of any sort. A system of diversity makes it difficult to devise and implement central policies.

We may have struck the core of what most people mean when they use the terms *centralization* and *local autonomy*. Indeed, it would not be unreasonable to simply define a centralized state as one that preserves policy uniformity and evidence of local autonomy as the existence of policy variation. However, to extend these definitions to other characteristics associated with these terms would be a mistake. For example, the maintenance of uniformity does not imply that all important policy initiatives come from the central government, only that the final resolution will be applied uniformly throughout the country. In a uniform system, local governments can make purely local policies only within a narrow domain, primarily local distributive policies. In any other area, a deviation from central policy becomes a national issue. Local governments cannot make their own policies without reference to national policies, but they gain access to the national agenda. When a local government in Japan enacts an innovative policy, it is national news, the policy is placed on the national legislative agenda, and it is a direct challenge to the central government. An innovative local policy in the United States is much more a local concern.

Another phenomenon associated with centralization, but not necessarily with systems that enforce uniformity is that some policies seem reasonable to the bureaucrat in the capital but are totally inappropriate in some parts of the country. Centralization conjures up images of rural schoolchildren reading stories that assume an intimate knowledge of the neighborhoods in the capital, of all farmers using a new seed that grows well only under specific geographical conditions, and of air conditioners being installed in the Arctic while furnaces are being installed in the tropics. One reason I chose Saga Prefecture was to search for this phenomenon. I assumed that central policymaking would focus on urban and industrial problems and that a rural agricultural prefecture would suffer from the "evils of centralization." I found no evidence of any. There are two basic reasons why the Japanese system can enforce uniformity and yet not produce these presumed effects of centralization. First, intergovernmental communications are remarkably dense and effective in Japan. Second, central control is exercised through impersonal rules and regulations.

Communication among various levels of government in Japan are so effective that local governments are seldom surprised by a central policy change. Normally, local governments know about a prospective change, have had the chance to express their opinion on it, and are prepared to implement it whenever it is formalized. The central government also knows a lot about what is going on in local governments. Many central officials have worked in local governments and have an accurate picture of how they work. They listen to regional complaints, because local governments serve as effective feedback mechanisms for the central administration. Even during intergovernmental conflict, communications are kept up. Central government officials knew about Tokyo's plans to enact a controversial pollution control ordinance in 1969. They expressed their opinion and even talked the Minobe administration out of some provisions. Even when MOHA slashed Tokyo's borrowing limits, Tokyo had been forewarned. Each side knows the other's position and can formulate its own position on the basis of accurate predictions about the consequences. Dense communications do not ensure agreement, but they do prevent gross policy stupidities and gross miscalculations of the other party's intentions.

Webman (1977) draws an important distinction between the French and British intergovernmental systems:

French institutions, because they provide for direct intervention and require joint action, facilitate direct and immediate influence by both central and local authorities. . . . British institutions, in contrast, permit national agencies considerable long-run control over the programs local agencies adopt but inhibit direct central intervention in the planning and execution of those programs. (p.70)

Japan is more like Britain than France, although its central controls are not as remote from local governments or as impersonal as Britain's. Japanese central officials know more about how local government works and what is going on in particular local governments because of the system of loaning central officials to the prefectures. Japanese central officials also use administrative guidance to participate more directly in local policymaking. Nevertheless, these forms of direct personal participation are much more a matter of communications than of controls. A central official on loan to a prefecture does not prevent that prefecture from enacting an ordinance of doubtful legality and seldom backs up administrative guidance with sanctions. The effective central controls are impersonal rules and regulations. As in Britain, these controls are quite effective, but produce a different style of intergovernmental relations.

A local policymaker in Japan lives in a stable, predictable environment. He is constrained by many detailed central regulations and is influenced by centrally designed financial incentives. There are probably more regulations than are necessary and those regulations are certainly more detailed than they need be. The incentives are strong and biased toward conservative policies. Nevertheless, the constraints and incentives are known ahead of time and remain stable over time. Proposed changes are known well in advance and local policymakers have some part in their formulation. Uncertainty has not been eliminated from the system, but the Japanese have gone a long way toward minimizing it.

Local policymaking in Japan is not autonomous in the sense of being generated internally only by local authorities. Neither is it impervious to central government influence. However, local policymaking is autonomous in the sense that it is made by local officials. The central government constraints, gives incentives and advice, but it does not make local decisions. Local officials make their own decisions within an environment created and manipulated by the central government. Indirect controls that allow local officials to make the decisions allow the application of local knowledge and keep the most ridiculous results of centralized policymaking from occurring.

Local Democracy. We cannot given Japan high marks for local democracy. In local assemblies politics is almost completely separated from policy. Urban areas, particularly Tokyo, are partial exceptions, but most assemblies are dominated by conservatives and conservative independents organized into personal factions. One-party noncompetitive politics produces an emphasis on distributive and personnel politics. Opposition parties have no systematic impact on policy, though they play important roles in aggregating and articulating citizens' complaints and in finding and publicizing cases of malfeasance or corruption. Corruption is common because the primary function of an assemblyman is to make certain his constituency gets its share of government benefits.

Local assemblymen represent their constituents in distributive politics, but do not seem to do a very good job of representation on the issues. This failure is most clearly revealed when a group of citizens band together to protest some government action. The normal pattern seems to be for assemblymen to be surprised and to avoid the issue. The government officials that deal with the protestors are bureaucrats (Minahan, 1977) or, if the issue is a big one, the local chief executive (Apter, and Sawa, 1984). Local assemblymen are strangely absent. I found an account of a hearing in Saga in which a prefectural assemblyman upbraided a bureaucrat because the bureaucrat had failed to uncover significant opposition to a project by the assemblyman's constituents (Saga Prefecture, 1976). The politician wanted the bureaucrat to take responsibility for reading and responding to public opinion!

With the exception of Tokyo and a few other cities, there is no possibility of the conservatives losing their majority in the local assemblies. Because there is no alternation of party control, assemblies provide no forum for competing party platforms. The conservatives have little incentive to present policy options to the electorate. It is smarter to concentrate on distributive politics. The only hope for competitive partisan politics is in gubernatorial and mayoral elections.

Presidential systems, whether at the national or local level, tend to produce two-party competition (Riker, 1982). The existence of the presidential prize is a strong incentive for cooperation among parties on a fragmented part of the political spectrum, both left and right in France (Wilson, 1980) and on the left in Japanese local politics. Presidential or gubernatorial elections can be competitive even when the distribution of party support in the electorate is unbalanced. In the same way that the Democrats could dominate the U.S. Congress and maintain a large lead in party identification during the 1960s and 1970s, and still lose the presidency, progressive governors in Japan have been elected in conservative strongholds like Kagawa or Oita. It is easier to defeat a single incumbent than to defeat enough incumbents to shift the balance of power in the legislature.

Gubernatorial and mayoral elections are the only elections in the Japanese system that produce alternation in power. Opposition parties win and are able to run a government and make a policy record. When progressives do win, they can have a major impact on both local and national policy, but the overall record of local democracy is not good.

Gubernatorial elections are dominated by incumbents. Since the 1960s incumbents have enjoyed a 90 percent success rate. Partly because of the strength of incumbency, many governors run virtually unopposed. Given the presence of independents, not all competitive races are left-right confrontations. Normally, less than half of the gubernatorial races include a viable progressive candidate. Progressives have a much better chance of winning a governorship than of controlling a local assembly, but the odds are against them in either case.[2]

Mayors and governors are primarily concerned with issue politics. However, the issue politics of local chief executives is normally not connected to partisan politics and elections. Local chief executives strive to appear above politics, to make policy on purely technical and administrative, not partisan or ideological criteria. The primary recruiting ground for gubernatorial candidates is the bureaucracy. At any given time, about 70 percent of the governors have had a bureaucratic background. This emphasis on being above politics accords with the wishes of the electorate (Steiner, 1965:445n; Toki, 1983:33). The job of governor is seen primarily as a matter of administration.

Governors try to project an image of being above politics in several ways. Most gubernatorial candidates run as independents even when they are supported by only one party. Once in office, governors typically try to broaden their base. Conservatives seek the support of center parties even when they do not need their votes in either the assembly or the electorate because it frees them from charges of partisanship.[3] More debilitating to competitive partisan politics, progressive governors often move to the center to get conservative support. Only about half of the governors originally elected as progressives face continuing conservative opposition. The other half become independents, receiving both conservative and progressive party support. Independents tend to be quite successful, often running unopposed and seldom getting defeated.

Local legislative politics is primarily distributive. Local executive politics is issue-oriented but rarely partisan. Although local chief executives can, and sometimes do, run on issues and win, the norm is one-party, nonpartisan, noncompetitive politics. The prospects for a vibrant local democracy are bleak. However, this bleak picture must be modified by two important qualifications. First, local politics seldom presents a pretty picture anywhere. My impression is that Japanese local politics would not look good on a scale of local democracy, but that it would not be far from the mean and would certainly not be an outlier.

The second qualification is that every once in a while a governor does win a partisan issue-oriented campaign and pursue innovative policies once in office. When that happens it can make a big difference. Progressive mayors and governors played a major role in responding to the challenge of pollution and that responsiveness is the basis of my overall positive evaluation of the Japanese intergovernmental system. Mayoral and gubernatorial elections are a major source of flexibility and responsiveness in the Japanese political system even under these seemingly adverse circumstances.

Perhaps the most important conclusion that can be drawn from this study is that an intergovernmental system does not have to be very good to be good enough. Local governments need not have much authority, much financial autonomy, or particularly democratic politics to be effective institutions. We must distinguish between what institutions normally do and what they can do. Japanese local governments usually do very little, but they can do a great deal. This transition from normally ineffectual institutions to active and effective policymakers under extraordinary pressures is triggered to mayoral and gubernatorial elections. In troubled times voters are dissatisfied and policymakers search for new ideas. These conditions increase the probability of a dynamic candidate running and winning the local chief executive election. A dynamic mayor or governor then activates the local government. An intergovernmental system does not have to be very good to be good enough if it possesses some triggering mechanisms that activates the system at appropriate times.

Notes

References

Index

Notes

Chapter 1. Influence in Intergovernmental Relations

1. Some subnational governments do represent natural communities and nearly complete social systems. Some regions are populated by distinct ethnic or cultural groups. These regions often demand local autonomy, but their demands are very different from those local governments that are integrated into the nation. Such regions demand partial sovereignty; they focus less on what policies are to be followed than on who shall decide. The case of cultural distinct regions will be ignored in this study. For one thing, Japan has no such regions. More fundamentally, when national integration is at question, intergovernmental relations takes on many different dimensions. I will limit myself to the simpler case of an integrated nation.

2. The federal-unitary distinction has been the object of some empirical research. See, for example, Cameron and Hofferbert, 1974.

3. Although all my research has been focused on industrial democracies, some of these generalizations may, with modifications, apply in other systems as well. Blair A. Ruble has found a several of these generalizations to be relevant to the government of Leningrad (personal communication).

4. This paragraph owes a great deal to my reading of Mark Kesselman (1967).

5. The two major exceptions are Ashford (1982) and Gyford and James (1983).

Chapter 2. Japanese Local Government in Comparative Perspective

1. The municipal and prefectural governments of Tokyo have been merged. Tokyo has no mayor, only a governor. The city of Tokyo has wards, like other designated cities, but other such cities also have mayors. Tokyo Prefecture

contains other cities with mayors, but the "ward area" is governed directly by the prefecture.

2. The constitution also contains a provision stating that civil and property rights shall not be abridged except by law. One could interpret this to mean that such rights cannot be abridged by ordinances. Such an argument was advanced in the 1954 case of the Nara reservoir, in which the authority of local governments to regulate land use was challenged. The court held in favor of the local government and since that time the dominant interpretation has been that the constitutional provision was meant to ensure that regulations only be enacted by democratically elected bodies. Local ordinances meet this requirement and are therefore laws in the constitutional sense.

3. The courts play a bigger role in all federal countries but particularly in the United States. In Canada the institution of federal-provincial conferences has evolved to handle many intergovernmental conflicts. In Germany the upper house expressly represents state governments. In Canada and Germany, there are alternatives to the courts not present in the United States.

4. Other bodies may be the object of agency-assigned functions, particularly legally established boards such as the board of education, but the controversy centers on assignment to mayors and governors. For a historical treatment of the development of agency-assigned functions during the occupation, see Takagi (1974).

5. I would like to be able to make many other comparisons of intergovernmental finances, but the data are not available. It is not even possible to estimate the percentage of expenditures made by each level because transfers among levels of government are handled differently in each country.

6. Samuels (1983) disagrees. He reports that "a fractured center produces duplicate central schemes" (p. 247). I am sure most Japanese scholars would agree that the grant system contains a shameful amount of duplication. I do not argue that no duplication exists, only that relative to other industrial democracies intergovernmental finance in Japan is highly systematized and has little duplication. The difference between my conclusions and those of Samuels is the base line of comparison. Samuels and most Japanese scholars take zero duplication as the base line, whereas I try to use a comparison with other industrial democracies.

My evidence is not particularly strong and my conclusion is based on a good margin of judgment, but it is my strong impression that a Japanese "horror story" of duplication and inefficiency is the grant process would be recognized as a common occurrence in the United States or Western Europe, but that an American or European horror story would bring cries of disbelief from a Japanese audience. To be more specific, the abuses reported in Hirose (1981) would not surprise an American reader but the case reported in Derthick (1975) would be impossible in Japan.

Samuels also gives a lot more weight than I do to *tatewari gyōsei* (he translates "vertical administration"; I translate "functional fragmentation"). Again, the difference is the base line. Samuels seems to think that this is a peculiarly Japanese phenomenon "little understood in the West" (p. 81), even though France has similar problems (p. 245). I think this is a universal problem and that Japan is less affected than most countries.

Only directly comparative research can resolve these differences but, in the meantime, we must do our best to use a comparative yardstick.

7. See Milch (1974) re France, and Ashford (1982: 281ff.) re Britain. The British system of intergovernmental finance has been undergoing changes toward stricter controls (Rhodes, 1984). If the central government is successful, British local governments may wind up with less long-run flexibility than Japanese local governments.

8. The Settsu case was actually somewhat more complex that this. Some of the facilities built by the city were not recognized by the central government and therefore received no subsidy at all.

9. Governor Kinoshita's progressive credentials are not clear. He defeated a conservative incumbent in his first election and faced an LDP challenger in his third election. In the second and fourth elections, however, he was opposed only by a token Communist candidate and thus had at least tacit conservative support.

10. MOHA may have begun to institutionalize the use of loan approval to discipline fiscally irresponsible prefectures. In 1982 Tokyo again gave its employees a raise MOHA considered excessive and MOHA again threatened to cut Tokyo's loan requests (*Yomiuru Shinbun,* February 19, 1982). It is also interesting to note that policies begun under the progressive Minobe administration are being continued in the conservative Suzuki administration, though at a lower level of publicity.

11. This explanation of the benefits of petitioning is based in large part on an interview with a former chief of the General Affairs Department of Saga Prefecture, July 29, 1977.

Chapter 3. The Evolution of Japanese Local Government

1. Governor Minobe retired from politics. Mayor Asukata became the leader of the national Japan Socialist party.

2. There is no evidence that progressive local governments were more active or innovative on the average. The election of a progressive does not seem to have increased the probability of activity, but Minobe and Asukata were leaders, even "stars," of the movement and progressives got a lot of the credit for the innovative policies.

3. Local assemblymen do not seem to know about protests or potential protests in their districts. They depend on the local executive branch to handle such things. For example, Brian Minahan (1977) found local assemblymen completely inactive in a dispute over the building of a garbage disposal plant in Hiroshima City. In Saga I was surprised to hear a prefectural assemblyman

asking a bureaucrat why opposition to a project had not been uncovered before the project was started. The clear implication was that uncovering potential opposition was the bureaucrat's, not the political representative's job (*Saga Shinbun*, October 7, 1976).

Chapter 4. Pollution Control Policy

1. Officials in all three prefectures agreed that resistance from industry was insignificant and even praised industrial efforts to control pollution. Officials suggested that there may have been more resistance earlier, but indicated that they had experienced none.

2. Chiba enacted a noise pollution ordinance in 1954. The 1963 ordinance was the first one to cover air and water pollution.

3. Governor Minobe was quite open in stating his expectation that the Tokyo Advisory Commission would "prove" the need for a stricter environmental standard (*Nihon Keizai Shinbun*, July 15, 1978), and his expectations were realized (ibid., February 20, 1979).

4. The Local Government Law lists monitoring (*kanshi*) under agency-assigned functions, but also lists measurement (*sokutei*) under entity-assigned functions. Officials at the EA professed to be as confused by this as I am.

5. One of the four factories has an agreement only with the city concerned, not with the prefecture.

6. Livestock wastes accounted for only 6 percent of the water pollution burden in Saga in 1975, but 21 percent of all pollution complaints (Saga Prefecture, 1976: 112, 4).

Chapter 5. Housing Policy

1. Mills and Ohta (1976) rate Japan's performance in housing construction positively using a comparative standard of judgment. Judgments made within the Japanese context tend to be much more negative. See Wada (1973, 1975).

2. These figures are *jūtakunan setaisu*, literally, "families with housing trouble." The figures are based on national housing surveys taken every five years. The standards are objective and minimal. Note that Yamaoka and Kyōsu (1976) may be considered an official publication, since the authors are the MOC Housing Division Bureau Chief and the Housing Planning Division Chief, respectively.

3. Several authors dispute the claim that the "quantity" problem has been solved. See Wada (1973) and especially Kishimoto (1977). The issue is primarily one of terminology and of what should be considered minimum housing standards. The government has, however, clung to its emphasis on construction. For example, the JHC did not change its policy of cutting back on quality before cutting back on the number of units built until around 1970 (Kurashige, 1977).

4. There have been some gains in the average size of Japanese houses, but this is due largely to the rising proportion of owner-occupied housing (Kishimoto, 1977).

5. The phrase "Saitama's Tokyoites" is *Saitama tomin* in Japanese, playing on the fact that Tokyo is a *to* and Saitama is a *ken* (both terms meaning prefecture). The images of these in-migrants is documented in Ushimi (1973). The author was head of Saitama's Department of Housing and Urban Affairs in 1975–1976.

6. Saitama uses *yokushi,* whereas Chiba and Kanagawa use *yokusei.* Although the dictionary definitions are similar, "suppression" or "restraint," *yokushi* has a connotation closer to "stopping."

7. Each prefecture also holds hearings to gather data and opinions from municipalities, but I did not investigate this part of the process.

8. These three prefectures are the only ones to have obtained priority for their citizens. Some cities in the Osaka region have obtained local priority on a city-level basis.

9. JHC officials do consult with the LDP on the proportions of rental and condominium housing.

10. The Kantō bloc prefectures demand that 20 percent of JHC projects' land be turned over for public housing. This means that JHC and public housing usually occupy the same sites. In one case in Saitama, the JHC project had only 33 applicants for 710 openings, but the public housing had 220 applicants for 250 openings. Unfortunately, the public housing cannot stand alone and will fail if the surrounding JHC project fails (*Saitama Shinbun,* April 8, 1977).

11. These percentages were taken from a report by the national Housing and Land Advisory Commission, attached to the Ministry of Construction.

12. This sensitivity to small, intense groups is reflected in the relative success of citizens' movements. Another way of stating the same fact is that the Japanese political system often fails to aggregate interests effectively (Richardson and Flanagan, 1984: 324ff.).

Chapter 6. High School Education Policy

1. The characterizations of the leftist and conservative positions presented here are my own interpretation, based on the painful process of familiarizing myself with the Japanese literature. Because of the high potential for controversy, discussions of education policy are often couched in highly abstract terminology. Some innocuous-sounding phrases can be code words for controversial positions, but may also be used sincerely. While I cannot claim to have completely penetrated the various smokescreens and ideological shadings found in the literature, I do claim that the freedom versus equality dimension discussed here is a key element in most of the policy conflicts in Japan.

The most helpful readings for the leftist position were Zenkoku Shinro Shidō Kenkyūkai (1974) and Sasaki (1976). It is harder to find informative statements of the conservative position. Arita (1976) purports to offer the conservative alternative, but a great deal of contextual knowledge is necessary to read this book intelligently. Two magazine articles state the conservative position very strongly, and may overstate their position: Ashita no Kyōiku wo Kangaeru Kai (1976) and Kawakami (1976).

2. The standard size of a high school class is forty students. The student population of a school can be accurately calculated from the number of classes.

3. I have no clear picture of the dynamics of adoption within the central government. The people I talked to in the MOE had not been in the relevant positions when the decision was being made. Moreover, MOE officials proved reluctant to discuss anything with political overtones, in contrast to officials of other ministries. Nevertheless, it does seem that once the budget request was made, MOE actively promoted the program. See, for example, *Naigai Kyōiku*, January 18, 1977, and *Asahi Shinbun*, December 9, 1975.

4. The math-science course was set up as an elite course in Toyama but not necessarily elsewhere. In Hokkaido the math-science course was the elite class of the school but not necessarily of the prefecture or district (Takeishi, 1973). In Tokushima the math-science course was used to bolster a lower ranking school (Ueda et al., 1976).

5. Test scores are kept secret in order to prevent a more precise operation of the ranking mechanism. I have found some tables using such data, but the only systematic use is in Hashizume (1976). This is the best article I found on the subject.

6. The 20 percent figure was given by a High School Teachers' Union official in an interview June 9, 1977. The debate is partially recorded in the Saitama High School Education Promotion Commission (1975).

7. In MOE statistics, small districts contain only one school, middle-sized districts contain from two to six, and large districts have more than six. The classification is one of convenience but the middle-sized category has proven popular.

8. This account is based on reports in *Saitama Shinbun*, September 7, 9, 15, 20, 22, and 27, and October 4 and 9, 1974.

9. The 20 percent refers to the number of seats in the school, not the total number of applicants. Thus, the top-scoring 20 percent of those choosing school A as their first choice go to school A, and the top 20 percent of those choosing school B go to school B, and so on.

10. The progressive candidate's progressive credentials were far from clear. He came to the prefecture from MOHA. He came as an outsider to help resolve a rancorous teachers' strike and to implement the comprehensive entry system. His success at both became his progressive credentials.

It is interesting to note that both candidates were Tokyo University Law Faculty graduates. The major difference is that the conservative candidate had gone into local government, while the progressive had a career in the central government (*Chiba Nippo*, April 4 and 13, 1975).

A review article in the *Chiba Nippo* (June 5, 1977) compares Chiba's experience with that of Aichi and Hyōgo. In all three cases, the superintendent of schools became a gubernatorial candidate after achieving a major reform of the entrance system. The ex-superintendent won only in Aichi.

Chapter 7. Conclusions

1. This use of bits of authority in ways that were never intended is also found in U.S. presidential-congressional relations. See Derthick (1972).

2. The elections of 1972–75 were exceptional. Only 15 percent of the incumbents ran unopposed. This was also the period in which seven progressives were elected (Reed, 1981B).

3. Although he attributes the phenomenon to different causes, Zariski (1984) finds a similar "consociational bias" in coalition formation in the Italian regions.

References

Abe Hitoshi. 1974. "Chihō Gikai no Kinō to Genkai." In *Gendai Shakai to Jichi Seido no Henkaku*, ed. Narita.

Aichi Prefecture Board of Education. 1973. *Atarashii Shokugyō Kyōiku wo Mezashite*. Aichi Prefecture.

Akimoto Ritsuo. 1975. "Jūmin Undō no Shokeitai." In *Jūmin Sanka to Jichi no Kakushin*, ed. Matsubara.

Amakawa Akira. 1974. "Chihō Jichi to Seitō." In *Gendai Shakai to Jichi Seido no Henkaku*, ed. Narita.

Anton, Thomas J. 1975. *Governing Greater Stockholm*. Berkeley and Los Angeles: University of California Press.

Aoki Iori. 1976. "Osaka-fu ni okeru Nyūgakusha Sembatsu seido no Kaizen ni tsuite." In *Kōritsu Kōtō Gakkō*, ed. Hyōdo.

Apter, David E., and Nagayo Sawa. 1984. *Against the State: Politics and Social Protest in Japan*. Cambridge, Mass.: Harvard University Press.

Aqua, Ronald. 1980. "Political Choice and Policy Change in Medium-Sized Japanese Cities, 1962–1974." In *Political Opposition and Local Politics in Japan*, ed. Steiner et al.

Arita Kazuhisa. 1976. *Nihon no Kyōiku wo Kangaeru: Atarashii Seki wo Hiraku Kyōiku e no Teigen*. Dai-Ichi Hōki.

Arnold, R. Douglas. 1979. *Congress and the Bureaucracy*. New Haven, Conn.: Yale University Press.

Asahi Shimbun, Utsunomiya Branch. 1982. *Chiji: Kenryoku to Ningen no Moyō*. Tokyo: Ochiai Shoten.

Ashford, Douglas E. 1975. "Theories of Local Government: Some Comparative Considerations." *Comparative Political Studies* 8 (April): 90–107.

———. 1976. *Democracy. Decentralization, and Decisions in Subnational Politics*. Beverly Hills, Calif.: Sage.

———. 1977. "Are Britain and France 'Unitary'?" *Comparative Politics* 9 (July): 483–99.

————. 1978. "French Pragmatism and British Idealism: Financial Aspects of Local Reorganization." *Comparative Political Studies* 11 (July): 231–53.

————. 1982. *British Dogmatism and French Pragmatism: Central-Local Policymaking in the Welfare State.* London: Allen and Unwin.

Ashita no Kyōiku wo Kangaeru Kai. 1976. *Bungei Shuniū* (August): 92–126.

Banfield, Edward. 1961. *Political Influence.* New York: Free Press.

Beardsley, Richard K., John W. Hall, and Robert Ward, eds. 1959. *Village Japan.* Chicago: University of Chicago Press.

Beer, Samuel A. 1976. "The Adoption of General Revenue Sharing: A Case Study in Public Sector Politics." *Public Policy* 24 (Spring): 127–95.

Braunthal, Gerard, 1984. "The West German Social Democrats: Factionalism at the Local Level." *West European Politics* 7 (January): 47–63.

Butler, David, and Donald Stokes. 1971. *Political Change in Britain.* New York: St. Martin's Press.

Cain, Bruce E., et al. 1984. "The Constituency Basis of the Personal Vote for U.S. Representatives and British Members of Parliament." *American Political Science Review* 78 (March): 110–25.

Cameron, David R., and Richard I. Hofferbert. 1974. "The Impact of Federalism on Education Finance." *European Journal of Political Research* 2 (June): 222–58.

Campbell, John Creighton. 1977. *Contemporary Japanese Budget Politics.* Berkeley and Los Angeles: University of California Press.

————. 1979. "The Old People's Boom and Japanese Public Policy." *Journal of Japanese Studies* 5 (Summer): 321–57.

Chiba Prefecture Citizens' Movement Liaison Council. 1973. *Chiba-Ken no Kankyō Hakai to Jūmin Undo.* Chiba Prefecture Local Government Problem Research Center.

Chiba Prefecture Land Division. 1976. *Takuchi Kaihatsu no Hensen.* Chiba Prefecture.

Chiba Prefecture unpublished materials. 1976. Available from the author on request.

Chihō Zaimu Kyōkai. 1975. *Naisei Kankeisha Meibo.* Chihō Zaimu Kyōkai.

Chubb, Judith. 1980. "Naples Under the Left: The Limits of Local Change." *Comparative Politics* 13 (October).

Crispin, A. 1976. "Local Government Finance: Assessing the Central Government's Contribution." *Public Administration* 54 (Spring).

Cummings, William K. 1976. "The Problems and Prospects for Japanese Higher Education." In *Japan: The Paradox of Progress,* ed. Austin.

————. 1980. *Education and Equality in Japan.* Princeton, N.J.: Princeton University Press.

Cummings, William K., and Ishido Kyōji. 1976. "Gakkusei Saikentō no Shiten: Shōgakku no Zehi to Kōkōsei Kyūzō Mondai to no Kanren." *Kōkō Kyōiku Tembō* (November): 12–17.

Curtis, Gerald. 1971. *Election Campaigning Japanese Style.* New York: Columbia University Press.

Dahl, Robert A. 1967. "The City in the Future of Democracy." *American Political Science Review* 61 (December): 953–70.

Dale, Jennifer. 1980. "Class Struggle, Social Policy, Central-Local Relations and Housing Policy, 1919–1939." In *Housing, Social Policy and the State,* ed. Joseph Melling. London: Croom Helm.

Davey, K. J. 1971. "Local Autonomy and Independent Revenues." *Public Administration* 49 (Spring): 45–50.

Davies, David. 1970. "The Concentration Process and the Growing Importance of Non-Central Governments in Federal States. *Public Policy* 18 (Fall): 649–57.

Derthick, Martha. 1970. *The Influence of Federal Grants.* Cambridge, Mass.: Harvard University Press.

———. 1972. *New Towns In-Town.* Washington, D.C.: Urban Institute.

———. 1975. *Uncontrollable Spending for Social Service Grants.* Washington, D.C.: Brookings.

Dolive, Linda L. 1976. *Electoral Politics at the Local Level in the German Federal Republic.* Gainesville: University Presses of Florida.

Duke, Benjamin C. 1973. *Japan's Militant Teachers.* Honolulu: University Press of Hawaii.

Elazar, Daniel J. 1967. "Federal-State Collaboration in the Nineteenth Century United States." In *American Federalism in Perspective,* ed. Wildavsky.

Feldman, Elliot J., and Jerome Milch. 1982. *Technocracy vs. Democracy: The Comparative Politics of International Airports.* Boston: Auburn House.

Fesler, James W. 1965. "Approaches to Understanding Decentralization." *Journal of Politics* 27 (August): 536–66.

Foster, James J. 1982. "Ghost-Hunting: Local Party Organization in Japan." *Asian Survey* 22 (September): 843–57.

Frieden, Bernard. 1979. *The Environmental Protection Hustle.* Cambridge, Mass.: MIT Press.

Fukumaru Keiichi. 1971. "Toshi Zaisei to Chiiki Keizai: Kagoshima-ken ni Miru Kaso to Bijion no naka kara." *Toshi Mondai* (August): 63–74.

Garlichs, Dietrich, and Chris Hull. 1978. "Central Control and Information Dependence: Highway Planning in the Federal Republic of Germany." In *Interorganizational Policy Making,* ed. Hanf and Scharpf.

Gary, Lawrence E. 1973. "Policy Decisions in the Aid to Families with Dependent Children Program." *Journal of Politics* 35 (November): 886–923.

Gourevitch, Peter. 1977. "The Reform of Local Government: A Political Analysis." *Comparative Politics* 10 (October): 69–85.

Greenstone, J. David, and Paul Peterson. 1973. *Race and Authority in Urban Politics.* New York: Russell Sage.

Griffith, J.A.G. 1966. *Central Departments and Local Authorities.* London: Allen and Unwin.

Grodzins, Morton. 1963. "Centralization and Decentralization in the American Federal System." In *A Nation of States,* ed. Robert A. Godwin. Chicago: Rand McNally.

Gyford, John, and Marie James. 1983. *National Parties and Local Politics*. London: Allen and Unwin.

Haider, Donald. 1974. *When Governments Come to Washington*. New York: Free Press.

Hanayama Yuzuru. 1972. "Urban Land Prices and the Housing Problem." *The Developing Economies* 10 (December).

———. 1973. "Toshi Keiei to Tochi seisaku." Iwanami Kōza 4: 263–96.

Hansen, Tore. 1981. "The Dynamics of Local Government Expenditure Growth: Local Finance in Sweden." *The Local Fiscal Crisis in Western Eurpoe*, ed. Sharpe.

Harada Naohiko. 1970A. "Kōgai Bōshi Kyōtei to sono Hōritsujō no Mondaiten." *Juristo* (August 10).

———. 1970B. "Kōgai Bōshi Jōrei no Genkai to sono Shimei" *Juristo* (November 15).

———. 1974. "Yoko Gyōsei no Hōteki Seikaku to Mondaiten." *Juristo* (January).

Hartley, Owen A. 1971. "The Relations between Central and Local Authorities." *Public Administration* 49 (Winter): 439–56.

Hashizume Sadao. 1976. "Gakkō Gun ni okeru Kakusa Keisei no Mekanizumu." *Kyōiku Shakaigaku Kenkyū* (September) 106–18.

Hayakawa Kazuo and Wada Yatsuka. 1973. "Jūtaku Mondai no Rekishi to Riron." In *Jūtaku Mondai Nyūmon*, ed. Hayakawa et al.

Hayward, Jack, and Michael Watson, eds. 1975. *Planning, Politics, and Public Policy*. London: Cambridge University Press.

Heady, Bruce. 1978. *Housing Policy in the Developed Economy: The United Kingdom, Sweden, and the United States*. New York: St. Martin's Press.

Heidenheimer, Arnold J. 1974. "The Politics of Educational Reform: Explaining Different Outcomes of School Comprehensivization Attempts in Sweden and West Germany." *Comparative Education Review* 18 (October): 388–410.

Heidenheimer, Arnold J., and Michael Parkinson. 1975. "Equalizing Educational Opportunity in Britain and the United States: The Politics of Implementation." In *Perspectives on Public Policy-Making*, ed. William B. Gwyn and George C. Edwards. New Orleans, La.: Tulane Studies in Political Science.

Hirose Michisada. 1981. *Hojokin to Seikentō*. Asahi Shinbun-sha.

Homans, George C. 1974. *Social Behavior: Its Elementary Forms*. New York: Harcourt, Brace, and Jovanovich.

Hough, Jerry F. 1975. "The Soviet Experience and the Measurement of Power." *Journal of Politics* 36 (August): 685–710.

Huddle, Norie, and Michael Reich. 1975. *Island of Dreams: Environmental Crisis in Japan*. Tokyo: Autumn Press.

Huntington, Samuel P. 1965. "Congressional Responses to the Twentieth Century." In *The Congress and America's Future*, ed. David B. Truman. Englewood Cliffs, N.J.: Prentice-Hall.

Hyōdo Yasuzō, ed. 1976. *Kōritsu Kōtō Gakkō Nyūgakusha Sembatsu Shikken Seido no Kaikaku ni kansuru Chōsa Kenkyū.* (Report of the 1974–75 Science Research Program.)

Ide Yoshinori. 1972. *Chihō Jichi no Seijigaku.* Tokyo: Tokyo University Press.

Ikeda Ryōji. 1977. "Jūtaku Kensetsu to Kōeki Shisetsu Futan Mondai: Jūtaku Kōdan no Baai wo Chūsin ni." *Juristo,* special issue (Summer): 329–34.

Imaihasi Morikatsu. 1982. "Jōhō Kōkai Jōrei wo meguru Hōritsu Mondai." In *Jichitai no Jōhō Kōkai,* ed. Imaihasi and Takayose.

Inoue Shinya, 1971. "Settsu Soshō no Haikei to Yakuwari." *Juristo* (March 1).

Ishiguro Seiji. 1975. "Chihō Toshi no Sabetsu Kyōiku—Toyama-ken no San-Shichi-Sei." In *Nihon Rettō: Chihō Toshi,* ed. Okuda et al.: 376–89.

Ishii Toshio. 1973. "Kōei Jūtaku Uneijō no Mondai: Chiba-ken no Baai." *Toshi Mondai* (August): 38–47.

Jennings, Robert E. 1977. *Education and Politics: Policy-Making in Local Education Authorities.* London: B. T. Batsford Ltd.

Johnson, Nevil, and Allen Cochrane. 1981. *Economic Policy-Making by Local Authorities in Britain and West Germany.* London: Allen and Unwin.

Johnson, R.W. 1972. "The Nationalization of English Rural Politics: Norfolk South-west 1945–1970." *Parliamentary Affairs* 26 (Winter): 8–55.

Jones, Charles O. 1975. *Clean Air: The Policies and Politics of Pollution Control.* Pittsburgh, Pa.: University of Pittsburgh Press.

Kamada Yoshio. 1973. "Kōdan Jūtaku: Sono Henyō to Kinō." *Juristo* (July 15): 35–41.

Kaminogō Toshiaki. 1978. "Naimushō no Fukkatsu." *Bungei Shuniū* (March).

Kawai Yoshikazu. 1973. "Hōritsu to Jōrei: Sono Tenkai Kateti Ron." *Toshi Mondai* (May–December).

Kawanami Yoshiaki. 1970. "Tokyo-to Kōgai Bōshi Jōrei." *Juristo* (November 15).

Kesselman, Mark. 1967. *The Ambiguous Consensus: A Study of Local Government in France.* New York: Alfred A. Knopf.

———. 1970. "Overinstitutionalization and Political Constraint: The Case of France." *Comparative Politics* 3 (October): 21–44.

———. 1974. "Research Perspectives in Comparative Local Politics: Pitfalls, Prospects, and Notes on the French Case." In *Comparative Community Politics,* ed. Clark.

Kesselman, Mark, and Donald Rosenthal. 1974. *Local Power and Comparative Politics.* Beverly Hills, Calif.: Sage.

Key, V. O. 1949. *Southern Politics.* New York: Random House.

Kishimoto Shigenobu. 1977. "Nihon Keizai to Jūtaku." *Juristo,* special issue (Summer): 55–60.

Kita Nihon Shinbun. 1975. *Yomigaere Chihō Jichi.* Keisō Shobō.

Koizumi Shigenobu. 1971. "Jūtaku gyōsei." In *Gyōsei Saishin Mondai Jiten,* ed. Isomura.

———. 1973. "Kōei Jūtaku no Henyō to Hyōka." *Juristo* (July 15): 42–49.

Kotaka Tsuyoshi. 1973. "Kōkyō Jūtaku wo meguru Hōritsu to Shomondai." *Juristo* (July 15): 28–34.

Krauss, Ellis. 1979. "The Urban Strategy and Policy of the Japanese Communist Party: Kyoto." *Studies in Comparative Communism* 12 (Winter): 322–50.

———. 1980. "Opposition in Power: The Development and Maintenance of Leftist Government in Kyoto Prefecture." In *Political Opposition and Local Politics in Japan,* ed. Steiner et al.

Krier, James E., and Edmun Ursin. 1978. *Pollution and Policy: A Case Essay on California and Federal Experience with Motor Vehicle Air Pollution.* Berkeley and Los Angeles: University of California Press.

Kurashige Tomoaki. 1977. "Nihon Jūtaku Kōdan Ron: Sono Hatashita Yakuwari to Kongo no Arikata." *Juristo,* special issue (Summer): 155–59.

Kuroda, Yasumasa. 1972. "Protest Movements in Japan: A New Politics." *Asian Survey* 22 (November): 947–52.

———. 1975. "Levels of Government in Comparative Perspective." *Comparative Political Studies* 7 (January): 430–40.

Kuze Kimitaka. 1973. "Tochi Taisaku ni kakaru Jōrei, Yōkō no Jittai to Mondaiten." *Jichi Kenkyū* (December).

Kyoto Prefectural Administration Study Group. 1973. *Sengo ni okeru Kyoto Fusei no Ayūmi.* Yubonsha.

Levin, Henry M. 1978. "The Dilemma of Comprehensive Secondary School Reforms in Europe." *Comparative Education Review* 22 (November): 434–51.

Lewis, Jack. 1974. "*Hokaku Rengō:* The Politics of Conservative-Progressive Cooperation in a Japanese City." Ph.D. diss., Stanford University.

———. 1980. "Civic Protest in Mishima: Citizens' Movements and the Politics of the Environment in Contemporary Japan." *Political Opposition and Local Politics in Japan,* ed. Steiner et al.

Lieber, Harry. 1975. *Federalism and Clean Waters: The 1972 Water Pollution Control Act.* Lexington, Mass.: Lexington Books.

Lowi, Theodore. 1972. "Four Systems of Policy, Politics, and Choice." *Public Administration Review* 32 (July): 298–310.

Maas, Arthur. 1959. "Division of Powers: An Areal Analysis." In *Area and Power: A Theory of Local Government,* ed. Maas. New York: Free Press.

MacDougall, Terry E. 1975. "Political Opposition and Local Government in Japan." Ph.D. diss., Yale University.

———. 1980. "Political Opposition in Big City Elections in Japan, 1947–1975." In *Political Opposition and Local Politics in Japan,* ed. Steiner et al.

Machin, Howard. 1981. "Centre and Periphery in the Policy Process." In *French Politics and Public Policy,* ed. Philip G. Cerny and Martin A. Schain. New York: Methuen.

McKean, Margaret. 1976. "Citizens' Movements in Urban and Rural Japan." In *Social Change and Community Politics in Japan,* ed. White and Munger.

———. 1980. "Political Socialization Through Citizens' Movements." In *Political Opposition and Local Politics in Japan,* ed. Steiner et al.

———. 1981. *Environmental Protest and Citizen Politics in Japan.* Berkeley and Los Angeles: University of California Press.

McLeay, E. M. 1984. "Housing as a Political Issue: A Comparative Study." *Comparative Politics* 17 (October): 83–105.

Masago Yasuke. 1975. "Chihō Kōkyō Dantai ni okeru Gyōsei Shidō: Takuchi Kaihatsu Shidō Yōkō wo Chūshin to shite." In *Gendai Seiji no Chihō Jichi,* ed. Adachi et al.

Matsubara Haruo. 1968. *Nihon no Shakai Kaihatsu.* Fukumura Shuppan.

Matsui Ichirō. 1976. "Nemawashi no Genkai: Nagano-ken no Sōgō-Sembatsu-Sei wo meguru Kengikai." *Jichi Kenshū* (July).

Merrit, Richard L., and Robert L. Leonardi. 1981. "The Politics of Upper Secondary School Reform in Italy." *Comparative Education Review* 25 (October): 369–83.

Milch, Jerome E. 1974. "Influence as Power: French Local Government Reconsidered." *British Journal of Political Science* 4 (April): 139–61.

———. 1978. "Urban Government in France: Municipal Policymaking in the Centralized State." *Administration and Society* 9 (February): 467–94.

Mills, Edwin S., and Katsutoshi Ohta. 1976. "Urbanization and Urban Problems." In *Asia's New Giant: How the Japanese Economy Works,* ed. Hugh Patrick and Henry Rosovsky. Washington, D.C.: Brookings.

Minahan, Brian. 1977. "Citizen Participation and Policy Making in the City of Hiroshima Garbage War." M.A. thesis, University of Michigan.

Ministry of Education. 1977. *Zenkoku no Gakushū Juku no Jittai.* Gyōsei.

Ministry of Home Affairs, Secretariat. 1974. *Chihō Kōsha Yōran.* Daiichi Hōki.

———. 1977. *Chihō Jichi Binran.*

Mitchell, Austin. 1974. "Clay Cross." *Political Quarterly* 45 (Summer): 165–78.

Miyahara Seiichi. 1975. "Nihon no Kōgai." In *Nihon no Toshi Mondai,* ed. Miyamoto. Chikuma Shobo.

Mladenka, Kenneth R. 1980. "The Urban Bureaucracy and the Chicago Political Machine: Who Gets What and the Limits to Political Control." *American Political Science Review* 74 (December): 991–98.

Mohr, Lawrence. 1969. "Determinants of Innovation in Organizations. *American Political Science Review* 58 (March): 111–26.

Mori Kiyoshi. 1970. "Kōgai Bōshi Jōrei no Enkaku to Genjō." *Juristo* (November 15).

Motoyama Shinichi. 1957. "Kōkō Dai-Gakku-Sei to Seito, Kyōshi, Oya e no Eikyō: Aichi-ken no Baai." *Kyōiku* (May): 45–57.

Narita Yoriaki. 1964. "Hōritsu to Jōrei." In *Kempō Kōza,* vol. 4. Gyōsei.

Narumi Masayasu. 1970. "Kigyō to no Kōgai Bōshi Kyōtei: Yokohama Hōshiki." *Juristo* (August 10).

Neiman, Max, and Catherine Lovell. 1981. "Mandating as a Policy Issue." *Policy Studies Journal* 9 (Spring): 667–81.

Neve, Brian. 1977. "Bureaucracy and Politics in Local Government: The Role of Local Authority Education Officers." *Public Administration* 55 (Autumn): 291–303.

Nishioka Akio. 1970. "Mishima-Numazu-Shimizu Ni-Shi Ichi-Cho Sekiyu Kombināto Hantai Undō." *Juristo,* exp. ed. (August 10): 117–21.

Nishioka Akio and Yoshisawa Mamoru. 1970. "Shimizu-Mishima-Numazu Sekiyu Kombināto Hantai Undō: Jūmin Soshiki no Hatten to Gakushū-kai." In *Kōgai Gyōsei,* ed. Nihon Gyōsei Gakkai.

Noguchi Yukio et al. 1978. "Chihō Zaisei ni okeru Ishi Kettei no Bunseki." *Keizai Bunseki* 71: 1–190.

Noma, Hisao. 1970. "Tokyo-to no Shin Kōgai Bōshi Jōrei." *Juristo* (August 10).

Ōhara Mitsunori and Yokoyama Keiji. 1965. *Sangyō Shakai to Seiji Katei: Keiyō Kōgyō Chitai.* Nihon Hyōronsha.

Organization for Economic Cooperation and Development. 1977. *Environmental Policies in Japan.* OECD.

Oshimoto Jirō. 1968. "Jūtaku Kōdan no Jigyō no Eikyō to Mondaiten: Kanagawa-ken Gyōsei kara Mite." *Toshi Mondai* (May): 25–34.

Park, Yung H. 1978. "The Local Public Personnel System in Japan." *Asian Survey* 18 (June) 592–608.

Pascale, Richard, and Thomas P. Rohlen. 1983. "The Mazda Turnaround." *Journal of Japanese Studies* 9 (Summer): 219–64.

Pempel, T. J. 1973. "The Politics of Enrollment Expansion in Japanese Universities." *Journal of Asian Studies* 33 (November): 67–86.

Peterson, Paul. 1971. "British Interest Group Theory Re-examined: The Politics of Comprehensive Education in Three British Cities." *Comparative Politics* 3 (April): 381–402.

———. 1981. *City Limits.* Chicago: University of Chicago Press.

Peterson, Paul, and Paul Kantor. 1977. "Political Parties and Citizen Participation in English City Politics." *Comparative Politics* 9 (January): 199–217.

Porter, David O. 1973. *The Politics of Budgeting Federal Aid: Resource Mobilization by Local School Districts.* Beverly Hills, Calif.: Sage.

Pressman, Jefferey, and Aaron Wildavsky. 1973. *Implementation.* Berkeley and Los Angeles: University of California Press.

Randall, Ronald. 1976. "The Consequences of Centralization for Welfare Policy." *Western Political Quarterly* 29 (September): 353–63.

Reed, Steven R. 1981B. "Gubernatorial Elections in Japan." In *Parties, Candidates, and Voters in Japan,* ed. Campbell.

———. 1982. "Is Japanese Government Really Centralized?" *Journal of Japanese Studies* 8 (Winter): 133–64.

———. 1984. "Factions in the 1978 LDP Presidential Primary." *Journal of Northeast Asian Studies* 3 (Spring): 31–38.

Richardson, Bradley M., and Scott C. Flanagan. 1984. *Politics in Japan.* Boston: Little, Brown.

Riker, William H. 1969. "Six Books in Search of a Subject or Does Federalism Exist and Does It Matter?" *Comparative Politics* (October): 135–46.

——. 1982. "The Two-Party System and Durverger's Law." *American Political Science Review* 76 (December): 753–66.

Roddewig, Richard J. 1978. *Green Bans: The Birth of Australian Environmental Politics.* Montclair, N.J.: Allanheld and Osman.

Rohlen, Thomas P. 1976. "Violence at Yōka High School: The Implications for Japanese Coalition Politics of the Confrontation Between the Communist Party and the Buraku Liberation League." *Asian Survey* 16 (July): 682–99.

——. 1977. "Is Japanese Education Becoming Less Egalitarian? Notes on High School Stratification and Reform." *Journal of Japanese Studies* 3 (Winter): 37–70.

——. 1980. "The *Juku* Phenomenon: An Exploratory Essay." *Journal of Japanese Studies* 6 (Summer): 207–42.

——. 1983. *Japan's High Schools.* Berkeley and Los Angeles: University of California Press.

Rose, Douglas D. 1973. "National and Local Forces in State Politics." *American Political Science Review* 66 (December): 1162–73.

Rosenbaum, Nelson. 1978. "Growth and Its Discontents: Origins of Local Population Control." In *The Policy Cycle,* ed. Judith May and Aaron Wildavsky. Beverly Hills, Calif.: Sage.

Rosenthal, Donald B. 1968. "Functions of Urban Political Systems: Comparative Analysis and the Indian Case." In *Community Structure and Decision Making.* Scranton, Pa.: Chandler.

Sada Masaki. 1975. "Keiyō Kōgyō Chitai to Minkankyōchō Hōshiki." In *Nihon Rettō: Chihō Toshi,* ed. Okuda et al.

Saga Prefecture. 1971–76. *Environmental White Paper.* The Environmental Agency.

——. 1976. *Saga Prefecture Assembly Record.*

Saitama Local Government Problems Research Center. 1976. *Saitama Kakushin Kensei no Genjitsu to Tembō.* Jichitai Kenkyūsha.

Saitama Prefecture Bureau of Education, Guidance Division. 1976, 1977. *Gakkusei to Sembatsu Hōho.* Saitama Prefecture.

Saitama Prefecture High School Teachers' Union. 1974. *Saitama no Kōtō Gakkō, Shōgaiji Gakkō Hakusho.* Saitama Prefecture High School Teachers' Union.

Saitō Hironshi. 1968. "Kōkō nyūshi 'kaizen' to Kyōiku no 'Seijōka': Hyōgoken no Baai wo Chūshin ni shite." In *Kōkō Kyōiku Tayōka,* ed. Miyahara: 59–90.

Sakata 'Tsukumo. 1972. "Jichitai no Sendōteki Yakuwari: Zainichi Chōsenjin no Kokuseki Mondai." *Toshi Mondai* (February).

Samuels, Richard J. 1983. *The Politics of Regional Policy in Japan.* Princeton, N.J.: Princeton University Press.

Sankei Shinbun. 1976. "1200-man-nin no Danchi." Serial, July 18–September 30.

Sasaki Susumu. 1976. *Kōkō Kyōiku Ron*. Otsuki Shoten.

Satō Astushi. 1976. *Tenkanki no Chihō Jichi*. Gakuyō Shobō.

Sbragia, Alberta May. 1974. "Urban Autonomy within the Unitary State: A Case Study of Public Housing Policies in Milan, Italy." Ph.D. diss., University of Wisconsin, Madison.

Scarrow, Howard A. 1971. "Policy Pressures by British Local Government." *Comparative Politics* 4 (October): 1–28.

Schafer, Gunther. 1981. "Trends in Local Government Finance in the Federal Republic of Germany Since 1950." In *The Local Fiscal Crisis in Western Europe*, ed. Sharpe.

Schain, Martin A. 1979. "Communist Control of Municipal Councils and Urban Political Change in France." *Studies in Comparative Communism* 12 (Winter): 352–70.

Scharpf, Fritz W., et al. 1978. "Policy Effectiveness and Conflict Avoidance in Intergovernmental Policy Formation." In *Interorganizational Policy Making*, ed. Hanf and Scharpf.

Schlesinger, Joseph A. 1965. "Political Party Organization." In *The Handbook of Organizations*, ed. March. Chicago: Rand McNally.

Schneider, William. 1980. "Styles of Electoral Competition." In *Electoral Participation: A Comparative Analysis*, ed. Richard Rose. Beverly Hills, Calif.: Sage.

Seidelman, Raymond. 1981. "Urban Movements and Communist Power in Florence." *Comparative Politics* 13 (July): 437–59.

Sharpe, L. J. 1970. "Theories and Values of Local Government." *Political Studies* 18 (June): 153–74.

———. 1978. " 'Reforming' the Grass Roots: An Alternative Analysis." In *Policy and Politics*, ed. Butler and Halsey. London: Macmillan.

Sherwood, Frank P. 1969. "Devolution as a Problem of Organizational Strategy." In *Comparative Urban Research*, ed. Robert Daland. Beverly Hills, Calif.: Sage.

Shiroya Yutaka. 1977. "Chihō Toshi no Jūtaku Mondai." *Juristo*, special issue (Summer): 70–74.

Simcock, Bradford L. 1974. "Environmental Politics in Japan." Ph.D. diss., Harvard University.

Smith, Gordon. 1982. *Democracy in Western Germany*, 2d ed. New York: Holmes and Meier.

Smith, W. Eugene, and Aileen M. Smith. 1975. *Minamata: Words and Photographs*. New York: Holt, Rinehart and Winston.

Snowiss, Leo M. 1966. "Congressional Recruitment and Representation." *American Political Science Review* 60 (September): 627–39.

Solesbury, William. 1976. "Issues and Innovativeness in Environmental Policy in Britain, West Germany and California." *Policy Analysis* (Winter): 1–38.

Stein, Robert M. 1981. "The Allocation of Federal Aid Monies: The Synthesis of Demand-Size and Supply-Side Explanations." *American Political Science Review* 75 (June): 334–43.

Steiner, Kurt. 1965. *Local Government in Japan*. Stanford, Calif.: Stanford University Press.

———. 1980. "Progressive Local Administrations: Local Public Policy and Local-National Relations." In *Political Opposition and Local Government in Japan*, ed. Steiner et al.

Steiner, Kurt, Ellis Krauss, and Scott Flanagan, eds. 1980. *Political Opposition and Local Politics in Japan*. Princeton, N.J.: Princeton University Press.

Strouse, James C., and Philippe Jones. 1974. "Federal Aid: The Forgotten Variable in State Policy Research." *Journal of Politics* (February): 200–07.

Sumita Shōji. 1977. "Jichitai Jūtaku Seisaku: Shichōson Jūtaku Keikaku no Teiki." *Juristo*, special issue (Summer): 167–73.

Takagi Shōsaku. 1973. "Gikai, Seitō, Gi'in Katsudō" In the *Iwanami Kōza* 3: 67–96.

Takayose Shōzo. 1975. *Chihō Jichi no Saihakken*. Tokyo: Keisō Shobō.

Takehara Norio. 1976. "Chihōsai no Shikumi to Chuō Tosei." In *Chihō Zaisei no Hanashi*, ed. Fujita and Monma.

Takeishi Fumito. 1973. "Hokkaidō no Kōkō Nyūshi Seido no Genjō to Kaikaku no Torikumi." In *Sembetsu no Kyōiku to Nyūshi Seido*, ed. Zenkoku Shinro Shidō Kenkyūkai.

Takizawa Iwao. 1977. "Hyōgo-ken no Sōgō-Sembatsu-Sei no Genjō to Tembō: Kōbe, Himeji de wa Jisshi wo Miokuri." *Kyōiku no Mori* (January): 64–67.

Tarrow, Sidney. 1977. *Between Center and Periphery: Grassroots Politicians in Italy and France*. New Haven, Conn.: Yale University Press.

Thurston, Donald R. 1973. *Teachers and Politics in Japan*. Princeton, N.J.: Princeton University Press.

Tobiki Tōru. 1970A. "Jōrei: Zenkoku ni okeru Jōrei Seitei no Genjō." In *Kōgai Taisaku*, ed. Satō and Nishihara.

———. 1970B. "Kōgai Bōshi Jōrei: Sono Zenkokuteki Gaikan to Mondaiten." *Juristo* (August 10): 262–65.

Toki Hiroshi. 1983. *Gendai no Toshi Seiji*. Nihon Hyōronsha.

Tokyo University Social Science Research Group. 1965. *Keiyō Chitai ni okeru Kōgyōka to Toshika*. Tokyo: Tokyo University Press.

Tomisawa Misao. 1970. "Yōsei ni yoru Gyōsei: Tokyo-to no Bai." *Juristo* (August 10).

Tsunoi Shin. 1975. "Daitoshiken ni okeru Tochi Mondai: Saitama-ken no Jittai kara." *Toshi Mondai* (June): 54–68.

Tsurutani Taketsugu. 1977. *Political Change in Japan*. New York: David McKay.

———. 1980. "The LDP in Transition? Mass Membership Participation in Party Leadership Selection." *Asian Survey* 20 (August): 844–59.

Ueda Manabu et al. 1976. "Tokushima-ken ni okeru Sōgō-Sembatsu-Sei no Chōsa Kenkyū." In *Kōritsu Kōtō Gakkō*, ed. Hyōdo: 77–92.

Ushimi Akira. 1973. "Jinkō Kyūzō Chitai ni okeru Kōkyō Jūtaku to Jichitai wo meguru Shomondai." *Juristo* (July 15).

———. 1977. "Kōkyō Jūtaku no Juyō Keikaku to Nyūkyo Kibōsha no Shin-koku Tōroku Seido." *Juristo*, special issue (Summer): 211–17.

Ushiogi Morikazu. 1974. "Hatashite Norikireru ka: Shinkokuka suru Dai-Niji Kōkō Shin-Zōsetsu Mondai." *Naigai Kyōiku* (November 15): 2–13.

———. 1975. "Jinkō Hendōka no Kōkō Zōsetsu Taisaku." *Nagoya Daigaku Kyōiku Gakubu Kiyō* (March): 51–67.

Van de Graff, John. 1967. "West Germany's Arbitur Quota and School Reform." *Comparative Education Review* 11 (February): 75–86.

Vidich, Arthur J., and Joseph Bensman. 1960. *Small Town in Mass Society*. Beverly Hills, Calif.: Doubleday.

Wada Yatsuka. 1973. "Sengo no Jūtaku Seisaku to sono Hihan." In *Jūtaku Mondai Nyūmon*, ed. Hayakawa et al.

———. 1975. "Kōkyō Jūtaku Kensetsu no Igi." *Toshi Mondai* (August): 3–14.

Walton, John. 1968. "The Vertical Axis of Community Organization and the Structure of Power." In *The Search for Community Power*, ed. Willis D. Hawley and Frederick M. Wirt. Englewood Cliffs, N.J.: Prentice-Hall.

Watanabe Seiichi. 1975. "Kōkyō Jūtaku Nyūkyosha Senkō to sono Mondai." *Toshi Mondai* (August): 26–37.

Webman, Jerry A. 1977. "Political Structure and Urban Redevelopment: A Comparative Study of Lyon and Birmingham." Ph.D. diss., Yale University.

———. 1981. "Centralization and Implementation: Urban Renewal in Great Britain and France." *Comparative Politics* 13 (January): 127–48.

White, Michelle J. 1981. "Self-Interest in the Suburbs: The Trend Toward No-Growth Zoning." In *New Strategic Perspectives on Social Policy*, ed. John E. Tropman et al. New York: Pergamon Press.

Wildavsky, Aaron, ed. 1967. *American Federalism in Perspective*. New York: Little, Brown.

Wilensky, Harold L. 1975. *The Welfare State and Equality*. Berkeley and Los Angeles: University of California Press.

Wilson, Frank L. 1980. "Sources of Party Transformation: The Case of France." In *West European Party Systems*, ed. Peter H. Merkl. New York: Free Press.

Yamagishi Kenban. 1973. "Nagano-ken no Kōkō Nyūshi Seido no Genjō to Kaikaku e no Torikumi." In *Sembetsu no Kyōiku to Nyūshi Seido*, ed. Zen-koku Shinro Shidō Kenkyūkai: 166–81.

Yamaoka Kazuo and Kyōsu Minoru. 1976. *Kore Kara no Jūtaku Seisaku*. Jūtaku Shimpōsha.

Yamauchi, Toshio. 1972. "Kikan Inin Jimu no Genjo to Mondaiten." *Gekkan Jichi Ken* (August): 6–43.

Yanagihashi Minoru. 1981. "The Perceptions and Attitudes of Japanese Candidates Toward Electoral Factors." In *Parties, Candidates and Voters in Japan*, ed. Campbell.

Yasue Kyōsuke. 1975. "Tokyo ni okeru 'Jichi' no Shuppatsu." In *Nihon Rettō: Kyōdai Toshi*, ed. Okuda et al.

Zariski, Raphael. 1984. "Coalition Formation in the Italian Regions." *Comparative Politics* 16 (July): 403–20.

Zenkoku Shinro Shidō Kenkyūkai. 1974. *Sembetsu no Kyōiku*. Minshūsha.

Index

Pitt Series in Policy and Institutional Studies
Bert A. Rockman, Editor